INDIA:
THE PEACOCK'S CALL

by

Aline Dobbie

Published by

**MELROSE
BOOKS**

An Imprint of Melrose Press Limited
St Thomas Place, Ely
Cambridgeshire
CB7 4GG, UK
www.melrosebooks.com

FIRST EDITION

Cover designed by Aline Dobbie

ISBN 978-1-906561-32-1

Chapters 1–14 of this book were previously published as:
Dobbie, A. *India: The Peacock's Call*. 2002. Serendipity Publishing, London.
ISBN 1-84394-010-8

Printed and bound in Great Britain by:
Biddles. King's Lynn. Norfolk

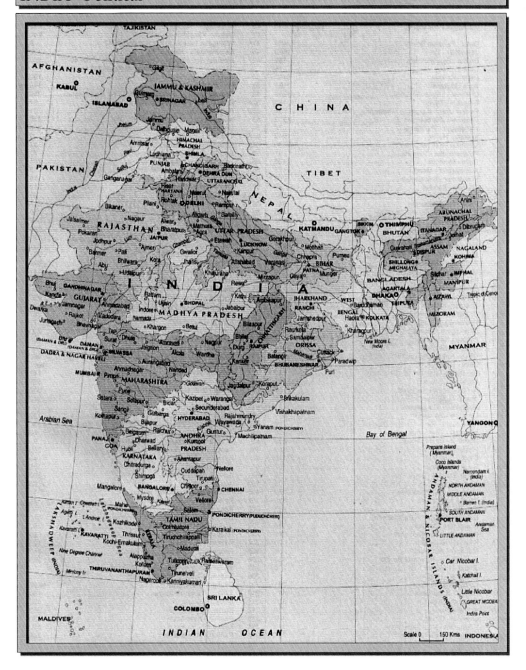

iii

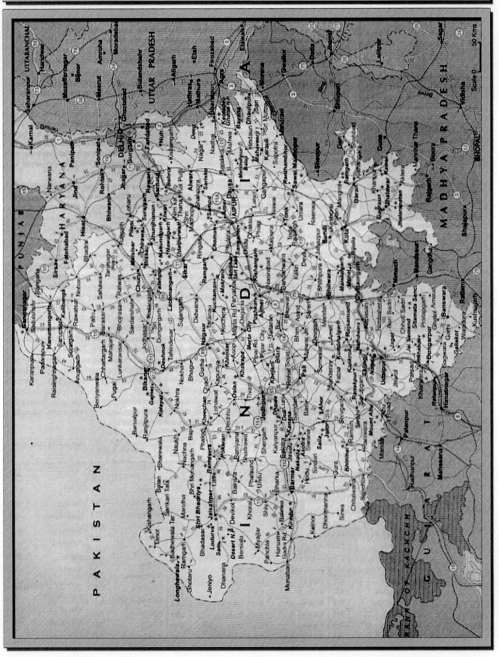

Foreword
by Martin Bell

The Anglo–Indian relationship is a love affair that did not end with divorce. Long after Partition and Independence, it has endured into the 21st century. It seems that the British and Indians, bound by ties of history and language, retain a certain natural affinity. It is not an uncritical relationship; sometimes we exasperate and chide each other, as we might a wayward relative. But there is a mutual fascination always, and never a moment of boredom. It has sometimes seemed to me, in my own travels in India from Simla to Poona and from Bombay to Calcutta, that the Indians are more British than the British. This applies especially to their military culture. If you seek the distillation of Britishness, visit an Indian Army barracks.

Aline Dobbie was born in one, or close by. Her father, Colonel Frank Rose, was a British officer in the IXth Jat Regiment of the Indian Army at Bareilly in Uttar Pradesh. He had earned the admiration of his men by leading a daring escape from Singapore as it fell to the Japanese in 1942.

Aline Dobbie left India at the age of 16 and returned thirty-five years later. *India: The Peacock's Call* is the chronicle of her return. It is more than a travelogue. It is the account of a personal pilgrimage – not so much a journey abroad as a return home. It is written with grace and affection, and a deep understanding of the Indians and their culture. She clearly belongs to the great tradition of indefatigable lady travellers who acquire their history by visiting it: throughout north central India, from Rajasthan to Uttar

Pradesh, one feels that there is hardly a temple or citadel left unvisited. Calcutta and Mumbai (Bombay) are also on the itinerary. Where a hotel's service is less than perfect, which is most rare, or she finds a place she doesn't like, she is not afraid to say so. Her husband Graham, on his first visit to India, plays an intriguing walk-on part. What is sometimes alarming to him is reassuring to her. She especially admires the Indians' dignity in even the most adverse circumstances.

Her book serves many purposes, not least to whet the appetite for a passage to India. There are many who will wish to follow her footsteps to some of the lesser-known destinations. *India: The Peacock's Call*, is an excellent travel guide for those who would venture beyond the beaten track. It is also a rare book of discovery.

Martin Bell

In memory of my father

Frank Rose

*His deep love and knowledge of India, the
land of my birth, was handed down to me
from infancy – he served India well*

Acknowledgements to Part I

I should like to thank my husband Graham for his encouragement and love and our sons for their interest and support which pushed me into writing this book. My affection and gratitude for friendship and hospitality in India I hope will be amply demonstrated within the book.

All of the photographs used in this work belong to the author's private collection. The photographs were taken by the author on her visits to India.

Contents

Illustrations

PART II

Part I

Part I

Chapter One

A Long-anticipated Return

As the great aircraft droned steadily towards its destination I sat back in my seat and thought back to almost thirty-five years ago. The tarmac at Dum Dum Airport, Calcutta and the tearful farewells to all who mattered in my life apart from my parents. Since a child of ten I had become used to frequent farewells when returning to Britain for schooling, but this was different. This was in effect goodbye to India along with farewell to all who had been so important in my life since I was a baby. As a teenager one is sufficiently realistic to know that this was a whole change in lifestyle and the future, though full of hope and challenge, would nevertheless be unfamiliar and therefore a little scary. Above all from the 1st April 1963 India would no longer be my beloved 'home'. Now as I watched intently the computer screen of the huge KLM aircraft the red line of the aircraft's path grew closer and closer to Delhi, my destination on this the first return trip all those years later on 1st November 1997. Graham, my husband, meanwhile was quietly watching me from time to time in-between bouts of chuckles; his book was *City of Djinns* by William Dalrymple, a hugely enjoyable read and to my mind almost obligatory if one is going to Delhi. We landed and I found a lump in my throat with the gentle cabin crew greeting of 'welcome to India' – for me it was of course 'welcome back'.

Indira Gandhi Airport is the modern Gateway to India and cannot honestly be said to have any real charm. It should be a showpiece but isn't. First impressions count and it disappointed me that trouble and attention to detail had obviously been spared when this building was constructed; still having travelled widely in developing countries, it seems that they often cannot appreciate the importance that travellers attach to their first perceptions of a country. As we were later to see, building a good airport is easily within Indian capabilities as Calcutta's internal airport amply demonstrates. The ensuing gentle chaos was extraordinary, not made any better by it being midnight. Four huge aircraft, fully laden, had touched down one after the other, disgorging approximately 2,000 people all desperate to extract their respective luggage and depart for their hotels or friends. For us it went on forever and truly ours must have been the very last item of luggage. By the time we emerged and blinked at the battery of people waiting to 'meet and greet', as it is called, there was pandemonium. It became obvious that our hostess in Delhi was not there and plan B needed to swing into action. A charming very well-dressed young man offered to help me and I gratefully accepted his offer whilst Graham looked after our luggage. He took me to a telephone and thank goodness our hostess Sarup Nehru had just arrived back at her house and was distraught at the idea we were there without her; she had somehow formed the idea we had not arrived on that flight. The portico at the international airport was a complete culture shock to Graham who was looking on bemused as Ambassador car after Ambassador car drove up to collect people, horns blaring; hordes descended on some long-awaited relative, children raced around, lazy policemen kept a watchful eye, taxi drivers touted for work and other passengers looked as shell-shocked as we felt! Our new-found acquaintance, having helped with the 'phone call, promptly summoned a pre-paid taxi and we gratefully climbed in, with him giving very explicit instructions to a compliant driver.

The drive into Delhi itself was an experience since neither of us was used to driving in pitch black without any lights on, which appeared to be normal practice for most of the vehicles on the road at that hour including our own. It soon became worryingly obvious that our taxi driver was not confident of where he was going and thus it fell to me to use my very rusty Hindi to ascertain directions. The various passers-by were amazingly helpful though I suspect not all that accurate, but the *durwans* (watchmen) of the residential colonies did their best. Eventually we realised that the driver was a '*bilkul gomar*' – not bright would be the kindest terminology and illiterate to boot, thus unable to read the street names be they in Hindi or English. Time was passing and we were increasingly worried with the driver becoming positively sulky because of course his fare had been pre-paid and this was eating into his profit! At last Graham and I worked it out which was no small feat, in the dark in a strange city without the benefit of a street map. Unknown to us the Prime Minister also lived in Western Avenue and when I firmly asked two sleepy policemen in a jeep for directions things began to improve. With relief and joy we finally arrived at Sarup's gate and were warmly received, but by this time the driver could barely speak to us; however my Hindi was coming on in leaps and bounds.

Thankfully after some very welcome tea and a short conversation we went to bed, with the familiar drone of the air conditioner. The late hour was fortuitous as it proved helpful in that we woke up refreshed in the correct time clock. The sounds of an Indian awakening were immediately familiar. We resolved in future not to use the noisy air conditioner but the fan instead since the temperature was very pleasant. Maharani Bagh in the morning is full of familiar noises – a man singing happily on his way to work, probably balancing a basket of wares on his head, the *mali* (gardener) clearing his throat rather ferociously, the purveyor of hot tea and *namkins* (savouries) shouting his presence to all and sundry, the hooting of the interminable horns, and close at hand the chattering of the seven sisters, the green parrots, the crows. I was back and the sounds of my childhood flooded in through the windows whilst I enjoyed a delicious and welcome cup of 'bed tea'. There followed a leap into the shower, some hurried dressing and then an exploration in daylight of Sarup's house and garden. There it all was, the *doob* grass lawn (different to British grass), the bougainvilleas riotous in colour, frangipani (the Temple Tree), oleander, crotons and, amazingly, the typical chrysanthemums in red terracotta pots. These are the horticultural symbols of winter's approach.

Surendar Singh and Kanti, Sarup's indoor staff, welcomed us and I engaged in some faltering Hindi but it was immediately understood and any mistakes gently corrected. Then ensued a friendly conversation about my roots and family and the fact that Stewart, our younger son, had been a guest in the home exactly a year previous. Stewart had backpacked throughout northern India and Nepal for two months the previous autumn and returned home with a journal full of stories and experiences. Now it was our turn. Breakfast was amusing as Graham was plied with rumble tumble (scrambled egg) minus chillies to Surendar Singh's obvious disappointment. Actually Graham became very enthusiastic about the odd bit of chilli in his omelettes as the visit progressed!

Meeting Chotu Nehru again was very special as we worked out that we had not seen each other for over forty years; our respective school days having intervened. We reminisced about happy times as children, the three Nehru boys and me and some of the gentle mischief we engaged in, happy Diwali parties, Balo taking us for ice creams to Kwality and the various golden moments of secure childhoods spent in the fifties. There stood Chotu, large and handsome and so like his father Balo, who like mine is gone from this world. His mother Sarup is deservedly very proud of him and her two other boys and his extrovert friendliness demonstrated to me why he is so successful in his chosen occupation. The rest of the family came in and were all enchanting. We agreed to meet up for dinner that evening but in the meantime our schedule called to us and we departed in the car to our travel agent's office.

Delhi in daylight! Well, yes, it has changed. The capital city of my youth was a superb place of wide vistas and avenues, grand buildings and historic monuments. These are of course still there but not quite so obvious to initial inspection. Delhi has become hugely overpopulated and this becomes distressingly obvious in a short drive. Leaving the leafy confines of Maharani Bagh, life is going on all around one, people, people and more people, dogs, pigs, cattle, buffalo, goats, hugely impatient traffic, flower sellers, fruit stalls, nut vendors, balloon wallahs, cyclists, motor rickshaws, scooters, buses, lorries, the cacophony of sound and visual culture shock is mesmerising. In a very short time one learns not to flinch at a vehicle six inches away from one's shoulder or the hawker shouting his wares through the window – and of course the very poor. Yes, that is arresting to the western eye. An air-conditioned car created a gentle barrier between the passenger and the spectacle, but on that first drive we were in an ancient Ambassador, hearing, seeing and smelling all of life going on around us. Graham had been prepared for some of what he saw, but nevertheless it is an unforgettable three-dimensional experience!

Our travel agent Amit welcomed us warmly and we sat down to finalise our arrangements. His attention to detail and good advice was going to prove immensely helpful. On hearing the debacle of our arrival he obviously firmly resolved that there would be no such glitches in the future – but this was India and one has, from time to time, to be prepared for unexpected developments. Patience is not a virtue in India, I would say it is an obligatory requirement, but then again a bit of judicious assertiveness works wonders too! A knowledge of Hindi proved situation-saving on a number of occasions. We resolved that early next morning Amit would accompany us to the railway station to procure tickets for the Kalka Mail from Varanasi to Calcutta, all efforts to obtain these tickets having failed through the normal channels. Foreign visitors who pay in foreign currency are supplied through a special quota.

Graham and I returned to Sarup's for some very welcome lunch. Our hostess was astounded we did not want to rest, but as we explained, here we were in Delhi with so much to see, rest could come later. I asked the driver to take us to India Gate. In the warm afternoon sunshine there it stood, India's answer to the Arc de Triomphe. For me, a daughter of the army, and very proudly the Indian Army, and the mother of a serving officer in HM forces, it was a natural act of homage to all those that had given their lives this century for King, Emperor and Country and then India Their Country. Eighty-five thousand men in the World Wars and North West Frontier, and an eternal flame to those killed in the 1971 war with Pakistan and the Unknown Soldier. When one pays respects be it in Edinburgh with personal relatives commemorated, or Paris or London; be it on a hillside

India Gate.

at Fiesole high above Florence, or the huge graveyards of Athens, this century's cruel marble mementoes along with Normandy and Verdun, one experiences that sad desolation of lives wasted – honourably and courageously given – but nevertheless wasted because of the jealousies, rivalries and greed of mankind. As the Remembrance Season approached I thought of our own family's fears for Hamish, our big son, in Bosnia last year and the fact that he escaped a mortar that fell on the house of his interpreter seconds before he arrived. I thought of India's conflict with China exactly thirty-five years ago in which I had become involved in a tiny way (helping to organise the evacuation of tea planters' families from the path of the invading Chinese in Assam). Young *jawans* (soldiers of the Indian Army) injured in hospital in Calcutta whom I visited, smelling of gangrene, their lives changed forever because of the injuries suffered. A family steeped in military history is probably the finest grounding for anyone looking back in the closing years of the 20th century. Civilians sometimes perceive us as a 'gung ho' bunch with an overeagerness to kill or brutalize. In my experience it is those with a military past who very well understand about commitment, ethos, self-discipline and sacrifice, qualities that would be of advantage in all walks of life. The modern soldier moreover has to be a compassionate diplomat as well in our peacekeeping armies. India can proudly claim the world's fourth largest army. As we were to experience in the ensuing few days they have every right to that pride. As befits the world's largest democracy their military forces are professional and first class, but with no thought of usurping the role of democracy.

Walking about in the sunshine, Graham was enchanted and interested as was I to observe Indians at leisure. Family groups strolling in the environs of India Gate all resplendent in their leisure finery, colourful troupes of young ladies, tiny infants, shy little girls, raucous little boys. Much to our amusement there were a group of youngsters splashing naked in one of the formal water channels on either side of India Gate. A good time was being had by all. I espied the familiar snake charmer and he played his instrument to coax the weary cobra to stand erect and spread his hood – what luck, the essence of India. The fruit juice and water sellers urged us to partake but we ever so politely declined! Then on to Rashtrapati Bhavan and the Secretariat Buildings. Their very grandeur dwarfs everything. The beauty and magnificence of the two colours of sandstone dominate but for the scampering of a troupe of monkeys playing on the porticos with the screeching of green parrots as they dart and fly around. On closer inspection there is a little chipmunk who observes one closely from his stone pillared perch. The fact that so many Indians are also promenading and enjoying the sights of their capital made it all the more interesting. Suddenly I would be firmly grasped and pulled politely into a group photograph and then would follow "Which your country?" I would answer invariably in Hindi to much delight and further curious questioning; little girls would sidle up and touch me and dart away when I asked "*Aap ki naam kya hai?*" A desire to communicate and learn was the overriding impression we gained. Naturally Graham and I were taking photographs and of course there were pleas to include them in the photos – which was a pleasure. A drive round Connaught Place and Jan Path which was looking rather shambolic in the aftermath of Diwali and a glance at Graham's face made me instruct the driver, "Imperial Hotel, please, for *chaai.*" This was a good idea. The old Imperial has been renovated and still retains its charm and ambience. Tea on the terrace is a time-honoured tradition. A charming bearer shimmered up and we ordered tea and *gulab jamuns* (Indian sweets). Excellent, Graham visibly revived and chortled over his *gulab jamuns*, declaring them to be the very best he had ever tasted. Then ensued a walk through the Aladdin's cave of the hotel shops. How can one refuse to buy with so many enticingly beautiful objects of varying prices to tempt one. Naturally we succumbed to the temptation! After this in the twilight we returned home to Western Avenue, very pleased with our first afternoon in Delhi.

Dinner that night was a family affair and immensely enjoyable but not before Kanti has silently appeared with an immensely welcome *taza*

Humayun's Tomb, Delhi.

nimbu – fresh lime. Oh! that was delightful, and several fresh limes later we enjoyed a superb meal along with three generations of the Nehru family. That was fun and very interesting. Youngsters the world over have the same aspirations and ways of expressing themselves. Sarup talked seriously of India and the family spoke of politics, their family's involvement and about the great and the good of the world whom it had been their privilege to meet. For me hearing recent Indian history from the 'horse's mouth' involving close members of the family, tragically now deceased, was fascinating. They too were very interested in our opposition-party political life in South Africa in the seventies. Interest in the British Royal Family is immense in India and I am impressed by the overall affection in which they are held, though with some perceptive observations nevertheless. The year's incredibly tragic events were still a major talking point all over India and particularly in Delhi following so soon on HM's visit and the Commonwealth Heads of Government meeting in our home town of Edinburgh. On the following evening it was again a major topic of conversation at a birthday party given for Chotuji's birthday (wife of Chotu). Having read *The Times of India* on the plane and hearing what various distinguished guests had to say from personal experience of the visit we sadly concluded that the British High Commission and the British Government had badly miscalculated this visit and allowed HM to unwittingly offend quite deeply. None of the anger or outrage was however directed at her personally, except for the bewilderment about the visit to Challianwallah Bagh. 'If you cannot bring yourself to apologise what is the point of the visit ...'

The following evening saw me rigorously questioned about Britain, its new government and the various personalities that comprise the cabinet. Indian social life never flinches from political discussion and I found it all very invigorating as did Graham. What a refreshing change to reserved Edinburgh dinner parties where nobody wants to be labelled as anything specific and thus insipid conversation about non-controversial subjects lurches on unless one is in the company of very close friends and relatives.

And so to bed after a full day with an even fuller one anticipated tomorrow.

Chapter Two

The Jat Regiment and Bareilly

The crack of dawn found two sleepy Dobbies preparing for a train journey to Bareilly in Uttar Pradesh. Bareilly was and still happily is the Regimental Centre of the Jat Regiment. At the time of my birth they were known as the IX Jat Regiment, meaning they were listed ninth in the British Army listing of Indian Regiments. Today in modern India they are simply the Jats but wisely the IX is retained on their distinctive insignia, but naturally no longer with a crown on the top. Driving through Delhi's early morning commuter/office crush is an interesting experience. Thank goodness for Balvinder Singh's excellent skills! One of the most charming spectacles was the little children all turned out in spotless uniforms patiently waiting with a parent or guardian for their respective school buses. Some of them appeared to emerge from a hole in the wall but nevertheless looked immaculate. I pondered on how those parents coped with all their duties in such disadvantaged conditions. I could stop being prissy and say horrible conditions but then I sound patronising and judgemental – to me they are horrible – but to them they are the norm and do not deprive them of their dignity. All over India I was struck by the individual's ability to simply maintain his or her dignity despite some punishing environments. Old Delhi railway station was a special experience, similar to others lodged in my memory but for Graham unique and almost overwhelming. The porter who carried our bags was very efficient and took us straight to the Bareilly train where our reservations appeared. We were ready for our adventure! On time the great train slowly pulled out past the Red Fort, Humayun's Tomb and other notable landmarks. Sadly the glass in the windows was dirty and therefore did not enhance the view, but still it was fun and oh so nostalgic for my umpteen childhood journeys in trains all over India. In those days we had a complete compartment to ourselves and travelled with all our servants inevitably – unless it was for a short holiday in which case only three! The first action my mother would take was to disinfect the lavatory with Dettol! If it was a night journey the berths would be made up and a meal prepared from the picnic ingredients we carried. The fans would be working at full speed to bring some relief from the heat. As an excited child I would have had my face pressed to the window looking out, because even in the dark there was plenty to observe. In the dark hours if one stopped at a major railway station the cacophony of sound continued, with hawkers shouting *garam chai* (hot tea), *piniko pani* (drinking water), etc. In the early morning light at a major junction there would be the spectacle of about 5,000 people starting their day with ablutions, exercises, coughing and spitting, selling glorious glass bangles and other exotic wares to the eyes of a small child. At the first real daylight stop my father's manservant would disappear up the platform to the engine and procure hot water for Father's shaving, the rest of us would wash in cramped surroundings in the en-suite loo/basin compartment and some form of breakfast would be eaten. Now in November 1997 my mind wandered back over all these wonderful memories and saw some ghosts, but then that is inevitable. My reverie was interrupted by Graham crowing with delight on spotting an elephant ambling by on a river's edge. There were the same fields, orchards, countryside, all looking very good after the rains, well tended and visibly supporting the often-heard declaration that India is now self-sufficient in food grains. The little hamlets, the bigger villages looked comfortable, Uttar Pradesh, India's most populous state, appeared to be prosperous. Crossing the Ganges and the Jamuna was for me almost spiritual. Those two rivers had been part of my life for the first sixteen years and I still catch my breath when I see the Ganges. There is something timeless about great rivers in all continents, but for me this time it was a feeling of Land of my Birth, lifeforce, Mother Ganga. We arrived at Bareilly on time after four and a half hours. After some slight confusion the Brigadier's personal car and driver arrived to collect us. Entering the cantonment in the Brigadier's car is an interesting experience. Everyone who can leaps up and salutes or acknowledges one. Interested eyes take one in, traffic stops. For me however a distant childhood memory was being revived. Long avenues of blue gums; well, here they were, long avenues of blue gums – everything immaculate in the afternoon sunshine at the start of an Indian winter. The Regiment was preparing for Raising Day on 17th and 18th November and everything that could be painted, polished, whitewashed, bluewashed, dug over, replanted or spruced up was having its annual makeover after the rains. The Jat Regimental Centre was looking sparkling and made me feel so proud. The Jat Regiment was raised in 1795 and celebrated its bicentenary in November 1995. Here again were the buildings so clearly remembered by my mother, depicted in faded black and white photos lovingly preserved by me. In fact we own several good photos of regimental occasions as well as family ones and I had brought them laid out in album pages. These were to prove fascinating to all who saw them and I was beseeched to leave them for the Regimental Museum, but I resisted as they are precious to me. From Brigadiers to Lance Corporal to Mess cook and servant they were intrigued, and of course the same buildings, even furniture featured – only the faces had changed. The photos of my parents with me as a tiny baby brought much enjoyment as they now could minutely observe the child grown up fifty years on! We had also put together a short 'brag book' of our family and thus regimental eyes could feast on continuity albeit in another distant land. The warmth of welcome was superb and for me the whole 24 hours was deeply moving and interesting. The hospitality was warm and thoughtful, with a whole suite provided for our comfort. The attention to detail is excellent, but because of the antiquity of some of the buildings and eccentric plumbing etc one could so easily imagine past generals, commander in chiefs and others all staying in these very rooms, set apart from the Officers' Mess for senior guests. On being shown round the mess dining room I pointed out that the chairs appeared to be the same as those in a photo of Daddy with fellow officers taken in 1947. Jat House has a lovely garden and Brigadier and Mrs Kumar are keen gardeners. Indeed the whole Centre and its environs looked beautiful. Sadly I wished that civilian India would take a leaf out of the Army's book. The Regimental Museum is so interesting and well kept and I presented a bound copy of my late father's story of his escape from Singapore to Ceylon in the company of several others on a flat-bottomed Chinese river boat called the *Wu Chang*. Father also wrote a brief history of the Jats as a people. Drinks with the 'Brig.' and his wife were excellent. Mess servants shimmered about with very enticing plates of hot cocktail eats. A visit to the actual mess was interesting to meet old officers and then look at regimental silver and try and identify for what purpose certain pieces were used. Indian messes keep to the time-honoured traditions as we were to experience shortly in Udaipur, but different cultures require different implements, or less of them. Finally we were served dinner in solitary splendour in our private dining room in the guest quarters. It was a fine meal beautifully presented and served with enormous friendship and warmth. Graham quietly observed that he was not used to being watched closely when eating. I explained that was the norm though usually done with discretion. The reason for the blatant curiosity was of course my origin and link with the Regiment. In-between mouthfuls I conducted a conversation in Hindi with Gurung, the very friendly and efficient Lance Naik, who was supervising our accommodation. Then in came a second mess servant and finally the cook. They all wanted to shyly converse about the past and what is our present. When we showed appreciation for the cooking the cook promptly went mad and produced fresh chappatis one after the other (indeed the very best way to eat them is hot and soft). Gentle questioning followed on our sons, their marriage prospects, what they do. There was evident pleasure that number one son is in the British military; indeed as we spoke, acting ADC to the General in Germany; they all agreed that was suitable for a Jat officer's grandson. The fact that his fiancée is also an officer in the army was a bonus. Number two son earned approval for having backpacked in India but why had he not come to Bareilly where they could have looked after him. We were admonished that we must all come again to Bareilly as a total family including 86-year-old 'Mummy' so that the Regimental family could look after us. I demurred that Mummy (*mataji*) was now *bahut purana* (very old) but they declared that an army doctor would be on standby! Indeed the next day I was assured that this would be the case by senior officers. Finally totally up to the brim with chappatis followed by sweetmeats we said thank you. Gurung wanted to know what we wished for breakfast, I replied papaya, *dulia* porridge (Jat porridge) and eggs. We retired to our enormous suite of bedroom, dressing room and simple but huge bathroom. Sitting in the bedroom looking at its colonial architecture made me think of the past one hundred and fifty years or so. How many men would have fulfilled their military duties here, reading and writing at the well-provided desk. Today there is a modern television with all of India's channels to educate or entertain, but not all that long ago there were only books. In my childhood how many times I had strolled into upcountry libraries in district clubs. Books very often partially eaten by white ants, or water stained, most of them without illustrations or eye-catching support material, just musty, stuffy and sometimes even boring books. Sometimes however there would be a gem and that would keep me from boredom on a long hot afternoon. Graham constructed the frame for putting on the *machardani* (mosquito net) and we finally slept. I took the precaution of leaving the bathroom light on. There was almost constant electricity but from time to time it could be heard switching over to a military generator presumably when the national grid failed. Visiting the bathroom in the early hours I found myself reacting as of years ago, stopping at the bathroom door to survey the floor carefully (thus the light) so as to avoid any creepy crawlies. These bathrooms have open run offs for the shower water, and open runoffs provide a welcome for sinister creatures like huge spiders, even scorpions and small snakes. My parents always ensured the outlets were secured with fine mesh to prevent such nasty surprises, but from time to time we had all experienced something unpleasant and potentially dangerous. Mercifully the bathroom was clear but the involuntary act of caution took me back over forty years.

The Indian dawn chorus is both wonderful and raucous. A huge noise really compared to our more melodic one in Britain. Chattering seven sisters, cawing crows, twittering parakeets, screeching peacocks, it was all there and in no time at all bed tea arrived with a smiling Gurung. There was too much to see and do and not enough time so we were up promptly. The curtains were drawn for privacy and I was chatting to Graham standing stark naked in the middle of the bedroom. Silly me! I had forgotten I was a guest in an army residence. These messes and suites are not accustomed to female visitors, thus the sergeant in charge of hosting operations had come to discreetly check on his visitors. He was accustomed to casting an eye through a small porthole in the closed door to the adjoining sitting room. He would normally have found a sleepy general or other. He had I am pretty sure never before encountered the spectacle of a white nude female, his VIP visitor, standing chatting in a relaxed manner in the middle of the bedroom. I suddenly became aware of the silent inspection and darted behind the dressing room door curtains. He attempted to move away discreetly. Graham and I fell about laughing but I knew it would present difficulties later; however we did not meet at breakfast and honour was saved by my careful countenance and complete 'ignorance' when we did.

Stepping out into the sunlit garden in the early sunshine was lovely. Graham and I took some photos which proved to be very successful and captured the morning mist and freshness of the early winter garden. After breakfast the jeep returned with a charming major to accompany us to meet the current residents of my parents' former house, the home to which I had been born. Number 4 Barrack Road has moved a little with the times but in essence is exactly the same. The current colonel and his wife could not have been more charming or welcoming. It was a moving experience for me and not made easy by the interested gaze of a television crew who were there to make a film on the dashing colonel's exploits as a microlight pilot. I reflected that a previous colonel (my late father) had also been a dashing young man, hero to his men in the fall of Singapore, keen shot and the man who brought the Regimental pipe band up to scratch after the end of WWII. Fifty years on here was a close family living in what had been a very happy home for my parents. They were enchanted to see the pictures of it as it was fifty years ago and Graham and I took pictures to show my mother what it looks like today. After visiting my old home we went to the Brigadier's office to receive an official welcome and meet the senior officers. Brig. Satish Kumar is a fine man running a superb outfit. There was enormous preparation for the forthcoming Raising Day when about

22 generals would be descending on the centre for the annual celebrations. It was interesting to see the amount of detail and also the warmth with which old officers of the Jat Regiment were welcomed. India had been independent for fifty years but the bonds between the British officers and the Indian officers and men were strongly present. All around us were the souvenirs of past times with photos of my late guardian Brigadier Bernard Gerty who had taken one of the Japanese surrenders at the end of the war. Having donated a specially bound copy of my late father's articles, I was given a beautiful leather wallet and purse with the Jat regimental crest, Graham was given a very elegant clock which now sits on his desk. Having declined to hand over my own treasured photos, I had that morning come across the brooch made out of a tiger's collar bone, mounted in gold. This tiger had been shot by my father in the winter of 1950. Today any form of shooting of big game is looked on in abhorrence, understandably, but that tiger had become a serious threat to a local village and was a cattle killer. Father had been asked to come back at Christmas and try and kill it. He had succeeded. In the last days of his life I recall vividly how he regretted killing two tigers and a leopard, but in those days of the 1940s and '50s cattle eaters were routinely despatched. Now India's huge population puts even more pressure on its wildlife and I am resolved to help in my own little way whoever seriously tries to save these wonderful beasts. The tiger collar bone brooch was not something I wore, but I had come across it when packing a few bits of jewellery for the trip. One essential item had been the Jat insignia in silver that had been made into a brooch for me from insignia off Father's uniform. Thus when I saw the tiger brooch something made me bring it too! Now here was an opportunity to present it to the Regiment. This gesture was hugely welcomed and immediate efforts were made to type out the caption for the subsequent frame in which it would hang. We were asked for our advice on the accuracy of the English and Graham told them it was called a clavicle. After the formal welcome Graham and I formally laid a wreath each at the Jat War Memorial. This was beautifully done with soldiers assisting us in full ceremonial dress and the protocol for doing this is outlined in every guest suite so we were well advised and prepared.

Remembrance season for any thoughtful person is a moving time, but here I was within hours of my birthday in the place of my birth laying a wreath. Half a century on it seems we have learnt nothing from all the supreme sacrifice. I thought of the Jat VCs, the extreme bravery of simple courageous men who helped their comrades in foreign lands. Young Jat soldiers who had never travelled previously suddenly catapulted into the horror of the Second World War, before that the Great War. What must these dignified but simple people have thought about their imperial masters waging war on this huge scale. The Jats are an ancient people with

The Jat Regiment War Memorial at Bareilly.

more than one dynasty in eastern Rajasthan and around Bharatpur. Their great ruler was responsible for the victory that resulted in the sack of the Red Fort at Agra and to this day at Deeg some of the spoils of war are still on display outside the beautiful but abandoned palace of Deeg with its 18th century gravity-fed apparatus to provide spectacular fountains to emulate a monsoon! There are those students of history that think it was entirely possible that the Jats as a race travelled in the distant past as far as northern Europe to the area we now know as Jutland in Denmark. Jats are farmers as well as warriors and the Regiment is justifiably proud of its origins. Now however Indians from diverse backgrounds choose to

15

serve in the Regiment.

I have a cameo memory of one of the superbly turned out ceremonial soldiers holding my handbag whilst I approached and paid homage at the War Memorial escorted formally by his two companions. Major Khulah took us into the Regimental shop and we purchased glasses, ties, swagger stick, insignia. The craft industry worked by soldiers' wives continues to flourish. We met the Regimental Sergeant Major and I conversed with him and thought of the famous Regimental Subadhar Major Hussein Khan who was RSM when I was born. My father was very attached to him and I grew up with a photo of Hussein Khan on Father's bookcase. He never spoke English to anyone, though people knew he could converse in English. His logic was that he had learnt English to speak to his King Emperor at the time of the coronation of George VI in 1937 when he represented the Regiment at his coronation – English was only for him and his King! This RSM was as proud and warrior-like as all his predecessors and we were glad to meet him. The major then took us to the hospital where I was born and we met the current doctors and saw that the hospital was flourishing with a sizeable birth rate, far in excess of the number fifty years ago. The last stop before lunch was the Church of St Stephen where I had been christened. This was a simple church built in the early 19th century and had undergone the violence of the Indian Mutiny or more tactfully renamed First War of Independence. The priest of the time had been murdered along with a few others and we stopped at their graves in the church garden. St Stephen's is now not an Anglican church but is used under Methodist or Baptist auspices. For years it lay in neglect, and indeed was disused at the time of my birth and my mother had to apply for special permission to use it for my christening – she just particularly liked the look of it. It is heartening to think that Christianity is still vigorous enough in Uttar Pradesh to justify renovating and maintaining it. All over Scotland now small churches are in decline and only used on a part-time basis or totally converted to secular use.

It had been a very pleasant morning but filled with emotion as well; Graham and I returned to the suite and changed for our return to Delhi, then we had a delicious lunch. At breakfast I had said we would like Jat Khana (Jat food) to the evident delight of Gurung and this was affectionately served. All too soon it was time to leave and everyone lined the steps to say their farewells. Army time is punctual and sadly I was saying thank you to each and everyone of them exactly 24 hours after meeting them. Major Khulah very perceptively told Gurung to jump into the jeep and we were on our way. No one was happy about this railway journey. The Army felt that they should have been allowed to organise it, they worried about the train – it was known to be 24 hours late on some occasions, moreover it originated in what is now a rather lawless part of India and security could be a problem. A box of provisions was thoughtfully provided with a picnic of food, snacks, beer and water to help us endure the journey. We arrived at the station and the major commanded the driver to drive onto the platform - an honour normally only allowed to the Brigadier and Generals. Major Khulah said he was going to leave Gurung with us in case we experienced any difficulties, but just as he said this, which we deeply appreciated, the loudspeaker announced the Delhi Bareilly express and the train arrived on time! The major was speechless with surprise; I was privately deeply relieved. We boarded the train with their strict instructions not to mingle with the other passengers. On our outgoing journey we had shyly but firmly started conversations with some of our fellow passengers, but as he pointed out that train started in Delhi with respectable working people travelling to Moradabad and Bareilly in the course of their work as well as a few families. Now we would be boarding a train that had started 24 hours ago in Bihar and Assam and could have on it all sorts of ruffians and pickpockets. Graham and I resolved to follow his advice faithfully. The train journey to Delhi was a time of reflection for me. For years I had wanted to make this sentimental journey – almost pilgrimage to the place of my birth, last seen but hardly remembered in 1950 when I was about 3 going on 4! Now I had been and was gone; I relived all these recent experiences with affection, the people we had met, the atmosphere, the buildings and wondered sadly if I would ever see it again. Little did I know that within four months I would be back to celebrate the festival of Holi with the Regiment. How strange life is, for years my beloved India had been a distant but vivid memory and then quite suddenly the opportunity presents itself for three visits within a space of seven months – truly life has its surprises.

As the evening turned into night and the daylight disappeared we had plenty of opportunity on this dreadfully slow train to observe Indian village life at dusk. Teeming thousands on bicycles, bullock carts, rickshaws, cars, buses, trains, elephants, buffaloes and cattle returning from the fields, herds of goats with minute goatherds and even a few camels though we were in the UP (Uttar Pradesh) not Rajasthan. The evening fires were lit, people crouched round cooking pots, children were playing in the dust and dirt. That train left Bareilly at about 4 pm, late, though it had arrived punctually, but it clearly was not going to arrive in Delhi on time! By about 9.30 pm it had arrived within a couple of kilometres of its destination but just sat on a shunting line for over two hours whilst other more important trains hurtled by. That was the dangerous time. Incarcerated in a full train when boredom can set in along with frustration among the rougher elements of the passengers, it was worrying; so finally when the train lurched into Delhi we were very relieved. Our driver was there to greet us on the platform. Thank goodness, the crowds were humungous and moving was a nightmare. Entire families were moving with their bedding and goods and chattels, little girls and boys all holding hands with their shy, tired-looking mothers. Curiosity is no respecter of time so why not engage in questions! Why was I there, where had I come from, to where was I going, how many children did I have? etc. Thankfully we threw ourselves into a clean, new Maruti car and were whisked away to Maharani Bagh. Arriving at Sarup's we were subjected to a severe scolding on the lateness of the hour, how dinner had been spoiled, what were we thinking of – it took some patience and courtesy to point out that not even we had any influence on the punctuality of the Indian railway system and yes, we were very hungry and exhausted. Sarup said Surinder Singh had even made me a special caramel custard; I gratefully ate it and told him the next day it was a favourite pudding. I reflected that when people have known one since extreme childhood they are inclined to forget the intervening years and make one feel as if a child of four once again!

The next day saw us visiting friends and then having a last lunch with Sarup and discussing all matter of things. How time passes, it would have been good to have a few more days, but hopefully we will see each other again quite soon.

Chapter Three

Land of the Rajputs

The evening saw us winging our way to Udaipur. Ever since I was thirteen I had wanted to visit Udaipur – there was a magic about the place for me with its lakes and palaces. The Maharana of Udaipur was to me a title imbued with ancient mystery. Indian Airlines provided a no-nonsense service to Udaipur and we were soon installed in our lakeside hotel. The following morning was rewarding. The slap, thud, slap of the rhythm of the women washing clothes on the opposite bank woke me and in no time I was photographing the early morning light. Our room had a balcony right on the water's edge from where one could observe everything. Women singing and washing, birds darting back and forth, the little kingfisher diving down into the lake for fish and returning to the moored boat just beneath me. Before we set off in the car to seriously sightsee we wandered about and took in the far-distant views of hills surrounding the lake basin, the brilliance of the bougainvilleas, the oleanders, early poinsettias, morning routines amongst the locals. After the smog of Delhi it was a real pleasure to be in a smaller place with the purity of colour. Udaipur's palaces, palace restaurants, art gallery of miniature paintings, gardens and temples are superb places with so much history and myth. The Udaipur Rajput title originates in the 8th century AD and thus has seniority amongst all the Rajput titles such as Jaipur, Jodhpur, Bikaner, Jaisalmer, Kota, etc.

An ancient land, a fascinating palace, a sparkling day with friendly experiences, what more can one want from a holiday? We were both in our element with the prospect of a fine lunch in a palace restaurant with superb views onto the lake and the various islands of the Lake Palace, Jagmandir,

The Jag Mandir island at sunset. Lake Pichola, Udaipur, Rajasthan.

etc. The beauty and tranquility of Lake Pichola envelop one best in the light of the setting sun; the boat trip to Jag Mandir was so worthwhile. To think that the fabled Shah Jahan as a young prince lived there in exile far outweighs the superficial fantasy of that over-egged James Bond film *Octopussy*. That evening we were guests of Colonel Gupta and 7 Battalion Jat Regiment. The Colonel sent a jeep with a young lieutenant as an escort. What ensued was pure comedy. Graham and I were formally dressed for an evening function and sitting bolt upright in the back of the jeep. The lieutenant rather shyly and stiffly conversed, the driver who of course was also a soldier was a tall solemn Jat, very serious about his duties. On attempting to leave our lakeside hotel, the jeep was surrounded by home-going traffic in the narrow lane. Traffic jams can be desperately frustrating, or simply amusing; this was a mixture of both – but only really for us. Picture if you will a smart white jeep with the large IX JAT insignia, self-important Indian officer and driver, two Europeans dressed in smart clothes sitting in the rear, whilst all around is chaos, noisy blaring total chaos, contributed to by immovable holy cows (the driver dare not touch or injure them), pariah dogs, countless men on bicycles, several on scooters, two or three rickshaws and hordes of pedestrians – all it lacked was an elephant or camel! Nobody would give way and everybody with a horn or bell used it ferociously to no avail, including the army driver. It was hilarious for us but we tried so hard to keep straight faces. The driver was incandescent with frustration and loss of face because he simply was not used to people holding him up. Usually the natural authority of a military vehicle cuts a path through the throng, but this lane was only about 15 feet wide at most, it was Friday night and the end of the week's frustration was evident on all concerned except of course the sundry cows chewing the cud who were really the reason for the chaotic jam initially. Finally we broke through and were on our way and when we arrived the Colonel and all the other officers and their wives were formally there to greet us. After the introductions the Colonel mildly commented on the longer than usual time it had taken. I could see it was going to be a little embarrassing for the young lieutenant who also did not want to admit that his wrong directions had added to the lateness; meanwhile the driver was standing stiffly to attention in the presence of Colonel Gupta. Fortunately I had the opportunity to turn and thank the driver and tell him his driving was *bharyia* (brilliant) – a useful idiomatic expression in modern Hindi. His face lit up and he threw an enthusiastic salute and everyone laughed and lightened the formality. Drinks on the lawn sitting in a large circle is an age-old tradition in India. Mess servants plied us with drinks and delicious hot cocktail eats. Conversation ranged over a broad spectrum and became quite heated at one point, with a young captain taking a verbal swipe at the British imperial past and the modern Royal Family and the tragic death of Diana, Princess of Wales. Throughout India there appears to be the theory that originated in the Middle East that the princess was murdered. It was a difficult conversation but courtesy ensured they listened to our views. However, Indian dinner parties are vibrant affairs as I have already mentioned and no one would just be content with trite phrases, nor indeed were we peddling them! Again the photos were of great interest, even here in this Jat mess hundreds of miles away from Bareilly. Dinner was a very formal meal with thoughtful hospitality and an official photographer. At the end of the meal came the *saunf*. This is based on aniseed and is how an Indian meal concludes with gentle ceremony, rather like an Indian equivalent of passing the port. Each household, mess, restaurant or institution will probably have its own individual mix of *saunf*. Graham and I found 7th Jat's mixture both refreshing and attractive, some can be a little too sweet. Thus Indian mess silver has its own unique vessels or salvers for this ritual. After dinner we took our leave and I thanked them all most sincerely for their warmth of hospitality and said it was quite obvious that as before in my babyhood the old cry '*Jat ki jai*' would hold true. This was well received. *Jai* is the word for victory, so the Regimental war cry is loosely Victory to the Jats!

Chapter Four

Ranakpur, Rohet and the Bishnoi

Leaving Udaipur for Ranakpur the next day had its challenges. Another lovely day, my birthday in fact but I had succumbed to some minor form of stomach bug which can present one with a challenge on a long car journey – and indeed it did, but Balvinder Singh was immediately sympathetic and would pull over in the wink of an eye for me to sort myself out! The only thing to do in the circumstances was to drink Coke and keep off food. The drive was enjoyable otherwise, travelling through the Aravalli hills with their semi-desert vegetation. Later I was to see this from the air in daylight and found it really wonderful.

Rajasthan is a dichotomy of ancient grandeur and modern technological wonder. Where else can one sit on a caparisoned elephant talking to someone on a mobile 'phone, or astride a camel as the sun sets and the stars come out and navigate with a satellite compass. More than half of Rajasthan is semi-arid and this desert belt is separated from the rest of the country by the Aravalli Range, geologically the oldest mountain range in India. People's perception of a desert state before experience does not include shimmering palaces on serene lakes. Intense winter cold is a few weeks later followed by blazing dry heat which we experienced in the summer of 1998 – the record was 49C. The wide skies of a desert night far from the glow of overburdened cities are clear black and full of twinkling stars, completely silent except for low-pitched human conversation and the grunts and chewing of a camel or two. In a period of quiet reflection

I thought of this land's ancestry dating beyond 2,500 BC. It is now generally acknowledged that the Indus Valley civilization had its origins in north Rajasthan. The Bhil and Milna tribes inhabited this area long before the Aryans thundered onto the scene around 1,400 BC. In the land that the present day Bishnoi are gentle guardians of was once the site of blood and battle interspersed with the gentle teaching of the message of Buddhism in the 2nd and 3rd centuries BC.

Afghans, Turks, Persians, Mughals followed the Aryan invaders, mixing their blood first in war then in peace and thus laying the foundations for the famous martial ancestry of the Rajputs. Whilst in the west in Europe and Britain as we now know them there was a steady decline of the Roman Empire and the fall of Rome to Alaric the Visigoth in AD 410, the Germanic tribes known as Huns, Visigoths, Ostrogoths and Franks were subjecting our northern lands, right down to the Mediterranean countries, to barbarism and what was to be known as the dark ages by writers such as Petrarch in the middle ages. Rajasthan from the 7th century to the early 13th century was enjoying a golden age. Thirty-six royal clans who had been successful in persuading the Brahmins of their Hindu faith to provide them with genealogies linking individual dynasties to the sun and the moon developed these competing kingdoms of Rajputs (sons of rajas), which led to Rajasthan's original name – Rajputana, Land of the Rajputs.

At Ranakpur is the beautiful, pure, clean white Jain temple at which we stopped and rested and enjoyed the beauty of a holy place. Alongside the temple is the *dharamsala* or resting place with cells for visiting pilgrims with its air of peace and tranquility despite nearby tourist buses and chattering crowds. Ranakpur is set in a peaceful wooded river valley and is a complex of temples founded in the mid-14th century. Chaumukha Temple has a huge walled complex covering 3,600 sq metres on a high stone plinth. Inside are 29 halls and 1,444 pillars carved from creamy white marble made translucent by the sunshine, each pillar is different. Scenes of daily life and images of gods and nymphs and elephants soar into glorious fantasy. The centre is dominated by a huge four-faced idol of Adinath, giver of Truth. The temple with its total aura of cleanliness thus easily leading one onto thinking purity was immensely restful. Divesting oneself of shoes is no problem for this holy place. A courteous Jain monk will give one a softly spoken background information and then leave one alone to enjoy and absorb the atmosphere. We found it very welcome as by this time my stomach complaint was venting its wrath upon me. Somehow this peaceful cool place gave me strength and we were loath to leave but the schedule beckoned. Near Ranakpur is a charming watering hole called Maharani Bagh where one sits and eats outside under attractive canvas awnings. The choice is varied and the service friendly. Graham enjoyed himself and I asked for papaya from a friendly bearer who immediately took some trouble for me. Fortunately the

Sunset at Rohert Garh with peacock roosting.

conveniences are excellent!! Since Balvinder Singh was also now refreshed we were soon on our way after briefly pausing to inspect a rather charming little flock of pink ducks.

The destination was Rohet Garh. This is a charming oasis. The Rohet aristocratic house runs their fort/mansion as a heritage hotel and everything was perfection. Arriving in time for tea on the lawn with the friendly family members, guests returning from riding sorties, the sun slowly setting is quite perfect. The buildings are well maintained and more renovations are obviously planned. The gardens are pretty with a plethora of bougainvillea, oleanders, hollyhock, green lawns, a most exotic courtyard pool right outside our suite and peacocks busily walking about. I very soon spied a little man with his assistants painting a mural in the outside dining area beside the pool. His art was charming and though not complete was obviously going to be the beautiful finishing touch to an attractive area. We conversed and he said shyly that he also painted in miniature, so naturally I asked to see some of his work. I bought a picture and then a little later saw him again in a part of the garden where he was obviously allowed to set up his art for the hotel guests. We bought some more paintings as presents for our sons and when I mentioned that this was my birthday he promptly gave me a painting that made a beautiful pair to the one I had originally purchased. His conversation was gentle and sweet, about his wife, how she also painted (in fact was the artist of the one given to me). Graham and I went up to the roof to watch the setting

sun. A tranquil scene of a small lake with island and trees, peacocks settling down to roost, the orange, red glow of the sunset, the gentle chatter
of birds at the end of the day, waving to little children at their dwelling
door, buffaloes and cows returning to their respective byres, what more
could one want.

Rohet was filled with French people. This could have been fun as we
love France and are well travelled in that country and also understand
enough French. It was however tiresome! The French talk loudly and
volubly and demanded their drinks' orders in French from a patient, shy
Rajasthani bearer – speak Hindi, or English, and he will leap to serve you
but to gesticulate and jabber aggressively in French was stupid. I know the
French are very proud of their language but this was taking it to extremes.
We watched the charade for a bit and then I murmured to the bearer what
was required, but the Frenchman simply glared at us and did not even
think to say thank you! Their guide was rather supercilious. Graham and
I kept our own counsel. Dinner looked perfectly delicious but since I was
by now feeling a lot better I did not tempt fate and ate a small amount
of rice and lentils. Sidarth Singh asked us if we would like the following morning to go out into the countryside and visit the villages and see
some wildlife. We said that was a lovely idea and after a pleasant night
were up very early to see the sun rise. The morning mist gave way to the
sun as the temple *pujari* made his morning calls. Standing on the rooftop,
all was still serene before the bustle of life took over. The horses in their
stables, Balvinder Singh cleaning his teeth, waving to me in reply to my
morning greeting, peacocks starting their raucous morning routine, men
coming out of their dwelling for their ablutions on the doorstep, stretching, yawning, praying. We visited the little painter in his room on the way
down from the roof. He showed us more of his work and I took a photo of
him and his assistants. Perhaps I will send him a copy along with one of
all his framed work on our dining room walls. Unsophisticated Indians are
always so delighted to be included in a photograph. Some of the painter in
residence's work was done on the back of ancient court manuscripts that
had been the accounts for the various royal households. Thus the back of
the painting is as interesting as the front and one therefore has to take care
in framing them, the quality of the paper is unique.

Our host's personal jeep awaited with driver and guide after breakfast
by the pool. The French party embarked in two other bigger vehicles and
we all set off but our driver did not just follow the others. As we left the
confines of the princely fort and navigated our way through the village
there was plenty to observe and it was difficult to imagine that it was a
Sunday, for nothing seemed to have quietened down – everything that
makes up Indian village life was taking place, except the children were not
in school uniforms. The drive out into the countryside was pure delight and

nostalgic in a way that is difficult to identify. Was it the dryness, the dust, the open plain, vegetation – certainly the vultures wheeling and resting on a carcass and a feeling of the primitive fundamental aspects of life? Here in the semi desert on the fringes of the Thar Desert which is the most populous desert in the world with some 84 people per square kilometre, life centres around watering holes and grazing areas for flocks of sheep or herds of camels. The Bishnoi, the most remarkable of desert people, are members of a sect who believe in complete non-violence to all living organisms, and they are the primary reason that desert wildlife still exists in the subcontinent. Bishnoi is an offshoot of Jainism and was founded in 1542 with the fundamental belief that all creatures have a right to life. Just over two centuries ago the Bishnoi defended with their lives their most sacred trees, the *khejri*. History recounts that in 1778 the Jodhpur administration sent men to cut down these trees to provide firewood needed for burning lime. The villagers defended the trees with their lives and paid the ultimate price with 363 Bishnoi dead. The mass slaughter resulted in a royal decree prohibiting the felling of any tree in a Bishnoi village, and a temple was later constructed at Khejarli in memory of the 363 dead, and every year thousands of Bishnoi arrive to commemorate the sacrifice of their ancestors. The Bishnoi even bury dead *chinkara* (the Indian gazelle) and erect stones to mark their graves. The *khejri* tree is particularly special because its leaves are essential fodder for livestock, its thorns help to protect the desert dwellers from wild animals and its pods are a vital foodstuff, and lastly the branches are lopped for firewood. Desert wildlife thrives around a Bishnoi village and a network of natural sanctuaries has resulted from beliefs rooted in the past that hopefully will ensure the survival of many species like the blackbuck and *chinkara* in the future.

The jeeps pulled up outside the mud walls of a village and all of us were invited to step inside the village compound. The villagers greeted us shyly and the French with their guide walked all round gesticulating loudly. It was an outrage in my view, they might as well have been in a zoo or safari park. Their manners evaporated and their noisy conversation appeared to us as arrogant and slightly disdainful. This village was as pure an example of Indian pastoral life as it is possible to find. I am not naive or unrealistic about India despite my passion for it, there is a strong possibility that Sidarth Singh of Rohet helps the village headman (the *sarpanch*) to maintain a perfect tourist attraction – I do not know, but I do know that it was their home, not a National Trust showplace which closes at five o'clock. I asked if I might photograph and they said yes, and then a village woman with a superb face invited me into a little house to watch her put on *kajal* round her eyes, whilst her teenage son looked on – all her simple strength and dignity looks out of my photograph. Her kitchen area was spotless and so simple. She made it courteously but firmly clear she did not want me to walk or stand

Two Bishnoi girls in all their finery.

A proud Bishnoi woman who invited me into her spotless village house.

near her hearth. Graham was interested in the livestock and I talked to the men in Hindi with which they were delighted. The usual questions ensued, was I married, did I have children – two sons met with approval. Then I introduced Graham and they understood and were delighted and talked further and wanted us to photograph them. Looking through a brick archway I saw two beautiful young girls superbly arrayed in Rajasthani village dress, and giggling quietly they posed for a photograph. Pulling water from the village water pump one young mother and child seemed to epitomise simple rural life, and then it was time to move on. We were guests in another village where the highlight was to participate in an opium ceremony. Foolishly, in my view, some of the tourists actually drank some of the distilled opium. Graham and I wandered away to talk to other villagers, the girls all wanting to know whether my rings were indeed gold. When we departed Graham and I had a quiet chuckle. Our driver considered that as he was driving the ruler's personal jeep he should be allowed to move off first – apart from ego the practical point was that he did not wish to see us covered in a pall of dust. In his indignation he decided to take a different route and that proved very successful for game spotting. We then found ourselves surrounded by a huge flock of sheep and goats, after which came a stately train of camels. All of this was a delight to us and we passed the time of day with the shepherds and camel herdsmen.

Rajasthan does have large flocks of sheep but in the desert where melons and bitter cucumbers sprawl out across the sand for a few short weeks the camel is king. Nearly three-quarters of India's population still lives a traditional life of subsistence farming. Most villagers are poor. They live in simple thatched huts, sleep on rope charpoys or on the floor, fetch water from communal wells and wash in nearby streams or tanks (man-made pools). Few have any education and medical facilities are patchy but most have just enough to eat and life while hard is not impossible. Living close to the land, nature is venerated and celebrated in a host of festivals marking the seasons. Driving along a dusty road in Rajasthan, with peacocks in the undergrowth and two or three supremely dignified women arrayed in bright red or orange attire, carrying pots on their heads, walking along the roadside, is in my mind's eye. I asked Balvinder to slow down sometimes and waved and made a *namaste* sign of respectful greeting to which they responded eagerly with beautiful grins and shy waves. It warmed my heart to see so many small children on weekdays in school uniform and eager to be there. Education is greatly prized in India; would that it were so in our disadvantaged areas of the United Kingdom.

I was to return to Rajasthan in the following March and then again in May just after the Indian nuclear test. The temperature reached a record 49/50C. The heat was so intense and dry that my face felt crackly and my hair as straw. I thought of the desert people that I had met briefly, those who had no refuge from this intense heat, their simple homes being engulfed by the harsh hot winds called the 'loo' that is a feature in April and May. In the towns there were booths set up on the roadside for people to be given water as they walked and went about their business. I wondered about the villagers we had spoken with and how they were coping and reflected that perhaps they would be equally appalled by the intense cold we suffer in northern countries. Certainly there were several fatalities this hot season. Indeed I found myself drinking at least four litres of mineral water daily to maintain a normal body temperature, and that was with the help of fans and air conditioning.

On our return to Rohet there were the usual sellers of rural fabrics and tourist items. One young girl shyly stood to one side with a cheerful red embroidered throw. It took our fancy and Graham wandered over to bargain – that started a minor scrum but in the end we considered hers was the most attractive and paid the required amount without demur. This was to astonish the sellers and they sweetly pressed us to accept two leather bracelets as well. In the meantime Balvinder Singh had obviously been chatting to all and sundry so several villagers engaged me in conversation and told me who I was – to my surprise. I should not have been however. In India *izat* is important, ie prestige, face, what you will. Balvinder had by now decided that he was not chauffeuring just another couple of tourists and that his passengers were worthy of interest. It is one of the endearing things about Indian life, though I suspect the reverse could be very ugly – if you treat people with courtesy but firmness then you receive it back. Friendship and taking an interest in their welfare, buying the third Pepsi, sharing some fruit, allowing time for rest makes for a happy journey with a contented driver. In India on those diabolical roads where anything goes that can be a life-saving essential!

The dust and dryness were best dealt with by a quick swim and change. All too soon we were leaving Rohet Garh, but I would recommend it to everyone as an oasis of calm and beauty with hospitable host and hostess with plenty of attention to detail. Jodhpur is a short drive away and we arrived at Ajit Bhavan in plenty of time for a light lunch in their enchanting gardens by the side of the pool. We had been allocated a 'rondavel' suite in the grounds and the hotel was completely full. A thoroughly charming place which is well maintained with courteous staff, Ajit Bhavan had been originally a princely palace which has been well adapted. Jodhpur is a pleasant smallish city with a large military contingent. The airport is minute and attractive and looking down from the Meherangarh Fort you survey a haze of blue houses; these are the homes of Brahmins, though I believe blue is being widely used now for its obvious attraction.

Swimming Pool at Ajit Bhavan Hotel, Jodhpur.

Chapter Five

Jodhpur, Osiyan, Jaisalmer and the Desert

Jodhpur was one of the greatest of the Rajput kingdoms, covering a huge 93,240 sq km. The royal family claim descent from the great Deccan Rashtrakuta dynasty between the 8th to 10th centuries and through them to their mythical origin, the sun! On the fall of the Rashtrakuta kingdom they migrated north to Uttar Pradesh, then west. Finally in 1192 Rao Siha moved into the Thar Desert and in 1381 Rao Chunda conquered Mandore. Thus was the desert kingdom of Marwar (Land of Death) and the modern Rathore dynasty born. Centuries ago Jodhpur was a staging post for camel caravans linking China and the Middle East. Today the city has a population of approximately one million but in Indian terms that is small and there are few facilities, though it is the legal capital for Rajasthan. Our guide was a charming articulate young Rajput called Sandeep who gave us an expert tour of the Meherangarh Fort. It is superbly maintained and extremely interesting; the princely cradles and exotic howdahs for ceremonial elephant rides were a highlight for me, whereas the handprints of the various maharanis who committed *sati* or *jauhar* are the most poignant. Some of these courageous women who lived three or four centuries ago fought like men and died by their own hand in self-immolation rather than be vanquished by the intruders. What made our whole afternoon so enjoyable was the interesting conversation with Sandeep, who though he speaks excellent English has his Rajput culture visible in his appearance which seems to lie easily with his young modern Indian approach to life.

Family life still is of the utmost importance to a man like Sandeep Rathore Singh, and he spoke with pride of his family of five brothers and their wives and aspirations. He is a proud father of a little girl and was dismissive of the boy child cult. The wives, however, one felt still lived a reclusive life steeped in Rajput convention, quite different from those in the bustling metropolitan cities. Sandeep was a friendly relaxed guide and introduced us to some wonderful shops in the Sardar Market. This market is a must to my mind for any traveller; a true microcosm of India with all of life going on in and around it. Naturally, faced with the enormous range of wonderful goods, Graham and I succumbed and bought. In fact I was to visit Jodhpur a second time and enjoyed it equally then when visiting the famous spice shop and as a guest of Sandeep in his rooftop restaurant with its simple hospitality.

However it is sobering and timely to remember that Phokran is not far from Jodhpur and the site of India's nuclear testing zone. In May immediately after the two nuclear tests, arriving at Jodhpur airport in the extreme heat of midday, there was an air of military alertness and readiness that had not been evident when I touched down two months previously in March. No one should become so enveloped in the faded grandeur of India's past as to dismiss her current military capability. Indians, be they generals, tourist guides or young thrusting Delhi wallahs were very defensive of their country's actions and made the point forcibly that India had not in fact instigated either war with Pakistan in the 1970s, nor indeed was she seeking to be warlike now. However the distrust of Pakistan and resentment at the help that country appears to have been given by the USA makes ordinary Indians become quite assertive. It is so sad to hear people in their seventies and upwards reminisce about life in places like Lahore before partition. Even now when Indians go to Lahore on a nostalgic trip, more often than not the shopkeepers hark back to the old days and what a beautiful place it was. They are only too well aware that Pakistan by most standards is a bankrupt country with little to offer the outsider.

From Jodhpur it is a short drive to Osiyan. Osiyan was a major trading centre on the camel caravan routes during the Gupta period (3rd–6th century AD). It is now a small market town surrounded by sand dunes. The largest of the Jain temples is dedicated to Mahavira with an idol made of milk and sand covered in 400g of gold and said to be 2,500 years old. We were en route to Jaisalmer and found the whole drive very enjoyable and interesting. The further west you travel into the desert the more dramatic it becomes and I enjoyed it all immensely. Starting after breakfast brings one to Jaisalmer by about 2 pm. Jaisalmer is a name and a place that caught my fancy way back in the '70s. Apparently Indira Gandhi went there to visit the troops in one of the Indo-Pakistan wars and realised its potential. Until that time it was slowly dying. She realised that the tourist potential of a medieval

Intricate carved detail on exterior of Haveli (mansion) in Jaisalmer.

fortress in its remote desert vastness was enormous and so the roads that had to be built to enable the military to function properly were doubly useful, followed by the Indira Gandhi canal which greatly added to the greening of this desert region and gives its population the essential life force.

As one approaches by car, there it is, a magnificent citadel rising from Tricuta Hill like a golden coronet from the desert plain. It is one of the oldest of the Rajasthani forts and was built in 1156 by Prince Jaisal who seized power from his nephew and made it his capital. Legend says the hermit who showed him the spot prophesied that the fort would be sacked two and a half times. Twice in the 14th century the inhabitants committed *jauhar* when faced with retaliatory attacks as a result of their own marauding.

We stayed two nights in Jaisalmer and though we enjoyed ourselves immensely we found our hotel, the Shiv Niwas, badly run by disagreeable staff. It is a fine building and there was no excuse for poor administration by disagreeable people. The food was quite awful. On our first evening we went to Bada Bagh, the royal cremation ground set between the desert and a rain-fed lake, built by Maharawal Jai Singh II. The memorial *chhatris* to the royal dead look superb in the evening light and it is worth it to wait patiently for the sunset. The notice at the Bada Bagh asking people to respect the site and refrain from doing various things is hilarious. The English is so poor that it makes the notice a 'must' to photograph as a modern day contrast to the elegance of centuries past. Sitting, chatting gently, watching the tourist crowds congregate is always interesting. Most of them simply ignore any requests for respectful behaviour. The following morning saw us up early and on the flat roof of our hotel to photograph the sunrise and discreetly observe the awakening in the village houses beneath us. Jaisalmer has turquoise as its predominant colour and in these little houses the daily tasks were being undertaken in-between washing and feeding livestock. The household goat would stand up and declare he was hungry, all the while behaving like a cockerel standing on a wooden chair in the courtyard; morning fires were being lit, old people came onto the doorstep for their ablutions, the *pujari* rang his temple bells. The *gawalior* (milk seller) would drive his cow from place to place followed by the calf – there was a curious subdued feel to it all. After breakfast we ourselves went with a guide to see the citadel. So much of it is impressive but I found it profoundly disappointing that the filth has been allowed to outweigh its charm. This did not prevent our enjoyment but in such a confined space, though we enjoyed our various meetings with locals such as the busy tailor in his little shop, or the housewife preparing lunch, the stench and effluent became overpowering. Other friends have said they are surprised because a few years ago it was still well maintained. What astounded me continually was the immaculate look of all the business men – their dhobis obviously have some magic touch to be able to provide

Gadi Sagar Lake at Jaisalmer.

that degree of freshness amongst the squalor.

In contrast the Gadi Sagar was a refreshing delight. Until 1965 it remained the city's only water supply having been built in 1156 and rebuilt in 1367 by Maharawal Garsi Singh. On a sunny November morning, standing on the steps at the water's edge, it was a serene spot with the vivid blue of the sky contrasting the golden sandstone. The idea of an all-powerful ruler being outmanoeuvred by a prostitute who built the impressive Tilon ki Pol – the palatial archway – was amusing. The story goes that the ruler was so horrified he wanted to tear it down but the astute woman called Tilon speedily built a tiny temple to Krishna on the top of the gate and that ensured the gate's survival. Jaisalmer has a lot to see in the way of architecture, and the various *havelis* are wondrous, we went inside three. One at least is a very attractive shop selling fabrics and *dhurries*. We spent a pleasant hour sipping tea and agonizing about which beautiful item to buy and naturally came out with two. So much of the workmanship is superb and the ethnic art coupled with some pieces of antiquity are breathtaking. Every time I walk into our dining room there are happy memories of that morning when I look at the antique sari bedspread sewn in an intricate panelled design, made out of old silver thread sari borders belonging to long-gone Indian princesses. We have hung this huge piece from a brass rod on an antique red wall and surrounded by Rajasthani miniature paintings from the different schools of art, ie Udaipur, Jodhpur and Jaipur, not forgetting our little friend at Rohet – the painter in residence, who was the only one we actually met. On the floor are two huge *dhurries* bought on a second visit to the famous fabrics' shop in the Sardar Market in Jodhpur. Now that is a young wideawake Indian with superb command of English who is a very persuasive salesman, but knowledgeable with it and not too pushy. When it is possible to take the time to sit down, drink tea and also discuss life with these people the whole business becomes such a happy experience. It is really quite easy to communicate through facial expression and body language when one is seriously not interested! I know that the guides invariably get a percentage commission on the sale, but why not, were it not for them we would not know where to go and provided no-one becomes too pushy everyone can be happy. Outright rip-offs do occur, and I feel we were the victims of one such in Delhi, but then no one pressed us – we simply got carried away with the excitement and ambience.

Lunch that day was a little strange but special and charming. I had read that the Dhola Maru hotel had a good restaurant, so we took the trouble to book a table for lunch and Balvinder duly deposited us there. We were ushered into a strange and enormous basement restaurant and were the only two customers. Graham and I became worried, wondering what was on offer, and since I was only just recovering from a gastric problem a little apprehensive. We need not have been; enthusiastic staff took our vegetarian order and disappeared. One waiter was left to potter around and keep an eye on us. This inevitably led to a conversation in Hindi, which so delighted him that he too rushed off to the confines of the kitchen and eventually the food arrived. It was superb, the delay had been caused by it all being painstakingly freshly cooked – thank goodness – and beautifully presented with enough to feed about six people. In-between mouthfuls the conversation had to continue but they were all delighted at our enjoyment. I am sure at night that restaurant would be a busy place but at lunchtime understandably the tourists were out and about. It proved a cool and friendly haven for us. That afternoon Balvinder and the guide drove us out to Sam Dunes, part of the Desert National Park to experience a camel ride and see the sunset. Our son Stewart had the previous year spent two days in the desert on a camel safari, but neither Graham nor I could have withstood that. It was not really necessary for me, just riding a camel for a short journey fulfilled my wish. Since a baby I have ridden on elephants, indeed even as a small child gently walked up an elephant's trunk to sit on her shoulders. They are the most intelligent creatures and so affectionate once they recognise one; however, camels have an altogether different reputation and I was slightly apprehensive. The camel owner was a cheeky youngster who was very helpful and friendly, his camel was called Kalu. Graham watched me mount and my obvious delight once up there, and then mounted his own beast. The smell was appalling. Camels fart with great vigour and I was downwind of Graham's beast! We were soon joined by a trio of musicians. All over Rajasthan there are musicians and dancers and after a while one can tire of this; I am sure it is the same for travellers who visit Scotland, the pipes must become quite boring along with all the tartanalia. This trio however were fun, they wanted to play, so I said in Hindi it would have to be a short tune as we wanted to get going; this so delighted them that they followed us for quite a distance and eventually we stopped and they sat down in the sand and played a couple of short songs. We applauded and said how much we enjoyed it and took their photo and distributed some money and had the inevitable *limca* drink from a bottle and parted happily. It was fun; just to have walked out to the edge of the desert would have been like going on a pony ride at the zoo when little, but our little troupe of people and the ensuing conversation made it amusing. Finally we said we had gone far enough and then dismounted and waited for the sun to set, all the while talking and laughing with others, mostly Indian who were doing the same thing. Our camel owners took us a little apart to enjoy the silence and the beauty. It brought back memories of another desert in another time. As a small child of five I recalled the sunrise on the edge of the desert at Basra, now in Iraq and a very 'no go' area for Europeans! On that occasion the aircraft in which we were returning to India from a home leave was diverted on the orders of the British Prime Minister to collect British personnel working in the oil fields that had been suddenly nationalised. It had been a remarkable journey as the aircraft had touched down in Cairo in the middle of a serious

Camels awaiting riders at Sam Desert Wildlife Park near Jaisalmer.

political situation and all of us passengers had been stranded at the airport throughout the day, then allowed into the city by bus, crouching under the seats to avoid sniper fire as we were driven. Hardly had we put our heads down in the old Heliopolis Hotel then we were instructed to get back into the bus and depart for the airport, our BOAC flight had been given permission to depart. As we droned on in this horrid Argonaut aircraft the captain of the flight was commanded to divert to Basra and pick up the British evacuees. I was very small but the memory of heat and uncertainty and then the bizarre waiting on the desert's edge by an old Nissan hut for an airport, sitting in wood and rattan chairs in the cold huddled up, just waiting and the sun rising was imprinted on my mind. Now I was watching the sun set and there was an opportunity to reflect on all that had happened in the intervening forty-five years. Memory recall does not actually take very long, but the silence with just a slight breeze stirring and Kalu endlessly chewing and swallowing and regurgitating (as camels do) was impressive. The two Indians had moved away to sit patiently; after all for them this was the equivalent of one of our desk jobs. It was a good experience and then we returned to the tourist car park, but on the way back the camels were frisky, obviously sensing that this was the end of their working day. The young camel owner told me of his young wife and how he planned to expand his business; he asked hopefully for any of my French perfume but I explained that I did not have any on me at the moment! He seemed to accept that readily and was equally pleased with the tip. Driving back to Jaisalmer in the dark with the moon now rising was companionable with the two Indians. We took leave of our guide and thanked Balvinder and said that he should go off and relax as we would find our own way for supper.

We walked through the quiet streets to the roof top restaurant. Walking on Indian streets requires a high degree of vigilance as apart from the traffic the road or pavement can be very messy and full of potholes and open drains. The shops of course were still open and doing business, but already the little households were obviously settling for the night. Our roof top venue was excellent with a superb view of the floodlit citadel. A party of westerners arrived, attired in full Rajasthani dress which we privately thought made them look completely foolish. I suspect that secretly the individuals thought so themselves. Fancy dress is something that is fun when a child, but to see grown hulking Americans decked out in turbans and tunics made it seem rather cheap and demeaning. I thought the world had moved on from the simplistic idea of donning Dutch clogs on a visit to Amsterdam! The food was delicious and as it had taken quite a while to serve us it was late and dark when we carefully descended and wended our way back to our hotel.

We had not brought a torch, but there was some dim street lighting.

However we needed to walk carefully in the little lanes. What followed was a charming experience. All the livestock of each household was tethered outside the respective dwellings. Thus you had to walk carefully between contented cows chewing the cud, bulky buffaloes, goats with their kids, often bedding themselves down on a piece of outdoor furniture. There was a curious serenity about it. Either there was no electricity to this particular area or the households were very frugal but somehow that quiet walk gave one a glimpse of the heart of India. Yes, this was Jaisalmer, the desert showpiece for tourists, but for these simple people it was their village street at night-time. Just as we had observed them that morning rising and preparing for the day ahead this was the peaceful Indian night and they were recovering from a day's work, as were their respective beasts. Tomorrow their routines would all start again.

Chapter Six

Bikaner and the Rat Temple

The next morning saw us up early for our drive to Bikaner. Bikaner had been another place that caught my imagination as a child when shown a photograph of the Maharajah of Bikaner who had formed the Camel Corps to help the British in the Great War. He had also been part of the British War Cabinet and finally been witness to the signing of the Armistice in 1918. Eighty years on to look at the photographs of all that generous loyalty to the British Crown makes one think of these splendid figures of history. Some of them had foresight and a sense of responsibility – others sadly seemed completely profligate and the epitome of decadence. The Maharajah of Bikaner was one of Rajasthan and India's bright stars. We arrived after an uneventful drive to stay in the Lalgarh Palace, still home to the present royal family but also a fine hotel. The Bikaner family were established after the foundation of Jodhpur. Jodha Rathore's second son, Bika, fought with his father legend has it, or more sensibly realised that a second son would not inherit the throne, and thus headed north deep into the desert. In 1488 he founded his own kingdom of Bikaner. Once again, a hermit prophesied that his dynasty would rule safely for four and a half centuries, and that is what happened since 1947 fulfils the time span. Maharajah Ganga Singh who lived from 1887 to 1943 was probably the most enlightened Rajput of his time. He created roads, railways, schools and hospitals and built the Gang canal which provided irrigation for 290,000 hectares of land. At Independence Bikaner became the first Rajput kingdom to join the Indian union. Today it is a thriving city with a medical school, veterinary school, camel breeding farm and a huge dairy industry which supplies the milk for a large proportion of India's sweetmeats that are manufactured throughout India, not just locally. The local clay is used for the manufacture of sanitary ware, and the hides from the beasts are made into leather. I wish in fact we had been able to spend more time, because not being on the eternal tourist route made it a very pleasant small bustling city.

Our suite of rooms in the royal palace was immense, and photographs showed that at one time they had been used by the current viceroy when visiting. To my mind staying in heritage hotels and establishments makes it all so much more enjoyable; after all one five or four star hotel in any country is much like another. It would have been nice to see the palace in better condition but from various refurbishments that were taking place that appears to be on the agenda. However, it is always difficult to achieve the perfect touch of maintained history, not overgilded restoration and country house hotel opulence. After a pleasant lunch we set off to visit the Camel Breeding Farm which had been set up in 1975 by the central government to research their habits and create a superior breeding stock. The Bikaner camel is a more robust larger beast than the camel seen around Jaisalmer.

Our guide was a charming man with a wealth of knowledge. It transpired that Vijay Singh's father, who is still alive, had been in the army and been honoured by the building of a roundabout at Jaisalmer to commemorate his heroic feats in the war between India and Pakistan in 1965. It is not normal to commemorate a living hero in this way but he is unique. Vijay Singh was obviously a man of influence in Bikaner with a few interests. His love of family and the ease with which he talked of daily life coupled with his vast historical knowledge made him a good companion.

The camel farm was interesting particularly for Graham who is a vet. We were able to meet one of the vets through Vijay's friendship and have a pleasant discussion. Graham has practised in his own small animal practice, lectured and researched and been a clinician at university and now he manages a large part of an animal charity. So often one meets foreign vets who come to the UK to study or attend conferences, but it is seldom we are able to see them in their own environment. We have a worldwide friendship or acquaintanceship with vets and many of the challenges they face are common throughout the world, but camels are not an everyday beast so proved interesting. It was to be the afternoon of animals, moving from a huge beast of burden to a small creature normally found under the heading 'vermin'!

The Karni Mata Temple at Deshnok is 32 kms south west of Bikaner and our very good friend Monu Basu had said we must visit it. Well we did, but even Balvinder seemed a bit queasy and admitted he had never been before. Vijay Singh however was full of enthusiasm and explained the legend. Durga, the goddess of war, came down to earth as Karni Mata for 151 years, six months and two days. She was renowned as a miracle worker and she married a member of the Charan family – the local rulers. Legend has it that the family members jeered at her powers, refusing to believe in her divinity, so she turned them into rats. The alternative version is that the family came to her when the young son of one of the brothers died. Karni Mata pleaded with Yama, god of death and the child returned to life, however in exchange all members of the Charan family have to live one life as a rat between human incarnations. Upwards of 20,000 rats at Deshnok are therefore treated with deference and fed by hand on sugar and grain because they are considered honorary humans. As one approaches the temple gates the odd rodent escapes and people lovingly shoo them back or scoop them up and return them. By now I was feeling extremely twitchy as going into the temple required taking off my shoes and walking about in bare feet. Graham's jovial veterinary approach I noticed was also leaving him rapidly but he too agreed to do it. Somehow Balvinder managed to enter the confines but hold onto his *chapals* (sandals). We however would not have managed that as we were the only Europeans present and thus under close scrutiny. The whole experience was not too intimidating, but when several rats come and sniff at one's bare feet on the filthy marbled floor it is difficult not to run back. Legend has it that if one is lucky enough to actually see one of the four white rats then good fortune will be round the corner. The place was dirty and literally covered in rats, with people eagerly wanting to touch them and stroke them. Graham thought he would

The Karni Mata Rat Temple near Bikaner.

pop his head into the holy of holies and approached the shrine, but just then a rat scampered over his foot and he had visions of it racing up his trouser leg and he beat a rapid retreat. I too was worried though wearing an ankle length skirt. Suddenly Balvinder thumped me on the back, in itself a remarkable gesture, because normally Indian men do not gratuitously touch women, and not in the driver to western passenger relationship. "Ma'am, come quickly," he directed, "I have seen the white rat," and so I did, almost slipping in heaven knows what. Yes, I did just see the white rat and showed proper pleasure and satisfaction. All around were over the moon. We duly left and retreated to the car. Graham and I were quite pleased with ourselves and we all chatted happily on the return journey. When we reached our suite I washed my feet vigorously in hot soapy water and sponged out my shoes as well, but no harm befell me or Graham. We were unadventurous and dined in the hotel which was pleasant though unremarkable. The great red sandstone building had been built in 1902 and encapsulates the royal Rajput slightly heavy look. Edwardian architecture in India, even if built for an Indian, inevitably had a westernized look to it, and quite naturally so if actually designed by a European. Standing in the moonlight on the sandstone terrace or plinth that probably had been designed to accommodate the Maharaja's band or visiting musicians, I could almost see the pomp and ceremony of a bygone era – perhaps a visiting viceroy for the shooting, or maybe a member of British royalty doing the grand tour of India; it is not difficult to produce these pictures in my mind's eye because I am fortunate enough to own a very rare copy of *The Face of Mother India*, the sequel to the book *Mother India*, both by Katherine Mayo. This book is so rare that even all our Indian friends pounce on it when given the opportunity. The narrative is factual and traces the history of the subcontinent, but it is the pictures that are archival and superb and capture the whole spirit of empire, dynasties, grandeur, pomp and the mystery and magic of India. The book does not seek to minimise the subcontinent's huge problems of poverty and segregation. To a young reader such as myself all those years ago it was mind boggling. Yes, I was living in India and took much of what went on around me for granted, but when I read the simple account of the reason and ritual I was appalled. My privileged childhood did not really expose me much to the harsh realities of unforgiving caste and inherent poverty or destitution. My ancestors had served the British Crown through both military and civilian life, theirs had been a privileged if sometimes difficult time; indeed some had played important parts in the subcontinent's history and been duly recognised. My grandmother Aline de Veria had been a schoolgirl with the girl who was to become famous as the Maharani of Cooch Behar, known to all as 'Ma'. Together they had written and illustrated (my grandmother painted the pictures) a book called *Bengal Dacoits and Tigers*. My great-grandfather William Rose had as his greatest friend the Maharajah of Patiala and they were neighbours up in Mussorie in the foothills of the Himalayas. Great–grandfather William had at Patiala's request built him a railway for his state, and been rewarded with beautiful mansions built to his specification. William had also helped Godwin Austin with the Survey of India as a much younger man. My grandfather Geoffrey Rose's eye had been shot accidentally by the Patiala heir when they were young teenagers. Grandfather wore a glass eye which was not even discovered by the army until he suffered a severe bout of dysentery and was hospitalised. On discovery he was honourably discharged from the army but by this time was a Lt. Colonel, who had served in the Middle East in the First World War. Both Roses, father and son, were engineers, and I thought of how that had leapt two generations to my own sons who are both graduate engineers, one serving in the army as I write, once more in Bosnia. In Field Marshal Lord Roberts' book *Forty-one Years in India* he diarized how the Commander in Chief, General Sir Hugh Rose, treated him with such kindness when serving as his ADC. In time when he himself became Commander in Chief William Rose was Lord Roberts' ADC.

Recently I had the pleasure of listening to a most distinguished Indian lady called Babli Bhagat recalling her early days as an army officer's wife. Babli also has the rare gift of clear memory and ability to recall defining moments. She lives in Mumbai with her charming husband 'Brig'. They are now senior in years but when they reminisce one is spellbound. Brig's younger brother won the VC at the age of 22 in Eritrea, Brig himself is a brigadier. Babli's early married life when she was only about 20 years of age gave her all sorts of opportunities. She had achieved a double Masters by the age of 20 but wartime India was still a very conservative place and there were only certain types of jobs open to a well-born Indian lady. Teaching was one of them but petrol rationing made it impossible for her to take up the position offered and so at the suggestion of her parents, who were distinguished in their own right, she joined the military, and was put in the women's arm of the Indian Navy. After six months she was commissioned and stationed in Calcutta. She recollected with clarity receiving the news that her first husband's brother had been killed in the Japanese theatre of war. This recollection was very similar to my own mother Barbara's upon receiving the telegram to say my father was missing. In fact Daddy had made an astonishing escape with his Indian men and helped to sail the Wu Chang all the way to Colombo and resume his wartime career. Babli's brother-in-law was not in fact dead but a prisoner of war of the Japanese. Babli was sent to London to represent the Indian Navy along with one or two others and this coincided with the end of the war in Europe and she recounted her memories of VE Day in May 1945. Everyone who was there must have unforgettable experiences, and Babli regretted that being so young she did not quite appreciate how historic the day was, but nevertheless she and her little band of friends had some splendid experiences, listening to Churchill, seeing him on the balcony and then later on the balcony of Buckingham Palace with the King and Queen and young princesses. Just finding something pleasant to eat was hard enough but these young women managed with her personality to find themselves tables at notable hotels like The Savoy for a sophisticated but swift meal. The alternative had been spam sandwiches laid on by their mess. Before departing for India Babli gave her two white silk saris that comprised Indian naval uniform for female officers to a good friend who made them into a very beautiful wedding dress.

Immediate post-war India was full of promise for eager, educated and well-born Indians and for me, a post war baby, it is fascinating to listen to them recalling events leading up to Independence and its aftermath. The prophet of Bikaner has said the dynasty would retain power for four and a half centuries. How true were his words. Within the space of a few months was born the world's largest democracy. In the last days of empire new names and faces would become household names, but some things go full circle; my mother told Field Marshal Sir Claude Auchinleck, "Commander in Chief, you are late, and because of that I have missed the parade I so much wanted to witness – I had to feed my baby ...". The Auk, suitably admonished, apologised profusely and insisted he did not make a habit of being late. That was at Bareilly for the Regimental Reunion of 1947 when several of the soldiers were decorated either posthumously or in person for their courage. I daresay he stayed in the suite of rooms we occupied fifty years later!

Babli recalls those early days of Panditji as Prime Minister. His gentle but firm charm when interviewed by her for a newspaper; yes, she came to breakfast at the instigation of Indira and enjoyed a relaxed family meal and was able to absorb the prime ministerial daily routine, but no, he would not be photographed standing on his head, that was a yoga position to be enjoyed in privacy. She recalls walking out to the car after breakfast and little Rajiv, his grandson, was holding his hand in the way companionable four-year-olds do. On being asked by his *nana* (maternal grandfather) which rose he should put in his buttonhole he would gravely choose one and the *mali* would cut it and fashion it for a buttonhole. Then they would walk to the car with smart attendant driver and guards, and Rajiv would say, "Nana going or not going?" the little face anxious and hopeful. Sometimes he was rewarded with the trip to the office as a treat by his grandfather.

On reflection I think India was the loser; if Babli had been able to enter politics as she longed to do she would have been a great influence for moderation and integrity, but as she had married at an early age to a potentially very successful army officer who later became General Sen,

DSO there was no question of it as politics would have crippled his military career. However her position as a senior army officer's wife gave her opportunities not open to others and she was able to use them constructively and form balanced judgements. Panditji, Indira, Rajiv, Sanjay, these are now the modern legends, and I have no doubt that somewhere there was a prophet who would have prophesied some of the tragedy that enfolded them.

Bikaner's Junagarh Fort is the only fort in Rajasthan that has never been conquered. Built in 1588 it has now been carefully restored and is filled with fabulous furniture and other treasures such as two World War I planes. Oddities abound like the Maharaja's bed which is so low on the ground to prevent assassins from hiding beneath and so short the Maharajah would presumably sleep with his feet on the ground – in readiness to stand up and fight. Bikaner has a wealth of interest but we were harnessed to a schedule that required us to leave at midday.

As we drove in the heat of the day Balvinder soon suggested we drop into a motel for a short rest and fluid intake. We were only too happy to agree and we stopped and had a cool drink whilst he ate a proper lunch. This odd little rest house was obviously on the side of the road but gave one an opportunity to wander in its grounds and the staff came to talk. It had been opened by Rajiv Gandhi, it transpired, a week before his assassination and his portrait was freshly garlanded in the entrance. The crop around us, I was informed, was peanut and there were the usual other semi-desert crops and an empty swimming pool surrounded by oleanders and bougainvillea. Again there was that peculiar peace one can find even in tumultuous India, with the sound of the busy raucous birds and the bells of some nearby goats. Having met Rajiv on a plane journey when we were both teenagers returning to UK I was still moved by his portrait with its fresh garland of marigolds. There had been a man on whom greatness and destiny had been thrust; he had not wanted it and thus perhaps was not trained to it, and yet honestly who could be wise enough to take up the reins of:

> '... the land of dreams and romance, of fabulous wealth and fabulous poverty, of splendour and rags, of palaces and hovels, of famine and pestilence, of dginns and giants ... of tigers and elephants, the cobra and the jungle; the country of a hundred nations and a hundred tongues, of a thousand religions and two million gods, cradle of the human race, mother of history, grandmother of legend, great grandmother of tradition ...'

and so it goes on, the famous quotation by Mark Twain made in 1897 from *More Tramps Abroad*. The only portion I could remember looking out on the fields was 'This is indeed India! the land of dreams and romance ...' but I resolved to look it up on my return. A hundred years on those words are as apposite as ever.

Chapter Seven

Dundlod and the Shekhavati Region

We were entering the Shekhavati area. The region between Bikaner Jaipur and Alwar was originally a province of Jaipur but it takes its name from Rao Shekhaji who lived in the 15th century. He declared Independence in 1471 but to this day there are no major cities and it has numerous small forts and palaces and was home to a remarkable group of Marwaris, who are merchants renowned throughout India for their financial acumen and resulting wealth. I recall some of the famous names in my childhood like Goenkor who were the billionaires of India. They had made vast fortunes in the last two centuries and some of them had spent money on building grand *havelis* in their respective home towns. For the most part these appear to be in disrepair, or run down, but are nevertheless interesting. A skeleton staff inhabits most of the properties and will show you around. There are still some fine frescoes depicting cavalries comprising elephants, horses and camels – martial expeditions appear to have been a favourite subject but since it is all so crumbly and shabby there is not a lot of charm. I wish the wealthy men who own these ancient buildings would spend some of their vast wealth on expert and sympathetic restoration, with an eye to cleaning up the little towns. As in other parts of India the countryside is beautiful but the towns fill one with sadness and some anger. Those who have been fortunate in life and in generational continuity should feel responsibility towards their place of origin. We continued on the small side roads that eventually led us to Dundlod. This was an intriguing destination. The exterior is like a fort with high, strong walls and little of architectural beauty. We drove up to the entrance gate and a servant came out to greet us. We were asked to sign in and then escorted up some old stone stairs to our suite. It was a place of character and charm, evidence of grandeur and history all around us. The bedroom was furnished in an old-fashioned style, and the bathroom had the most enormous marble bath that made me think of a tomb. We had requested tea and the cheerful staff member had said, "Yes, of course." I heard him talking to someone so I left the room and went on the roof terrace. There was a courtly gentleman who welcomed me and said, "Ah, you must be Aline Dobbie and you were born in Bareilly!" "Yes," I responded, "but how did you know?" "Well," said Thakur Ranbir Singh, "your driver is very proud of you and trumpets your arrival!" A charming story but I suspect the wise old *thakur* quickly makes a beeline for the recent arrival's driver and gives him the third degree, or maybe a cross between the two possibilities. Staying at Dundlod is a charming respite and one could not want for a more interesting host. Four more guests joined us in due course; they were Swiss and good company. Suddenly the electricity failed which was inevitable but tiresome as it left some of us with wet hair. We all sat in the dark on the terrace and hoped the current would resume in time for dinner. Mercifully it did and we went down into the dining room for the meal. It was good but not memorable. Where there is a hostess the cuisine reaches higher levels. However the Dundlod family were charming as I was to meet them subsequently in Jaipur at their town house. Ranbir Singh's conversation ranged over all the famous princely houses to whom he was related and we were able to have an excellent conversation about people and events over the past forty years. He is also related to the Patialas and thus was interested in my family's connection there and he pulled out some wonderful old black and white photographs going back to 1911 and the Delhi Durbar. All his uncles had been polo players and some of them had been friends with my late father. Ranbir himself is a playwright and author and considers himself a 'leftie', but he is sufficiently aware of his lineage to be able to recount the past and its glories vividly. The following morning we were up early and in time for the sunrise and the *pujari's* call to worship. I looked down on the sleepy little town from the fort's high walls and beyond its boundary – there was Balvinder making ready for the day, he always managed to look smart and fresh and I realised how blessed we were to have him as our driver. The previous evening both Swiss couples had recounted horrendous stories of their respective drivers' recklessness. Driving is to my mind the only way to see and experience Rajasthan but one does want to reach one's final destination in one piece.

Ranbir told me there were eleven schools now in Dundlod and that was satisfying. Hopefully some of those immensely wealthy *marwaris* channel some of that money into educational and medical improvements if not town planning and renovation. Certainly the aristocracy no longer has the money, nevertheless they possess the dignity. Dundlod is charming but desperately in need of sympathetic refurbishment and indeed maybe that will take place soon as I notice Dundlod features in many advertised itineraries for Indian Grand Tours. We breakfasted on the terrace which was a delight but sadly Graham began to feel really ill (it was a heavy cold probably caught on the flight out), and we resumed our journey to Jaipur, which was not far.

Chapter Eight

Jaipur on Three Occasions

Jaipur (City of Jai) was built by Maharajah Jai Singh II, ruler of Amber and a man ahead of his time. Aged 11 years he was the protégé of Aurangzeb (son of Shah Jahan), a most terrible man if you consider what he did to most of his close family. Jai Singh II was responsible for building the new

Amber Palace on the outskirts of Jaipur.

city following the Hindu principles of perfect architecture with a grid of nine blocks (two occupied by the palace). Main roads were 33m wide and side roads 4m. The local aristocracy and merchants were directed to build courtyard style *havelis*, and the streets were built with colonnades providing shade from the sun to pedestrians. Sadly these have all been inbuilt now and the charm has faded, but for an early 18th century builder his ideas were superb and the 'old pink city' remains intact. Jai Singh II was building his new city before Edinburgh's New Town was conceived. How I wish the present City of Jaipur would embark on a restoration programme and restore it to the jewel it must have been. When Rajputana became Rajasthan, Jaipur became its capital and is now a city of about two million inhabitants.

Having visited Jaipur three times recently I have been fortunate enough to have enjoyed each visit, though none of them were long enough. On each occasion I had the company of an excellent guide who became a friend, Veni Madhaw Sharma. Sharmaji is well educated and knows his history and was a good companion on the first afternoon. Graham retired to bed in the very welcome four star hotel run by Clarks. Being ill in India as a traveller is not funny and a comfortable bed, en suite bathroom and efficient room service and well stocked 'fridge with bottled mineral water is a haven. I set out in the company of Sharma and Balvinder to see the city. The first stop was Jantar Mantar. This literally means 'instrument to make calculations' and it was built between 1728 and 1734. The Jaipur observatory was the largest and most ambitious of five astronomical observatories constructed by Jai Singh II. He became an astronomer. It has 18 different instruments used to plot the movement of the sun, stars and moon, and calculate time, date, season, the monsoon and the signs of the zodiac. Sharma showed me the Jantar Mantar in detail and when we checked the time on the hour clock with my battery watch, it was precise and correct to the second! Sharma has to take hundreds of visitors so he asked me to go up the world's largest sundial by myself. I did but decided that coming down was no joke as one can only move sideways to one side holding the wall which pulls a muscle in one leg descending the steep steps. However the climb had been worth it for the photographic viewpoint of the whole Jantar Mantar and the rear of the Hawa Mahal. From there we progressed to the City Palace. This was built at the same time as the pink city and is immensely interesting. Probably the most interesting of all the items were the huge silver urns weighing over 340 kg which were commissioned by Madho Singh II, who filled them with Ganges water to take for his visit for the King's coronation in 1902 in London. Jaipur is the city of jewels and so Sharma took me to a huge jeweller's where I saw gems the like of which I have never seen before. I was looking for a pair of emeralds and was shown several but in the end they could not find me a perfect baguette cut pair. The price was

Jantar Mantar.

Jantar Mantar Observatory at Jaipur.

completely reasonable and in the end I bought garnets which are the local stone for family members. The jeweller agreed to make up a necklace of pearls and garnets in an 'opera' length designed as a gift for my daughter-in-law to be. Her birthday falls at the end of January and the garnet is her birthstone. Visiting these jewellers is worthwhile and people should not think they will be exploited. Provided you know what you want and have some idea of the costs in the West you can make a good bargain. I would stress however that these are large reputable jewellers with sophisticated showrooms, mercifully air-conditioned, with cool bottled drinks on hand!

The evening was not a total success. Graham had made a determined effort and showered and changed and I did likewise. The prospect of the Rambagh Palace Hotel was enticing. Built by Ram Singh II, this superb palace was home of the Maharajahs and had its own polo ground. It is superb and sumptuous but not overdone. We had decided to dine and were disappointed that the grandest of the three restaurants was booked out – as it happened, fortuitously so! Graham was still feeling awful but enjoyed a drink in the famous Polo Bar. I lapped it up because the photographs on the walls in this elegant room were all in my memory. Jai, the great glamorous polo player, was known to me from countless polo games in the 1950s and early '60s. Looking at the pictures and trophies, I reflected that it was fitting that he had died from heart disease at the end of a polo match in England. A sad and shocking end for his grieving wife but a wonderful way to go for him! I chose a cocktail which included cream as an ingredient. It seemed delicious, but within minutes I was feeling very odd – since I had decided on non-alcoholic, I knew it was not liquor causing me problems. We went into dine and in no time at all I was feeling seriously unwell. Stupidly I ate and then without a word disappeared to the ladies. Doubtless the elegant fellow inmates of the ladies' cloakroom thought I was another foolish woman who could not hold her drink. I was too busy to care! When I returned to the restaurant Graham said I was a pale shade of green and we both laughed weakly. What else to do, we had looked forward so much to an evening at The Rambagh, one of the great hotels of the world, only to both feel seriously unwell and incapable of enjoying it. When the resplendent doorman called up our car, Balvinder asked had we had a lovely time, so we replied weakly had he, since he too was dining with a friend and fellow driver. "Oh yes," they replied, "an excellent meal." I declined to elaborate on our experiences.

The next day found us both feeling much better and eager to see Amber. Sharma arrived to collect us and we set off for the Fort. It lives up to one's expectations. Built in 1592 the Kuchwaha family reigned here since the 11th century and the surrounding hills are covered in ruins. The ruler Bihar Mal married his daughter Jodhbai to Akbar who built Fatehpur Sikri. Here was a family that not only agreed terms of coexistence with the Mughuls but married into the Mughul dynasty. The waters of Moata Sagar reflect in the bright sunlight the brooding vastness of the fort, and it is fitting that we travel the final few hundred metres by elephant. It was so long since I had ridden an elephant and Graham never had. We had fun and enjoyed ourselves, but I was also sorry to see the great animals so exploited; however that is India and one should be grateful that the tourist trade enables these elephant owners to make a reasonable living. I have a lovely picture of an elephant in downtown Jaipur, perfectly framed through the car window, juxtapositioned with an ancient cycle rickshaw. Somehow that picture encapsulates India, pedestrians, rickshaw wallahs, elephants, car passengers and scooter riders. Sharma gave us a most comprehensive tour of Amber and also treated us to tea in the shade for a rest. On the return journey we paused and looked at Jal Mahal in the centre of the Man Sagar, which I notice Ford are using as a backdrop for their advertisements in western newspapers. There is a great deal to see like the Gaitor and Maharani-ki-Chhatri (Kings' and Queens' cenotaphs) and Jaigarh Fort, which is another magnificent mountain stronghold dating back to the 11th century but rebuilt by Jai Singh II in 1726.

On a second visit to Jaipur in March I stayed with the Nawab and Begum of Loharu at Loharu House. They run their city mansion as a charming Pay and Stay establishment. The welcome is very personal and the attention and service could not be improved. I personally greatly valued my conversation with the Loharu couple and revelled in their household of atten-

Jaipur's ancient means of transport.

tive friendly servants and the feeling of family that took me back to my own childhood; excellent food with little details like homemade jams and chutneys from the garden produce. The garden is large and well maintained with an orchard area and back garden. Loharu is a small place north of Jaipur, technically in Haryana, but like Dundlod and Mandawa. The Nawab is a parliamentarian and at the time of my visit thinking deeply on the new Indian Government and its widely publicised religious beliefs and trumpeted intolerance of other religions. We both hoped that it was part of the rhetoric of general elections and that their more pragmatic personalities would have a benign influence. The Nawab was very well travelled and over the years had met many world-famous people who were all captured in photographs positioned round the drawing room. We did not in fact sit in this room, preferring the verandah, but it was irresistible as a photo subject with its great stuffed tiger standing in the centre. On this occasion I had driven from Jodhpur to Jaipur and resolved firmly to never do such a dangerous thing again. That particular stretch of road is part of the main Delhi to Mumbai highway and a constant stream of heavy overladen lorries travel night and day at breakneck speed, with total disregard for other road users. We were pushed off the road on three occasions and had our car's driver's side mirror ripped off. All along the road there are wrecks and obvious signs of fatalities. On this occasion we did not have the trusty Balvinder and were the poorer for his absence. Indian drivers are very good if one considers the driving conditions and overpopulation, but some are either lacking in imagination or anxious to reach a further incarnation.

On my third visit to Jaipur on business in May we stayed at the Rajputana Sheraton and were very thankful for its air conditioning and elegant facilities. The Welcome Group, who own the various Sheraton hotels such as the Maurya in Delhi and others in all the major cities, have a special place in my heart as the company is part of the great ITC Group, one of the huge conglomerates that bestride the Indian industrial and commercial scene. Indeed one of our greatest friends, Monu Basu, had been its managing director, but in my teenage years he had been a junior executive to my late father. This was the start of a great friendship and to this day both Monu and Champak Basu are inclined to remind me that they have known me since a child of 12 if they think I am getting above myself. I in turn recollect that their very talented daughter Srila, who is India's only glass-blowing artist, used to leap into my lap as a tiny child in 1962 and demand to know how many babies I had and who was my 'uncle', ie husband. I would say no babies and no husband – which was a relief all round considering I was only 15, but Srila would leap off in disgust and my standing in her eyes was ruined!

The heat of May was truly stunning and I would not recommend that time of year for purely tourist activities, however there were many from Spain and France and I wondered how they could endure the heat in the various tourist attractions and outside. We had flown into Jaipur on this occasion and the day had reached a record temperature which made the aircraft's landing particularly difficult for the lady pilot with all the thermal currents. I had again been saddened as it was the anniversary of Rajiv Gandhi's death and all the papers were full of commemorative photographs, and here we were on an Indian Airlines aircraft, which in his vital days as a young man he had probably captained himself. Jaipur like Jodhpur has a good airport and is well maintained. My strong recommendation to travellers would be to arrive by air or rail or perhaps from the north by car, but on no account from Jodhpur by road. In the extreme heat the importance of colour seemed to strike me more forcibly. Colour has great significance in traditional Rajasthani dress. Only Rajput men can wear yellow turbans, those who are Brahmins can wear orange and yellow, while businessmen wear orange, lower castes dark red, and farmers and those in mourning, white. The younger women wear saris or embroidered skirts and bodices of pink, red, yellow and orange; those in black, blue, green, grey or white are widows.

On this last occasion we were able to visit Anokhi and see some of the wonderful hand-printed clothes, soft furnishings and accessories. They now have shops in many countries but Jaipur was the origin and the shop is a delight. Now in two of my bedrooms the bright and cheerful colours of Rajasthan are reminders of a happy time. Lovers of blue and white would find it particularly worthwhile. The last two days in Jaipur in May were enjoyable as we were able to relax a little and were treated to some excellent and friendly hospitality by the manager of the Rajputana Sheraton, George Verghese. George originates in Kerala and extolled its virtues to us. Indeed I already knew because Hamish, our eldest son, and his wife Vicky went there for their honeymoon at the end of 1997 and had a glorious time. They had rented a villa close to Kovalam beach and also visited Cochin, and experienced a backwaters' journey on a houseboat, with glorious food and a gentle mode of transport. They had managed to fit in a visit to Periyar and ride elephants and help to bathe them, and their photographs are truly beautiful. George did not have to persuade us too much that Kerala should be our next destination in India. Indeed Babli Bhagat urges us to fly out to stay with them in Mumbai and then all of us should go down to Kerala to a friend's house – yes, that indeed would be special. Being a houseguest in India is so relaxing. Indians are famous for their hospitality and justifiably so. Nothing gives me greater pleasure than to be enfolded in the heart of a large Indian family and enjoy their spirited conversations and leisure pursuits, golf being high on their agenda.

This essence of family I had further experienced in Bareilly in March. Had someone said to me that after thirty-five years I would be back in Bareilly twice in five months I would have laughed, but so it was. We were able to share their Holi festivities. The traditional Hindu festival of colour celebrates the end of winter, the destruction of the demon Holika and the veneration of Kama, god of love, and his wife Rati, goddess of passion. People mark the day by bombarding each other with coloured water, dye, or in poorer villages watery clay and cattle dung and by drinking marijuana-based *bhang*. In various cities there are also accompanying festivals like in Jaipur which has its Elephant Festival. However as a guest of the Commandant of the Jat Regimental Centre we played a rather dignified version of Holi, with, I am glad to say, pure colour powder with no adulterations that might be harmful. We arrived at 8.00 am having left Delhi on a nightmare drive at 4.00 am, to avoid roadside revellers. Even in the darkness one could see people lighting the spring fire and winding themselves up for further merriment. Our journey suddenly became very dangerous because we drove into a pea soup fog and the driver and I decided to proceed with extreme caution as there was nowhere on the roadside where we could stop safely; no one else thought of stopping and the idea of a huge lorry driving into the back of us was appalling. However we suddenly drove out of the fog into the sunrise and Bareilly on Holi day awaited us. Satish and Saroj Kumar were still in their nightclothes but welcomed us warmly and the telephone started ringing with everyone calling to wish 'Happy Holi' rather as we would say 'Happy Christmas'. The Jat House staff were happy to see me again and plied us with sweetmeats and sweet tea. We were shown to our suite and chose the one adjacent to the previously used set of rooms. Gurung, who was in excellent form, arranged some fruit for breakfast and then we changed for the Holi party. The officers and their families all came in old and shabby clothes, but we had not brought our gardening togs and anyway I suspect it would not have met with approval had I arrived in some faded dungarees! We were driven to Jat House and the moment we arrived the young officers who recognised me from my previous visit covered us in bright yellow and red and orange powder. The obvious affection and friendship was heart-warming and I loved it all. To be in Bareilly, my birthplace, on a clear beautiful spring day with the Jat House garden ablaze with flowers, friendly people hugging one and smearing one's face and hair, well, that is a unique experience and one of my most treasured memories. Food was laid out as a buffet and we gorged ourselves on further *namkins* and sweetmeats. Gurung was the most attentive of stewards, and how I wished Graham could have been there along with our two sons. This was a regimental family in the Indian Army enjoying itself on one of its special days. Tiny tots ran around and were scooped up and plastered with yellow powder, the Brigadier was having a wonderful time as were the young men, then Colonel Vijay Singh arrived and I was so pleased to see him and meet his wife, who was so gentle and murmured that she was fasting for the day. Having been a guest in British Army messes with our son Hamish, it was lovely to experience the present buzz and exuberance of their counterparts in the Indian Army. Lunch was to be at the Officers' Mess and I cleaned up a bit for that. The officers and their families were going to play Housey Housey and we joined in, it was amusing. Finally lunch was served and I was invited to help myself to food along with the Brigadier's wife. There was a glorious array and silence gradually reigned whilst we all ate with enthusiasm. Brigadier Satish and his wife then said they would leave and that was the signal that we would all disband. A welcome shower was in order and a scrub of the clothes I had worn – mercifully the cleaning agent with which I always travel now made short work of the garments, but curiously it took much longer to rid oneself of the colour in the hair and skin, though by the next day it had completely disappeared without any allergic reaction. Sitting on the verandah outside our suite, I saw Gurung cycle by, off-duty now and ready to play Holi with his fellow soldiers. Shyly they would come and chat to me whilst I wrote a letter home. These young soldiers and their older brothers in arms are fine people, with an eagerness to learn and communicate. This time I had brought them the colour photos of Hamish and Vicky's wedding and they were delighted with that as it showed the ceremonial uniforms of the British Army and all the colour and tradition of a big wedding. In-between the chat was that peculiar silence again, interspersed by the call of the peacock on the wall, some chattering monkeys and the noisy seven sisters' birds. I was weary after my pre-dawn departure and the stress of the car journey, but I did not want to sleep and miss any of the experiences on offer. Fortunately the photographs of that happy day have developed beautifully and will always be a memento.

Above Left: Aline Dobbie covered in colour playing Holi with Jat Regiment officers.

Above Right: Brigadier Satish and his wife, Saroj.

Left: Army Officers' children.

61

Chapter Nine

Chandra Mahal, Deeg and Bharatpur

When we said farewell to Sharmaji that first time in November we left for Chandra Mahal Haveli at Pehersar, just within the boundaries of Rajasthan, very close to Bharatpur and Deeg. This is a Jat area and the Jat farmers constitute a small percentage of population and are chiefly concentrated in areas close to Delhi and Haryana. Rajasthan had two Jat kingdoms, Bharatpur and Dholpur, but it is believed by some that the Shekhawati region was also held by the Jats. Our host at Chandra Mahal is a Jat with an illustrious father who in his young days had been Commandant of the Governor General's Bodyguard to Lord Mountbatten. Our host is married to a beautiful woman from the Jodhpur royal house and together they run a superb establishment in their ancestral home. Young Amit, our travel arranger, had wisely thought to book us in here, and we were so pleased with the arrangement. Munna and Giri Singh are charming and the house is beautifully but simply appointed and one is invited to feel as a personal guest. The cooking is a celebration and the rooms are simple and attractive. The architecture of the mansion-cum-fort is very heavy on the exterior but true to the *haveli* tradition there is an inner courtyard off which there are verandahs and suites of rooms, with narrow little stairs taking one to the flat rooftop from which there is an excellent view into the village surroundings. The gardens are a picture, and since I was lucky enough to be a luncheon guest in March as well, I know that they provide a colourful haven throughout the tourist months. Indeed Giri's hollyhocks were to be envied and when we remarked upon them in November she imme-diately directed her *mali* to provide me with some seeds. I thought that a few in an envelope would be forthcoming, but in fact I came back with a full plastic bag and today there are hollyhocks from Rajasthan growing in Peeblesshire. That first evening I ran up to the roof to see the setting sun and try to photograph it, but in fact I had to be patient until the sun-rise because the light had gone very quickly. In the morning light it was enchanting watching yet again Indian village life at the start of the day, with the little children waving and calling greetings. The buffaloes were coming out of their byres and a village woman was busy sculpting cow pats into cakes to dry on the roof to make fuel for her family. A peacock was busy pecking at a pumpkin plant that was growing nearby on the roof and the road sweeper was making a faint effort to clean up the main mud thoroughfare.

We left Chandra Mahal to visit the Keoladeo Ghana Bird Sanctuary at Bharatpur. Today it is world famous for its bird life but before Independence its fame was more generic. Bharatpur was the premier Jat state and is a legacy of Churaman, a Jat overlord whose forces were a source of con-stant irritation to the Mughals in the late 17th century. The Mughals retali-ated by destroying the Jat villages but they later regrouped under a leader called Baden Singh who firmly entrenched himself in the region beside the Jamuna river between Agra and Delhi. Baden Singh built the fort and pal-ace of Deeg in 1725. A short time later his son laid the foundation nearby of the fort at Bharatpur. Bharatpur's fort was never taken by the British though they laid siege to it several times. The fort was made impregnable through the simple device of surrounding it with massive earth walls and a moat. Today Bharatpur has little charm, in my view, but is a must to visit for the bird sanctuary. Deeg however is a showcase of Jat architecture and has several trophies of war including a marble swing that belonged to Shah Jahan and was taken by Maharaja Suraj Mal in his successful sack of both Delhi and Agra forts.

We started our day by a visit to the bird sanctuary. Upon arrival a large problem emerged. We had sufficient funds in travellers' cheques and credit cards but we appeared to be very low in Indian currency. There was a small entry fee to pay and then the rickshaw wallah to pay and it is not a good idea to be without small change in India at any time. Balvinder sweetly offered us some money and a young rickshaw wallah came up and asked us to use his services. We said yes but that we had this problem with a cash shortage. Devi Singh was his name and he confidently said that it would be no problem and we should go with him. It is lovely once one enters the park as only authorized vehicles are allowed and everyone else has to use a cycle or a cycle rickshaw. The atmosphere was peaceful and relaxing and already the heat of the day was increasing. Devi Singh first of all took us to the Forest Lodge Hotel to exchange our travellers' cheques, but it was Sunday and they would not do so under any circumstances as we were not residents. So Graham and I thought, well, we must simply register as hotel guests and pay for a day's tariff. No, said the clerk, he could not offer us a room as he was fully booked. Interestingly there was almost no one around. We replied that we did not need accommodation but would be happy to register and pay the tariff and thus be allowed to cash our cheques. He said that could not be done and would look odd in his book-keeping so we had to come away defeated and a little worried. Devi Singh said not to worry he would find some British tourists and maybe we could exchange some sterling. Fortunately I had £20 in my purse. The first cycle tourist turned out to be an American who though sympathetic could not help, and then along came a pair of British who understood our dilemma and were happy to exchange a ten pound note for Indian rupees. Thank goodness, neither of us knew how we had allowed this situation to develop but it could have put a blight on the day until we arrived at our hotel in the evening. Devi Singh was very knowledgeable about the birdlife and we began to enjoy it. On another occasion we hope to spend a couple of days and rise very early and watch the birds on the marsh as well as in the trees. The sanctuary has 360 species of bird and among the bulbuls, doves, egrets and ducks are seven species of birds of prey, several species of heron, stork and owl and a migrant population of rare Siberian cranes. There are also animals including chital, *sambar*, *nilgai*, blackbuck, jungle cats and python. In 1733 the Maharaja dammed several small rivers to create marshland breeding grounds for ducks. These would provide sport for the famous Bharatpur duck shoots for people like the Viceroy when they came as guests. Two hundred and fifty years later it became a national park.

The conversation with Devi Singh ranged over life and his aspirations as a family man, that he needed a greater income than what was on offer from being a rickshaw wallah – after all that is very seasonal and when we left him we took his address and have kept in touch. I later met Devi Singh again in Agra in March when he came to my hotel to meet me. Sometimes India is so frustrating for the Westerner. The Devi Singhs of India are hard-working simple people who would dearly love to have second and third incomes, but it needs someone to find the opportunity for them and bureaucratic India can make that very difficult by obfuscation and delay.

At the gates of the park there are the usual fruit sellers and we were tempted by the papaya (paw paw) vendor. He had some huge papayas and now we had the cash with which to buy a couple. Graham and I tried always to have a fresh papaya in the car because it provides a moist and delicious snack which is hygienic provided one does not put any of the skin in one's mouth; moreover should one have an irritable stomach papaya will actually help to soothe and cure the malady.

Deeg is a short drive from Bharatpur and well worth the detour. The actual citadel was built in 1730 and dismantled by the British in 1804 and now only the 28-metre-high wall remains. In 1768 the Maharajah built himself a stunning summer palace of yellow stone. The central building, the Gopal Bhavan, is flanked on either side by barge-shaped pavilions. In front are laid out large gardens, which today are not very well maintained, and at the rear is a huge green tank (man-made lake) which is the water supply for the locals. That Maharajah had an obsession with water. The gardens and the buildings on the water's edge are filled with nearly 2,000 fountains, all designed to create an artificial monsoon. The Keshav Bhavan pavilion used jets of water to roll stone balls and recreate the sound of thunder and for the Maharajah's birthday the fountains' pipes would be filled with dye and the fountains flowed in rainbow colours. Sadly nowadays these water extravaganzas only take place for three days in the year. We were the only Europeans present and the resident guide caretaker came forward and invited us in and took us round the palace, which is extraordinary in that it has been left as it was with stuffed tigers, elephant's foot furniture, sofas, chairs, pianos, beds and other memorabilia. The atmosphere is not eerie but odd, as if one has walked into a faded palatial stage set. We both enjoyed the experience and when it came to saying thank you I realised that once again we were short of cash, having paid Devi Singh the money owed to Balvinder and the papaya seller! So I proffered a tip and explained in Hindi what had happened. The caretaker was so kind and said no, memsahib must not be without money and he would not dream of taking anything and leaving us in a difficulty! However I pressed it on him, saying his excellent guidance could not go unrewarded and we parted friends. Much to my annoyance the film in the camera at this point unknown to me had not wound on properly so I have only one photograph of Deeg and none of Kaleodeo Bird Sanctuary. From Deeg we had to retrace our drive to Bharatpur and Balvinder said we should stop for a rest. He chose an awful place which confirmed my worst nightmare about Indian-style lavatories.

In fact when well maintained these are extremely hygienic and not at all a problem provided one wears a longish skirt. Trousers for obvious reasons could be a big problem, and especially if there are some evil-looking fluids swilling around. It is curious that a race that tries whenever possible to take a great interest in personal hygiene and appearance should have so little interest in lavatories. After all that is a place we all have to visit, and indeed the five star hotels and other institutions have marble floors and gleaming sanitary ware with gold-plated taps and attendants. Middle of the road hostelries have less attractive facilities of both western and eastern design and the rest are just simply awful, including those on the train. When I emerged out of this example Balvinder looked very sheepish and apologised and I brushed it off to save him embarrassment, but then men do not most of the time have quite the same requirements!

We very soon reached Agra, and on the way saw the outlines of the fabled Fatehpur Sikri. We had to press on however because Taj (as it is called) is closed on a Monday and therefore we needed to visit on the Sunday afternoon and then again at sunrise on the Tuesday morning. On the Monday we planned to visit the Red Fort at Agra and anything else and then drive back the short journey to Fatehpur Sikri. The plan worked superbly and we went straight to the Taj Mahal on arrival in Agra. It was a beautiful afternoon, bright and clear and cool.

Chapter Ten

Agra and the Sublime Taj Mahal

O Soul, thou are at rest. Return to the Lord, at peace with Him and He at peace with you. So enter as one of His servants. And enter into His garden.

That is the 89th chapter of the Qur'an, engraved above the Great Gate of the Taj Mahal.

In the Persian/Urdu script the word for garden is the same as the word for paradise. It is thought that Shah Jahan is suggesting that God speaks thus, ie '... and enter into His paradise'.

These days the approach to the Taj is down a road that ends in a large car park to which there is no alternative. At the park one can take an electric minibus or horse-drawn carriage or rickshaw. The journey is very short and one is deposited outside the boundary at the ticket booth. Once one has obtained the ticket then the path takes one forward into the huge enclosed courtyard area where people have to queue for entrance, which is controlled for security purposes. In the afternoon sunshine this was no great problem until we saw the size of the queue and despaired; anyway we joined it and actually it moved quite quickly, but I observed others jumping the queue and was highly indignant. However on my second visit four months later that is exactly what I was able to do which made me feel guilty, but the reason is that on the first occasion we had not met up with our guide through a slight misunderstanding. The second time around I went straight to the hotel to meet him and then on to Taj. The security search is a good thing

The beautiful red stone Gateway to the Taj Mahal at sunrise.

The Taj Mahal.

but I doubt they would actually detect anyone seriously determined to damage. As I emerged from the gateway I was nervous that I would feel underwhelmed and disappointed, but it was not so. For all the pictures and all the words the Taj Mahal has its own special serene beauty, and the hot frustration that I had felt at queuing melted away and I just gazed. Of course there were hundreds of people but apart from the odd irritation they did not spoil the experience. In fact we delighted in so many Indians visiting their great national treasure. We remained for as long as possible and I would urge people to make more than one visit. The atmosphere alters with the changing light, see it in sunshine then at sunset and if possible, as we did, at sunrise.

Built over twenty-one years (1632–53) and with twenty thousand craftsmen this ultimate symbol of Mughal extravagance was built as a memorial of love by Emperor Shah Jahan for his wife Mumtaz Mahal who died giving birth to their fourteenth child.

The tomb is within a marble monument standing on a raised platform, topped by a huge central dome and four smaller domes. On the corners of the platform stand four lofty decorative tapered minarets, so cleverly constructed as to lean slightly to achieve a perfect perspective. The formal gardens are quartered by water courses in the *charbagh* (traditional Islamic) design. It is surrounded by a high sandstone wall with three gates. On either side of the central platform are identical red sandstone pavilions that on the left (west) is a mosque, the one on the right is a copy built for the sake of symmetry; the Urdu architectural name was the word *jawab*,

Carved panels on the Taj Mahal relief carving and Pietra Dura work on dado.

meaning echo or reply. The mausoleum is constructed from white marble brought from the area between Jodhpur and Jaipur and the entire building is inlaid with semi-precious stones such as carnelian, lapis lazuli, red, yellow and brown jasper, turquoise and jade. The carving is quite superb and so intricate and even the carving in the marble panels is so fine and accurate that all the flowers are recognisable, not just stylised emblems. That first afternoon Graham and I were by ourselves, and though on the Tuesday morning we had an excellent guide with whom we had become friends, on that Sunday afternoon it was just wonderful to take one's shoes off and walk on the surrounding plinth and sit on the parapet and look out on the Jamuna and watch the light change gradually. At the mosque devout Muslims said their prayers when the hour approached, but the rest of us just walked around or sat and lingered and drank it in. Then we retreated to the lawn area from where I judged the best sunset pictures would come and they did. Despite the throng we had a restful memorable experience and left reluctantly.

Now I read that the Taj Mahal is endangered by the 10 million visitors annually and the decades of industrial pollution that have taken their toll. Agra is proud of its efforts to control pollution. To western eyes it would seem 'what control and how much effort?' but much more will have to be done and India should not be too proud to ask advice and seek solutions from others faced with the responsibility of conserving world-famous tourist sites. It is infuriating for those of us who care to watch whilst bureaucrats make cosmetic gestures. On Monday Taj is closed, apparently to help limit the numbers and to do any restoration work, but on Fridays it is free to everyone. Having in the same year spent several days in both Florence and Venice, two magnificent cities under tourist siege, it is quite obvious to us all that authorities will have to have the courage to take measures to preserve these world-famous sites for posterity. In the case of the Taj Mahal the Indian Government should spend a sizeable amount on cleaning up Agra and maintaining it as a show case city with Taj as its jewel. If they are frightened of loss of revenue they are mistaken. Were serious measures implemented to clean and restore the whole city and preserve Taj, Indian tourism would grow, but not in a cheap fashion. Instead the true travellers and lovers of art and history would visit rather than millions of 'cheap seven days away' visitors who have a rather superficial interest.

Apparently 1999 has been designated 'Visit India Year'. I pray that someone with courage and foresight will speak up and demand a millennium pledge to clean, restore and maintain all of India's great architectural history. They have the manpower, and the communication system through television to educate, and I have no doubt would also receive sponsorship that acts as advertising. How wonderful if the youth of India could marshal itself with this resolve.

I have however read a suggestion in the British papers that raising the fee for entry to Taj would help. Yes, it is minimal and that would be a good idea if the revenue was purely used on maintenance of the Taj and its environs, but then the fee should be structured to allow Indians to see their national treasure at a realistic figure relevant to their incomes. Those of us who visit India and continually mentally convert into our own respective currencies find it very cheap, but that is not so for the thousands of ordinary folk who come in their family groups to also enjoy their heritage. Therefore all foreign tourists should be required to pay a figure that is double that paid by the country's inhabitants.

We stayed at the Clarks Shiraz in Agra and found it very satisfactory. On occasions the management could be rather ineffectual but if one firmly remonstrates they act quickly to rectify the fault. There is a curious habit that one encounters at Indian hotel check-in desks. People come up and interrupt one's registration and conversation and the desk clerk seems to think it in order. On the second occasion when I stayed at the Shiraz I had yet another experience of this but decided to firmly and forcefully tell the clerk what I thought of this behaviour and it worked a treat, and what is more the offending gentleman actually apologised. It could be that Indians because of their heavily populated country have so little personal space when outside their respective homes that they do not see this behaviour as offensive I resolved that I would not let people invade my personal space whatever the reason.

The Shiraz has some bedrooms with a beautiful view of Taj and I was fortunate to have one of these the second time. The gardens are pleasant and the swimming pool is a welcome relief in the hot weather as I was to experience in March. There is also the most charming masseuse in the beauty parlour and she does wonderful massage with herbal Ayurvedic oils. The food is good with a choice of several restaurants and room service. It is quite interesting to visit a place both as a tourist and then again on business. I noted the second time that when I had entertained some people at the poolside and then said goodbye to them and was wanting to settle the bill the waiter was very surly. I realised that in fact he was showing his snobbishness and had felt that I was consorting with people beneath the social order that usually frequented the hotel. This was unacceptable so I told him in no uncertain terms never to approach me again without a salver on which the bill lay instead of just handing it to me, and I told his manager that I was not impressed with his supervision. If this sounds over the top it is not. Because of all the hierarchical intricacies and caste system plus the snob element brought in by westerners and the relic of the British rule it is vital to treat staff with courtesy and friendliness, but if they overstep the mark in any way show firm command of the situation. Particularly for a woman doing business in India this is essential otherwise respect will evaporate and exploitation take over. In any country in the world people are apt to look for a vulnerable area to exploit, but in India where there is still huge chauvinism and male dominance women should be alert to the necessity of maintaining respect. It is therefore essential that one dresses appropriately – how often did I hear the sneering asides in Hindi from Indian youths when they saw a scantily clad western girl with her bottom hanging out of her brief shorts and her chest visible through a transparent blouse. 'Eve-teasing' is the term used to describe harassment of women and a lot of this has arisen from the multitudes watching western films with all their sexual candour. Our Indian friends think that Bollywood with its gratuitous violence endlessly depicting rape, followed by savage murder and bloodbaths, has led to the huge increase in the crime rate and most especially of rape. Most Indians sadly agree that India is a much more violent place now than thirty years ago.

The following day Anil Sharma, our guide, took us to the Red Fort. This is well maintained and so impressive. Anil was a knowledgeable man and with enthusiasm instructed us in its history. The Red Fort at Agra is so much more impressive than that of Delhi, though possibly that is the fault of the British, who in revenge for the 1857 uprising decimated it without any thought for history. Indeed when I consider what we as a race did in our arrogance, or tried to do, if you recall that Lord Bentinck planned to

The Red Fort at Agra.

dismantle the Taj and auction bits off!

Those of us in the West talk volubly about pollution but we were the original polluters and looters and though we should invite everyone to learn from our mistakes we cannot afford to sit in judgment without at least finding solutions. Indians are very scornful of Americans particularly when the subject of pollution or exploitation rears its head. Americans are very judgmental about India and reduce most comments apparently to 'well, it was nice but so filthy ...'. Just recently the USA has again declined to cuts its own pollution levels yet it is one of the world's great offenders. I encountered quite a number of Americans in my Indian travels and they seemed to view everything in a sad superficial light. As a student of history myself I wondered if it is because they are such a young country comparatively and thus have no national folk memory of culture and history upon which to draw and of which to be proud, thus they frantically travel the world to view its antiquities but quite often miss the depth and vision that is a result of antiquity. It is not fair to generalise, I know, but again and again one meets them in both Europe and the East.

In fact Akbar's fort in Agra shares a number of striking features with that built by Shah Jahan in Delhi – it was evidently the model for the latter. Akbar (1556–1605) was the greatest of all the Mughuls. He came to the throne aged 13. He conquered massive new territories including much of Rajasthan, he created a proper administrative system, introduced standard weights and measures, tax structures and a sort of police force. He

Fatephur Sikri near Agra.

73

was married to at least seven wives. Among them was Jodhbai, you may remember, the daughter of the Maharajah of Amber as he then was, Jaipur not having been established as yet. Quite simply the Red Fort at Agra is worthy of a whole morning in the company of a good guide.

All Mughals were capable of patricide and even fratricide, as we know with Aurangzeb, but standing in the octagonal tower at the window which overlooks the Taj Mahal on the banks of the Jamuna in the distance one cannot help but feel sorry for Shah Jahan, the old man destined to spend his last eight years as a prisoner of his third son Aurangzeb, looking wistfully at his beloved wife's memorial, even deprived of writing paper and books. Aurangzeb murdered the rightful heir, Prince Dara Shikoh, and presented his severed head on a platter to his father. What must his memories have been? In *The Padshanama* – the chronicle of the Ruler of all the World, which was his title at the zenith of his power, there is an exquisite pictorial record of some of his reign. I was glad that earlier in the year I had been able to go to the Queen's Gallery at Buckingham Palace and see that beautifully presented exhibition. The detail of the painting is superb and so interesting because each one depicts an important event in Shah Jahan's life, from his early days as a prince to his accession and the adult lives of his sons. One can fancifully even imagine the resentment in Aurangzeb's face that his wedding celebration is not as magnificent as his brother Prince Dara Shikoh's because he is not the eldest and favourite son. Prince Dara Shikoh's marriage took place quite soon after the tragic

Fatephur Sikri with the Panch Mahal to the right.

death of Mumtaz Mahal who had been apparently instrumental in the planning of it; that too has a poignancy. The Royal Collection is indeed lucky to have one of the very few copies of *The Padshanama* and apparently the only one to be fully illustrated with a portfolio of 44 illustrations. It was given by the Nawab of Oudh via the British Ambassador to King George III and was overlooked when King George IV gave his late father's collection to the British Museum, thus the Windsor Castle collection still retains it and it was made the subject of a beautiful exhibition to commemorate the fifty years of independence of both India and Pakistan.

After a thorough inspection of the Red Fort we had tea and *gulab jamuns* with Anil at the Fort's cafe. Without him I doubt we would have ventured into the cafe but Anil is obviously a friend of the owner and ensured we were given the freshest of sweets and we remarked on how delicious they were. A hoopoe meanwhile started pecking at the lawn very close to us and both of us were delighted. You do not see many of them these days but for each of us, growing up in India and Africa, they were a familiar sight. Agra has so much to see that it is a question of priorities which inevitably are subjective. By this time it was midday so we set off for Fatehpur Sikri which is 35 km south-west of Agra on the Jaipur road. This was the culmination of a dream for me as somehow since a teenager I had been entranced with the idea of the Emperor Akbar. At school in England history was taught quite naturally with Britain as the focal point and I realised that Akbar was a contemporary of Queen Elizabeth I; he and his palace city were objects of fascination to me.

Akbar, despite remaining illiterate throughout his life, was truly a man before his time. He very quickly realised, despite his extreme youth, having succeeded his father Humayun after the latter's death as a result of falling down the stairs from his library, that it was a lifetime's folly to try and subjugate the Hindus in 'Hindustan' and he concentrated on winning their loyalty by benevolence and trust. He had a host of Hindu advisors and administrators and he abolished the *jitzya*, a tax on Hindus that the Muslim rulers had introduced. He became deeply interested in other religions and started dialogues between all religions and provided the opportunity for Muslims, Hindus, Jains, Zoroastrians, Jews and Christians to talk about their fundamental beliefs and differences. Orthodox Muslims must have found it very distressing, but this broad religious tolerance was very helpful politically and his marriages to Rajput princesses ensured that the various Rajput princely houses became very loyal and provided him with the bravest of warriors. Thus within a peaceful empire the arts, literature and music could begin to flourish. He employed scholars and artists and in his newly created library there were texts from Turkey, Sanskrit chronicles and Latin gospels. The arts were now established and so the Emperor turned his attention to architecture.

There was however, the story goes, one vital aspect about which Akbar was desperate; he had as yet been unable to produce a surviving heir and he asked a Sufi mystic, Sheik Salim Chishti, for help, and shortly afterwards his son Jehangir was born. In gratitude Akbar built a massive 7.5 sq km administrative capital around the Sufi mystic's home between 1570 and 1582. The palace complex was inhabited for about sixteen years and then it is thought that Akbar felt threatened in his kingdom and moved to Lahore, the better able to deal with the threat. There is a myth that the city was abandoned because of a shortage of water, but this is unlikely.

The court historian Abul Fazl wrote: 'Inasmuch as his exalted sons had taken their birth in Sikri and God-knowing spirit of Shaikh Salim had taken possession thereof, his holy heart desired to give outward splendour to this spot which possessed spiritual grandeur. An order was issued that the superintendent of affairs should erect lofty buildings for the special use of the Shahinshah.' Here was erected a huge mosque and courtyard and an intricate palace complex and in time the tomb of Sheikh Salim Chishti. Following Akbar's conquest of Gujarat in 1573, he put a prefix to the name of his new city, ie 'Fatehpur', or 'City of Victory'. As the nobles and courtiers took his lead and also built houses in the vicinity, it rapidly grew into an impressive new centre. Moreover, it is recorded that in its heyday the road between Fatehpur Sikri and Agra was flanked by continuous markets. Indeed English travellers of the time remarked on the size and magnificence, but by 1685 Akbar had transferred his capital to Lahore and by the early 17th century the city was crumbling and returning to vegetation and even the principal buildings were falling into decay. Nevertheless Fatehpur Sikri remains today one of the most remarkable architectural conceptions and is still a bit of a Mughal puzzle.

Anyone visiting should not do so without a guide. They are very knowledgeable and can explain the whole sequence of events and tell one so much about the age and architecture. Of course you could just visit with a reputable guidebook but the place comes alive with a guide such as Anil or one of his colleagues.

After enjoying the architecture, Graham and I walked in the small garden which is well maintained and in seconds the *mali* (gardner) was by our side. We had an interesting conversation on the various shrubs, one of which was really quite special as the flower turns into a completely different colour and I am ashamed to say I have forgotten the botanical name which tripped off his tongue, and I mean Latin botanical name! *Malis* are not merely men working in a garden, they are for the most part knowledgeable and have pride in their accomplishments. Congratulate the *mali* if appropriate wherever you are and he will be delighted and take you round the garden be it large or small. My childhood hours were often spent in the company of the *mali* and he always took time to explain things. Father had a small *khurpi* (Indian form of hand tool) made for me and I would earnestly try to help. Something must have worked because I won a prize for my larkspur and cornflowers at one flower show, and some snapdragons at another.

The best time to enjoy India's horticultural heritage is about February and March, when the winter spectacle of western flowers looks impressive and the indigenous spring flowering trees are coming into bloom. In the monsoon months there is a paucity of blooms, mostly balsams and zinnias, and of course the extreme heat of the hot weather has killed everything else except perhaps some cannas. At Fatehpur Sikri the *mali* asked me to take a photograph of him and promise to send it to him; this I was able to do by handing it over on a second visit to the area.

On our return to Agra we talked about India and her present-day politics. In actual fact Anil talked and we listened to a very worthwhile explanation of what was upsetting the average young family man such as himself, and his aspirations and ambitions were really no different to any of us here at that time of life – stability, financial security, good education for his little one and access to healthcare. He was however interested, being a history graduate, in our recent history so I explained what I could of the last fifty years since the Second World War very briefly and how it had impacted on India. He was intrigued; interpretation of history can be fundamentally different, we all know, but some of the finer detail was unknown to him and made events more understandable. The Queen's recent visit and the change to a Labour Government were again the major talking point; he could not understand why the Government would be either so arrogant or so naive as to think the Indo–Pakistan conflict could be settled by a few trite words of encouragement and became impassioned, and it soon became clear that he was an adherent of the BJP, the Bhratiya Janata Party, which since March 1998 has become the Government of India, though because of all the horse-trading a very ineffectual one.

Akbar's mausoleum is at Sikandra and he began building his own tomb in 1602. It is decorated by Muslim, Hindu and Christian symbols, ie the round Hindu cupola, the minarets of Islam and the Christian cross; he was obviously determined to have his religious tolerance in life reflected in his death very wisely. The mausoleum is on the Mathura road, 15 km north of Agra.

Mathura is the birthplace of Lord Krishna and therefore immensely important as a centre of pilgrimage; indeed the whole area is littered with small temples that do not have architectural significance but are associated with key events in the god's life.

The tomb of Itimaud-ud-Daulah is superb. Composed of pure white marble inlaid with precious stones and covered with filigree screens, it has an air of fragility. It was built between 1622 and 1628 by Nur Jehan (wife of Jehangir, Akbar's longed-for son and successor) for her Persian father,

Mirza Ghias-ud-Din Beg, and it stands in formal *charbagh* gardens. Lastly there are the Ram Bagh gardens laid out by Emperor Babur in 1528. This is the earliest surviving example of a Mughal garden, but is disappointing now and the authorities should recruit some serious *malis* and allocate funds to renovate it back to its former beauty. Indeed were the Uttar Pradesh Government to decide to clean up Agra and impose restrictions on the building proliferation and sympathetically undertake conservation, I am confident the area would become a tourists' Mecca, and not something that has to be endured to see the Taj Mahal. Situated on the banks of one of India's sacred rivers, the Jamuna, with the wealth of Mughal architecture and history, the entire city should really be a World Heritage Site and in the winter months could become a destination of delight, whereas at the moment the normal reaction is one of awe at Taj but shock and disgust at Agra.

We visited the Taj Mahal again at sunrise and were so grateful for that opportunity. Naturally the crowds are quite minimal if one is early enough and one's patience is rewarded by the sunrise and the possibilities for photography. There are some tiresome people who talk volubly about 'a Diana pose' but it is easy to ignore them and hopefully all that in time will fade away to a sad memory. It is however worthwhile having one of the local photographers take a picture of one as an individual or couple because he will bring the results to the hotel a couple of hours later and they are good and inexpensive. It captures the mood for you at the time when it is still

Aline Dobbie sitting in front of the Taj Mahal during sunrise.

foremost in the mind. On the way back to our hotel we watched in amusement all the cycle rickshaws weighed down with small children going to school. Yet again they were beautifully dressed and neat and attractive; what alarmed us was the fact that each rickshaw was overcrowded and we worried about possible accidents. That evening, to our horror, on the national news was the account of a most horrible school bus accident in Delhi in which countless children had died and been injured. The scale of the tragedy was immense, and all due to an aggressive driver at the controls of an overloaded bus – we grieved along with the rest of the country, who were also very angry. It spoilt the end of what had been a superbly interesting day.

If leaving Agra to return to Delhi, I would suggest using the Shatabdhi Express which leaves at 8.00 pm arriving in Delhi at about 10.30 pm. It is inexpensive by western standards and efficient; under no circumstances consider returning by car. In my case on both occasions the driver returned to Delhi on his own in the early morning to avoid the danger of night travel. We however on the first occasion were travelling south-east and so that afternoon we flew from Agra to Khajuraho in Madhya Pradesh. The security at Agra airport was intense, and further reinforced by the arrival of the American Secretary of State. In fact the Taj was closed that afternoon for her privileged viewing which must have been hard on the countless tourists who would not have known about that trip in their planning.

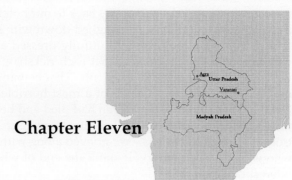

Chapter Eleven

Khajuraho and Madhya Pradesh

The trip to Khajuraho is short and pleasant and it is a superb destination. A small neat comparatively clean place with many excellent hotels and just the two sets of temple complexes to visit. Madhya Pradesh is the heartland of India, and literally translated means 'Middle Land'. It is India's largest state and covers approximately 450,000 sq km. The next largest state is Rajasthan and that is about 100,000 sq km smaller!

Geographically Madhya Pradesh is very diverse. The northern part of the state with Gwalior as its largest city lies in the Indo–Gangetic plain whereas the rest is upland plateau and hills interspersed with deep valleys. Some of the finest of India's forests are in this state with deciduous hardwoods such as teak, *sal*, Indian ebony and rosewood. Bamboo is prolific and the fruit and flowering trees are wonderful. Rudyard Kipling's famous *Jungle Book* was sited in the Mahadeo Hills of the Satpura Range and here you will find tiger, panther, Indian bison and the whole spectrum of herbivores.

Ashoka, the great Bhuddist emperor, had Malwa, the old name for Madhya Pradesh, as the centre of his Mauryan Empire and the most important relics of his reign are at Sanchi where there is a Buddhist centre. This is a small place but well worth a visit for its charm and obvious antiquity. However to get there you would need to travel from Bhopal; for us on the recent trip it was not possible and we had to content ourselves with Khajuraho which is easily reached by plane. However on a future occasion we shall add Orchha, Gwalior, Mandu and Pachmarhi to our itinerary. There are also several wildlife reserves here which from recent accounts are worth visiting but travel in the interior of Madhya Pradesh is not as

80

Khajuraho Temples.

easy as on the popular tourist trails and the traveller would have to con-
tend with long car and train journeys and be both patient and tolerant and
not too demanding about accommodation standards.

Khajuraho has a population of under 10,000, at least that is what my
research has discovered, so in Indian terms it is a minute place and compa-
rable to Peebles, our local market town here in the beautiful Borders region
of Scotland. Its size makes it a most delightful place to rest and recharge the
batteries. The temples are fascinating and well maintained in attractive garden areas and moving around is easy with so little traffic. I imagine, given
more time, cycling would have been attractive. We stayed at the Jass Oberoi
which was both elegant and comfortable with very nice staff. The grounds
are beautifully maintained with a delightful pool and sitting area and one
can see why Khajuraho has become a honeymoon venue for young couples
or a weekend destination since the other hotels are equally well appointed.
Because Khajuraho is difficult to get to other than by plane the airline seats
are reserved well in advance and sadly there is not yet sufficient competi-
tion in India's internal airlines to challenge the somewhat mixed reputation
and monopoly of Indian Airlines.

Khajuraho was once a great Chandela capital; this was a dynasty that
lasted for five centuries before falling to the Mughal onslaught. The tem-

ples almost all date from a burst of creativity that started in AD 950 and lasted one hundred years. The puzzle is why? Khajuraho, as we have seen, is difficult to get to so was presumably even more difficult a thousand years ago and though charming does not appear to have any special quality as a venue for massive temple construction. Moreover in the hot weather it is extremely hot and dry and dusty. For us seeing it all on a pleasant couple of days in the cool of November almost gives a false impression, but one with which we were very content. Because of its remoteness possibly, the Muslims did nothing to destroy what in the early days of Muslim invasion was regarded as 'idolatrous' and for that we must be grateful.

With a good guide you will see the carvings as a celebration of all aspects of life, not simply erotica. In fact it is believed to have been the depiction of Tantric life in which sexual activity can be used to eliminate the evils of the world and achieve final deliverance. In the quest for nirvana, Rhoa, which is physical enjoyment, is rated as highly as yoga, which is spiritual exercise. Our guide was a very serious young man and he had found that the way to have a discourse on these matters in the presence of women was to talk whilst looking at the carvings and then looking down, ie not catching my eye. Since there are some very saucy depictions it seemed a satisfactory way to conduct matters! Had Graham and I been alone I am sure we would have had a good giggle. However the guide was almost apoplectic when he overheard what another guide was putting forth; I don't know what so enraged him but he had a quiet tirade on the dangers of exploitative guides who told innocent westerners a lot of nonsense.

The temples comprise the Western, the Eastern and the Southern groups and they are easy to walk around and contemplate and photograph. I was not so much interested in the erotic positions of humans as the delicacy of the carving of some of the female attire and little details of the maidenly conceit, plus the roguish look in the eyes of some of the animals like the elephants and camels. We were scheduled to fly onto Varanasi but had we had the time I should have liked to visit the Panna National Park about 32 km away and the Ajaigarh and Kalinjar fort which are about 80 km from Khajuraho. The former was a Chandela building but the latter Kalinjar is much, much older, built during the Gupta period and technically inside Uttar Pradesh.

Just as we had settled down beside the pool to have a rest and some lunch, fate took a hand and we saw the little man who was the local representative of our travel agent approaching. He announced that there was an airport controllers' strike and thus our flight was very delayed and rather uncertain. We were dismayed. If we did not return to Delhi by the morning our continuing schedule would be affected and there was something important that we needed to accomplish in Delhi. We asked Badli Alu to do his utmost to make sure we were on the next aircraft when it arrived.

Amazing carvings on Khajuraho Temples.

Khajuraho Temple carvings in exquisite detail.

In the meantime I began to notice that the hotel lobby was filling up with impatient-looking Americans. It occurred to us that if all the people who were now milling around in our hotel wanted to embark on the same aircraft, plus similar numbers in the other hotels, life would become rather stressed and hectic, and someone would have to lose out! I determined it would not be us so went and asked for a telephone. Naturally several other people had the same idea and very soon the telephone lines to Delhi were jammed. In the meantime I heard the local agent, who was senior to Badli in managerial rank, having a telephone conversation I asked him to please ensure we were able to leave. His attitude was unattractive, but as I was speaking in English he had no knowledge of my Hindi and so when he started a conversation and told the person at the airline end of the telephone that he would fob some of us off, I simply 'phoned the Delhi head office and explained very angrily what I had heard. This can happen in India, and even the people you least expect to let you down or deceive you will do so; they are inclined to tell you what you want to hear, regardless of the consequences and that you will in turn discover their deception. I made it clear that any nonsense would have serious repercussions with the managing director. If it sounds like one person jumping up and down having a tantrum, it is, but without the jumping up and down!

It all became quite funny as time wore on because we could all hear the little aircraft arrive and then take off – apparently the same one, which had flown from Delhi to Agra, then Khajuraho and on to Varanasi then back to Khajuraho then back to Agra, return to Khajuraho and once more to Varanasi and so forth! By the late evening the Jass Oberoi very kindly laid on a buffet supper and young Badli Alu, who was by this time worn out, came back to assure us we were on the next flight but having to go to Varanasi and then to Delhi. Badli looked exhausted and when we asked when if at all he had eaten he said at about 5.00 am prior to going to work. He lived some way away and his young wife was at her parents' house with their firstborn (which is the customary way for young first-time mothers in India). I said he must have something to eat and he was very embarrassed. Again it was the case of the lower class, with insufficient status, to even think of eating in the Jass Oberoi. "Enough," I said, "you will be our guest and everything else can wait," and I ordered him a bar meal of his rather shy choice with tea and cool drinks for us. The barman looked down his nose and made very little effort to progress the order so I went to the bar and said in Hindi that this was my order for my guest and he better believe it! The meal arrived and the young man wolfed it down despite his shyness. He was so humble and so eager to please and he did his utmost to ensure everything else went smoothly. However, Graham had decided that as we were independent travellers despite Badli's assurances we would go to the little airport in good time, not totally trusting the airline clerks who with an innocent stare may well have switched the names around were we to turn up at the appointed time. Our hunch paid off, and we also positioned ourselves near the door of the transit lounge. True to form the clerks had given up on the problem and issued everyone with a boarding pass, but there were no allocated seats. I have never seen so many middle-aged American, German and Japanese tourists swarm to the narrow door and all try to get out at the same time. Graham and I had worked it out and were a little ahead of the game. Thankfully we sat ourselves in the first pair of seats near the rear door.

When that aircraft revved its engines and started its take-off truly I prayed to my own God, Lord Ganesha in the Hindu deity and the Sufi Saint of Fatehpur Sikri. It somehow felt as if the little machine was totally exhausted and not wanting to leave the ground – oh, I know this was fanciful but it really felt like that sitting in the extreme rear of the aircraft! The flight to Varanasi was uneventful and after refuelling we were thankfully on our way, having flown about 1,000 km out of our way. We arrived at Delhi's internal airport at midnight, totally exhausted but thankful, and were met by Ajay and Balvinder Singh. We were taken to the United Services complex where they operate a sort of hotel rather like a military mess. There are no frills but it is clean and the staff are pleasant and the whole complex is very interesting, as we discovered once we had had a good night's sleep.

Chapter Twelve

Delhi in Diverse Detail

Within the last twelve months I have been able to spend nearly three weeks in Delhi but fortunately spread out through three of the seasons beginning with our November visit, following on in March and culminating in May. Winter, in which we first arrived, is the most pleasant season in Delhi, sunny and cool but the minimum temperature drops sharply in late December and January and every time there is a heavy snowfall in the mountains icy winds blow down from the north. In March there is a brief change of season between winter and the hot weather. Spring lasts only a few weeks in February and March but it is attractive because it is the season of new leaf – many of Delhi's indigenous forest trees are covered in vivid green and this is followed by the vibrant colour of the ornamental flowering trees. The Hindu festivals of Basant Panchami and Holi celebrate this season, known in Hindi as Basant.

In the Indian tradition there are six seasons – Grishma, Varsha, Sharad, Hemant, Sheet and Basant. They correspond approximately to Summer, Rains, Post-rains, Early winter, Winter and Spring. The most famous literary work on the theme of seasons is the *Ritusamhara*, literally the gathering of seasons, written in the 5th century by the Sanskrit poet Kalidasa. The credit for planting indigenous forest species in Delhi is shared between Lutyens, the architect of New Delhi, and William Robertson Mustoe, who came to India in 1919 from London's Kew Gardens. Indeed just this summer the Royal Botanical Gardens of Edinburgh held an exhibition of exquisite paintings of Indian trees in bloom with meticulous line drawings showing the early discoveries by the various plantsmen who went to India

Lutyens's New Delhi.

and began the great plant collections for the various botanical gardens and private estates. The Calcutta Botanical Gardens, which in their time were superb, were featured as were the Agri-Horticultural Gardens of Calcutta where so much early work was trialled.

It was a pleasure to see again the Gulmohur flower in shades of fire red and orange, the Bauhinia in delicate mauve, the Laburnum festooned with racemes of gold, the Jacaranda which becomes a delicate filigree of mauve and blue, the Champa, or Temple Tree, which has exquisitely textured and scented flowers and interspersed with all these the ancient Pipals, the most common of the *Ficus* (fig) species, and the Neem. Neem provides dense shade and its medicinal and germicidal properties have been known for centuries but have recently come to the attention of the West. In places like Bareilly we were able to briefly walk in orchards of mangoes and guavas, though it was not the season for fruit, and there too were the *Lagerstroemia,* or Pride of India, with blooms in shades of deep pink or mauve, and closer to winter, the Rusty Shieldbearer, or *Peltophorum roxburghi,* stands out with its copper-red oblong seed pods and sprays of yellow flowers touched with rust.

In the third week of February it is customary for the Mughal Garden at Rashtrapati Bhavan, the Residence of the Indian President (previously the viceroy's palace), to be opened to the public for about two weeks and this is beautiful, but the inevitable security checks have to be endured.

The building of New Delhi created a garden city but wisely did not tamper with the old parks and thus it is possible to see some of the old garden remains from centuries before. Now, however, fifty years on from Independence, Delhi's population has grown hugely and it is now a mega-metropolis. I have heard the figure 30 million used in conjunction with Delhi and its various satellite towns like Gurgaon, Noida, Ghaziabad, Shadara, Faridabad and Rohini. This has put a severe strain on civic amenities and the environment and the power utilities.

I had been told that when Indira Gandhi was in power she had decreed that Delhi was never to be without power and water. It is the capital of India, and of that the country should be justifiably proud and therefore even if it meant taking from the other interstate electricity grids the capital was never to be deprived of power. Sadly because of that arrangement not enough has been done to provide Delhi with sufficient electricity and water when the hot season arrives, and this year there were large demonstrations with hundreds if not thousands of Delhi residents showing their frustration and displeasure.

It is so foolish to just keep trying to 'make do'. India has huge talent in scientific and engineering skills. If a courageous government would just commission new environmentally friendly forms of power stations and provision for water very probably the rest of the world would help them financially, provided that whoever was appointed in charge of such huge building projects had sufficient integrity and complete authority to oversee it without corruption. Indians become very defensive about their massive environmental problems, but they need not be. It seems to me that all of us in the West are only too aware of the logistical problems they face, but it requires honesty and with honesty and integrity they will clothe themselves in dignity, which is quite naturally important to the nation as a whole. When I left India thirty-five years ago there were about 500 million people, now it is close to one billion. To see beautiful Delhi under such strain is heartbreaking and there are no easy solutions, but face-saving cosmetic legislation provides no lasting solution.

We were fortunate enough to stay at the India International Centre in both March and May as temporary members. It was visualised as an international centre for exchange of ideas among scholars. The architect was J. A. Stein and he built a typical 1960s' building but it captured the soft quality of light through the use of traditional *jaalis* (screens). There are a library, an auditorium, conference rooms, restaurants and a beautiful garden.

J. A. Stein was also responsible for the Ford Foundation building in 1968, the Memorial Plaza, the Lodi Greenhouse, UNICEF Headquarters, the World Wide Fund for Nature – India, and the India Habitat Centre as recently as 1994.

The great advantage of staying in such a charming club-like institution

India International Centre – New Delhi.

is that one is able to see Indians at work and leisure. If you are in the very sophisticated five star hotels, beautiful as they are, the predominant hotel guests are foreigners. In the International Centre it is quite the reverse and very nice too. There is now a recent annexe which is equally well thought out with its own restaurants and theatres. The food in the various dining rooms and lounges is good and inexpensive and it makes it much easier to entertain for business and pleasure. In May we had a lovely suite with its own balcony, sitting room, bedroom area and bathroom overlooking the Lodi Garden.

The garden was laid out around the beautiful tombs of the Lodi and Sayyid sultans who ruled north India in the 15th and 16th centuries. There used to be a village where the garden now exists but it was relocated in 1936 when the garden was then called Lady Willingdon Park. It was renamed Lodi Garden in 1947 and was relandscaped by J. A. Stein and Garrett Eckbo in 1968. Depending on the season the garden is very pleasant. In January and February and perhaps March the flower beds are full of English country garden flowers but by May the heat is intense and only the flowering trees and shrubs give colour. It is a favourite garden for Delhi picnickers, mothers with babes in prams and the jogging fraternity. Early in the morning before the heat takes over we would observe the earnest Delhi jogger or walker of all ages. We decided to join them but at a very leisurely walk. The scene was attractive and interesting – the young perhaps using the opportunity for flirtation, the military types walking in

Lodi Tombs in Lodi Gardens in cultural New Delhi.

stern fashion, whole families out to take the air, humble youths playing simple cricket – all this going on daily around the tomb of Mohammed Shah who died in 1444, or the Bara Gumbad and Masjid erected in 1494 and the Sheesh Gumbad which is decorated with tiles in two shades of blue, giving it a glazed appearance. That same blue pottery is still made in Delhi by one family nowadays, Hazarilal – we have a most beautiful lamp in the classic shape and a vase and plate to match. Those items are only forty years old, bought by my parents, but it is amazing to think that they are being manufactured in the same way as those tiles of centuries ago. A special mix of powdered quartz is used to make the stoneware base which is then glazed blue, with ingredients which were used for the pre-Mughal and Mughal domes. The tomb of Sikander Lodi built in 1517 resembles Mohammed Shah's tomb but there are no *chhattris* along the dome. Each morning when I walked out of the International Centre's gates into the Lodi Garden there was an extraordinary feeling that here I was in modern New Delhi built by the last great imperial invaders but if I looked through the early sun's rays I would catch a glimpse of folk who had lived and worked in the intervening centuries since the tombs had been built five hundred years ago.

There is so much to see in Delhi that it would take a stay of several weeks to do it justice. Critics of Delhi dismiss it and say that it should be just a jumping-off place, but that is usually extreme youth in its arrogance and ignorance talking.

Indraprastha in 1400 BC was the ancient Delhi on the banks of the Jamuna; the legendary Pandavas of the Mahabharata are said to have ruled from here in the eastern part of the city. The last Hindu kingdom in north India was ruled from an area in South Delhi. Delhi remained a capital city almost throughout the period between 1190 and 1526, of a state whose boundaries kept shifting and which include Afghanistan and the Deccan. The Mamluks were succeeded by Khaljis, Tughlaqs, Sayyids and Lodis.

Not only was Delhi the site of royal power but after the fall of Baghdad in 1358, when the Caliphate shifted to Cairo, it became the capital of Islam in India. Along with Ajmer in Rajasthan it was a major centre for Sufism – a popular form of Islam which came close to Hindu mysticism.

Delhi's architecture and opulence were famous and breathtaking in the medieval world and became a magnet for all – merchant adventurers, devout pilgrims – and marauders like Timur. In 1398 Timur and his armies ransacked Delhi – in similar fashion to the actions of the Crusaders in Constantinople in 1204.

Vasco de Gama, the ultimate merchant adventurer, was to land on India's shores at Calicut and the Portuguese proceeded to behave in a barbaric fashion in the name of Christendom; that was exactly five hundred years ago. Thirty years later Babur of Samarkand, descendant of Timur and Genghis Khan, challenged Ibrahim Lodi and was successful. Babur's diary is a most valuable document because he details his opinions of the newly conquered land and writes with complete candour and in some detail. His description of the elephant, which hitherto he had not encountered, is enchanting, as are his details on the fauna and flora of 'Hindustan'. The Mughals, as we have seen, were an immensely successful dynasty, but by the 18th century the empire began to crumble following the death of Aurangzeb in 1707.

The Maratha Empire followed, stretching to the north and east from the Deccan, but by 1750 they too had been defeated by Afghan invaders. By the end of the century the Rajputs turned to Britain to help rid themselves of the Marathas, and thus British Rule came into existence. The Regulating Act turned the East India Company into a British administrative agency and Warren Hastings was appointed the first Governor-General of British India. By 1815–18 the Marathas had finally been vanquished and almost the entire subcontinent was now under the direct rule of the British. In 1857–58 the Indian Mutiny, or as I prefer to call it, first Indian Revolt, took place, sparked off by a false rumour that bullets were greased with cow and pig fat thus offending both Hindu and Muslim soldiers. The Rajputs allied themselves to the British and after intense fighting, with severe atrocities committed by both sides, the British finally won.

In the mid-19th century imperial arrogance and ignorance were equal partners and though lessons were said to have been learnt, Indians were to continue to feel the yoke of the overlord. In 1877 Queen Victoria was pro-

Raj Ghat Gandhiji's Memorial.

claimed Empress of India and from that moment India was governed by a viceroy and an Indian Council. In 1885 the Indian National Congress held its first meeting and the seeds of the movement to free India from British imperial rule were sown.

The British had changed the capital from Delhi to Calcutta but in 1911 the decision to return to Delhi and construct a whole new imperial capital was taken and Sir Edwin Lutyens was commissioned to design and build the capital fit for an Empire. This was in line with the building that had taken place in South Africa and other dominions.

Fifty years after Independence Delhi is a teeming city state, fully mindful of the seven cities that have gone before but full of their legacy and now interacting with the whole world. Countries vie with each other to gain a market share for their respective manufacturers, others send their skilled engineers to persuade the government that they too should be allowed a manufacturing base within the subcontinent; world-renowned designers fly to India to find inspiration for their next season's collections, and professional bodies invariably find Delhi an exotic venue in which to hold world conferences, be they on human medicine, veterinary medicine or other world-encompassing topics.

Waking up one morning in March feeling incredibly weary from an overnight journey, I heard the muezzin's call from the great Jama Masjid (Friday Mosque). For one night I was staying at The Park Hotel and therefore within range of the sound. It reinvigorated me and as I looked out of the window I saw the wheeling flocks of pigeons swoop and fly in circles with the sound of the muezzin floating like a benediction across this great teeming place. It filled me with hope for Delhi and for India – some things never change, God willing, and that continuity will always bring strength to a vital people who will find a way to go forward, building on the centuries of heritage.

As I have already said, there is so much to see but the way to do it is to pace oneself and if time permits arrange for a guide and hire a car with driver which works out cheaper and a great deal more convenient than endlessly hailing a taxi. Moreover should a shopping excursion present itself then the shopping can be safely stowed in the car until the frenzy has passed! Frankly you could shop until you drop, but seriously there are so many wonderful things to buy – Kashmiri carpets, fabrics from all over the subcontinent, jewellery, brass and silverware, leather goods, objets d'art across the spectrum from simple village to gallery sophistication, artwork, books, furniture that can be shipped overseas and clothes. Nowadays an immense proportion of the world's clothes for both genders are manufactured in India and sold under well-known brand names in western countries, and probably the east as well. On our journey to Bareilly we met two young men who were quality controllers for leather and brassware travelling to Moradabad, the large city one stop before Bareilly. It seems that Uttar Pradesh has become the manufacturing base for all the wrought iron work that is currently so fashionable along with the metal/aluminium look in the West, and Saharanpur further north in the same state is a centre for furniture made out of *sheesham* wood. As a child in the 1950s I had lived in Saharanpur so the idea that exporting to the West has brought prosperity to the local artisans is a happy thought.

Eating out in Delhi is also an adventure and visits to the various five star hotel restaurants can be very enjoyable. We particularly enjoyed the Bukhara and the Dum Phukt in the Maurya Sheraton – the food was outstanding in attractive surroundings. Way over in South Delhi there is The Village Bistro which is a huge complex of eight restaurants including Continental, South Indian, North Indian, Chinese and kebab and tandoori specialities. Lunchtime is very well catered for by The Imperial which is so central and has the added advantage of Thomas Cook to hand, besides what could be nicer than sitting out on the hotel's terrace overlooking the green lawns on a winter's afternoon. Inside there is an Indian buffet and much entertainment to be had just earbending to the various tables around one where so often parliamentarians are thrashing out some political strategy. In November we were fascinated by the horse-trading going on at the table next to us and as the Government was in danger of falling it was doubly intriguing. An election was called very soon after that occasion. At the Santushti shopping complex, originally started by military officers' wives, there is The Basil and Thyme bistro. This is a very popular lunch-time venue where the young and fashion conscious like to be seen. The shopping complex itself is at the sophisticated end of the spectrum and interesting in a beautiful garden setting.

Best of all however is the warm hospitality extended by Indians, old friends or new acquaintances. Anybody can travel the world and view each new place from the poolside or shopping mall of a glamorous hotel, but to begin to understand a country it requires visiting in the homes of the locals. I have happy memories of several such visits across the social spectrum.

Chapter Thirteen

Calcutta and Memory Lane

Graham and I flew on to Calcutta, arriving at night, but on my second trip I arrived in the early morning sunshine and was able to see this vast city sprawling beneath me. Much has changed, and only some of it is an improvement. There are new road systems which curiously serve to condense the distances, or is it that my teenage memories have distorted the reality – a bit of both, I suspect. We were on both occasions guests of dear friends Monu and Champak Basu and I had last entered their house in March 1963. It was as elegant as ever but they had made some minor changes upon which I commented. Champak seemed amazed that I should recall it so clearly. They had visited us in Edinburgh in 1996 and been special guests at my mother's 85th birthday, but it was lovely to catch up with them in their own surroundings and I looked forward to meeting Srila again and seeing their little granddaughters for the first time. Like all close families the grandchildren play an important part in their lives and the family circle brings that special relaxation. The youngest grand-daughter was to celebrate her fifth birthday on our last full day and prepa-rations were busy and fraught. The little one was to be dressed in a new dress especially ordered by her 'Nani' and to prevent her elder sister feel-ing left out 'Nani' was hurriedly making a matching skirt – this suddenly became a last-minute problem because a chubby seven-year-old does not have a defined waistline, but frantic improvisations were a success. Early in the morning we sat and drank tea on the first-floor terrace, surrounded by exotic blooms, with the calls of the various hawkers floating up to us and Calcutta's snarling traffic already making its presence felt. In the east the early morning is a special time and a quiet cup of tea and glance at *The Statesman* – Calcutta's national newspaper – was a pleasant way to relax and chat.

Calcutta was a British creation. The exhibition at the Victoria Memorial takes one through from its creation to the present day. Job Charnock stepped ashore from his ship in 1690, having sailed down the river from Hoogly which was the little port and factory site for the East India Trading Company. He chose the area between three villages, Kalikata, Govindapur and Sutanuti, as the new site for the enlarged factory for the company, and thus was Calcutta born. It therefore has none of Delhi's antiquity and heritage, and though it went on to become the capital of India, second city of the Empire and a world centre it went into decline after World War II. Today it strikes one as a city in decay and sadly so many of the fine build-

The Memorial to Queen Victoria in Calcutta, West Bengal.

ings of a century ago are being allowed to crumble and add to the air of decrepitude.

With Partition at Independence Calcutta had to withstand the onslaught of hundreds of thousands of refugees from what was East Pakistan and then again as a result of the Indo–Pakistan conflict of 1971 and the creation of Bangladesh when it broke away from Pakistan. It was already suffering from a population explosion but this was to deal it a body blow and put the city's utilities under severe strain. However, it appears that some of these problems have been overcome and in many ways Calcutta enjoys a stability that places like Delhi do not. Nor should one endlessly harp on about its disadvantages because Calcutta, though a city of over 12 million people, has a warmth and friendliness about it that is recognised throughout the subcontinent.

Kipling rather sneeringly wrote 'From the midday halt of Charnock ... More's the pity grew a city, as fungus spreads chaotic, from its bed so it spread, Chance directed, chance erected laid and built on the silt. Palace, pyre, hovel, poverty and pride Side by side ...'.

There is now a metro and a second Howrah Bridge to complement the original built in 1941 by the British. Some said that the Victoria Memorial was built to rival the Taj Mahal. Well, it does not in any way do that, yet it stands imposing and serene with its reflections mirrored in the surrounding ornamental pools on a sunny day. I had never entered it before and found the present exhibition well presented. It was encouraging to see so many local visitors and in fact we were the only Europeans present and thus asked to pose with numerous groups and families for photographs. This building had also held a fascination for me but when I was a child it had nothing of worth inside to encourage a visit, I was told. Indeed Mother recalls vividly how it had to be camouflaged during the war to prevent Japanese bomber pilots using it as a marker in their raids over the Kidderpore docks a few miles away. I had heard that serious renovation of the various oil paintings in the interior is being undertaken and this will enhance a fine building. Indians are mature and now with a half century past since Independence see the relics of British imperialism in their perspective. I truly hope so and I do hope they will conserve the other buildings around BBD Bagh (previously Dalhousie Square).

For me Calcutta is a place of family history; my paternal grandparents were married in the Roman Catholic chapel of Fort William, which today is still a military establishment though I believe the chapel is now a library; my maternal grandparents were married in the Scots Kirk of St Andrew in Dalhousie Square. Grandfather Ord had been an elder and was the treasurer to the kirk session. My own parents were also married in St Andrew's, three days prior to Father going off to war in the Malayan campaign. My own confirmation took place in the Cathedral of St Paul by the Metropolitan Bishop of India, Burma and Ceylon in April 1961. This building was consecrated in 1847 and is in a Gothic style painted a pale shade of grey. The steeple fell during an earthquake in 1897 and there was further damage in the 1934 'quake and it had to be rebuilt. St Paul's is still very much in use but sadly St Andrew's is only opened about twice a year for services. My mother sometimes indulges nostalgia by visiting the Kirk of St Andrew and St George in Edinburgh's George Street as this was the model for that church so far away which is its exact replica with curved interior and elegant simplicity. Were she to go back to Calcutta there would be too many ghosts. My maternal grandparents are buried in the now famous Park Street cemeteries as are other relatives, but that was a pilgrimage from which I refrained. The sepia photographs of them in my family album are altogether happier reminders.

As a girl I would ride my pony, Miss Muffet, on the Maidan (great stretch of green) and then canter or gallop round the Race Course. Very often the Commissioner for Calcutta Police, Mr P. K. Sen, would kindly ask me to accompany him. In my mind's eye I see a small pigtailed girl astride a bay mare, keeping up gamely with a large man confidently riding a huge magnificent black horse called Fujiyama. Because of his status those around would wish to show deference but 'P. K.' would chat to me and encourage me to ride without a saddle to enhance my horsemanship. After these early morning rides P. K. would presumably go off to his office and I would go home to bathe and change and go to school. Sometimes if it was a holiday my mother would suggest we go to Flury's for breakfast and this was a huge treat. Flury's still exists but I think in a different form. In the '50s and '60s it was the place to go for coffee or tea and cakes and pastries and savouries. Moreover the Swiss manager with his charming jovial manner would be only too pleased to make special birthday cakes and tiny marzipan figures with which to grace a birthday table. Calcutta in those days could produce the most memorable Sachertorte or other delectable patisserie and the detail of the icing and marzipan work could rival anything in Vienna or Geneva! Very often dinner party hostesses did not even try to concoct sumptuous desserts, they just went in advance to Flury's and could be confident of a showstopper!

Club life is very lively in Calcutta and it was a pleasure to once again sample the freshness of Tollygunge. How many times have I swum in that old-fashioned pool and then sunned myself on the racecourse outside. In those days Tollygunge had its own small racecourse and it was possible to have tea on the lawn, play golf and watch horse racing all at the same time, Oh! and have a game of tennis as well if the opportunity arose. Sometimes it seems that was the end of an era, but like all of life it has simply evolved and now the well-to-do Indians are all, I am glad to say, doing similar things. Calcutta needs these distractions as it is a cultural city but with little opportunity for rural leisure. The city and country clubs give an opportunity for relaxation and socialising. Golf is now a major status sport.

In other aspects of life there is also continuity. The little Basu grand-daughters attend school at La Martiniere, a private establishment, and that is where my mother started her school life before going back to Britain in the 1920s. Before I left India for boarding school in Winchester I attended Miss Scrimshaw's in Alipore and then Miss Martin George's in Camac Street. Indeed I recall vividly writing my 11 Plus exam for entry to Saint Swithun's in the classroom of the nursery folk. Miss Martin George was quite a martinet and very annoyed with me subsequently. The English paper asked the pupil to describe the room in which he or she was seated for the examination. I did just that, but with a child's no-nonsense eye described it without frills. Miss Martin George had through middle age lost the ability to see the room with its peeling wall pictures and shabby schoolroom furniture, she presumably still saw it in its pristine colours of yesteryear! Now in Camac Street there is another school, I believe, run by the Charity Future Hope. In this school no one is privileged or returning home at the end of the school day to parental mansions of affluence. The pupils are gathered from the street children of Calcutta and it is the brain-child of Tim and Erica Grandage. Through education to be able to change the aspirations of some of these children who have been hardened by the harshness and deprivation of their lives is a wonderful opportunity and one I would dearly love to help. The Grandages have registered their char-ity in Britain and operate from a London address in W11.

Calcutta does not require intense sightseeing but for the energetic there is plenty to choose from; however for me it was a journey of nostalgia and such happy memories. Yes, it is a shabby, decrepit, overpopulated city but there are still some rare instances of great beauty and special experiences.

We required to buy a birthday present and where else to go than the New Market, formerly the Sir Stewart Hogg Market. This is a huge sprawling conglomeration of shops under cover. Part of it was burnt down in 1985 but happily it was rebuilt. In childhood a visit to the New Market was always an exciting way to spend a couple of hours. Now seen through the eyes of a well-travelled mature adult it still has charm, but one would need to be very selective. However, everything you could possibly ever want is on sale in different shops which are laid out rather like a European indoor market in France or Italy. As you leave the car a porter (or coolie) approaches – I signalled my acceptance of him and said that we needed a toy shop. The man strode ahead and I followed with Graham bringing up the rear. Unknown to me he was thinking 'Fancy Aline remembering the way after all this time ...'. I had not of course but was confident of our leader! At the toy shop we inspected everything with the help of two assistants and finally decided on a globe. Having made the purchase, I put it into the coolie's basket and Graham queried it and said he would carry the item and tried courteously to dispense with the man. I explained that that was not how things are done and to trust me. After toys we wanted the florists; I would try to find the flower shop where my mother used to shop and have them make a bouquet of flowers for Champak. We were led to the arcade of flowers and duly ordered the bouquet, comprising gladioli in subtle shades. Gladioli are very popular in Indian flower markets all over the country but I would not allow any old mixture of colours. This required time and care. The three of us stood waiting and watching the preparation. I was beginning to wilt from the heat and humidity and the coolie and I had a conversation which ranged round my childhood, parents and now my own children. I said that they were now grown men in their twenties and that I missed them. Then transpired a superb monologue – it would be generous to describe it as a dialogue. The old coolie said of course that was the way of life, children are precious but they grow up and become men but in your heart they are always your babies. So much I understood but my rusty inadequate vocabulary was letting me down. I found all that he said so moving and translated for Graham who agreed vigorously with gestures and several "Hahs". He talked about Calcutta and his life and then when we left for the car he naturally followed with our purchases. He bade me look for him again when I come and that he would see me. We parted with that spontaneous affection that can just happen in India and I gave him what I hoped was a generous tip – it apparently was. All around the poor were begging – young girls, old women, mothers with babes in arms; we tried to give something but truly one needs a bottomless purse and that we do not have. We returned to the Basu home, contented with our outing but troubled by all we saw around us. However, some superb home cooking and pleasant relaxed conversation after a much needed shower were very enjoyable.

Calcutta still has Armenians and Chinese communities tucked away in little corners of the city centre. Somehow they cling to their ancestral identities and cultures. The Armenians were a large community in my youth and several well-to-do children were in prep school with me a huge proportion of the Armenians seem to work as railway drivers and in management, and as craftsmen. The Chinese continue as they have always done but I think their standing was affected by the Indo–Chinese war of November 1962 which I clearly recall. Certainly the Chinese hairdresser that we all went to in the early 1960s, very near to the New Market, was discovered to be a listening post for the Chinese Government and the owner and some of her girls were arrested. Since I was only 16 at the time I was duly very impressed with the idea that my hair had been dressed by a spy! Images of black and white movies with Trevor Howard admonishing one that 'careless talk cost lives' came to mind.

In March there was a curious feeling I experienced that I was part onlooker and part player in an Indian game. I was in Calcutta on business and required some legal advice. Having been driven to the building near the High Court, I had to make my way through the throng on the pavement and find the right office on the fifth floor. It was astonishing. The sheer magnitude of the crowd, the endless hawking, talking, bargaining going on all around me. The lift was under pressure so I elected to walk up the stairs, which were unfinished and dirty. As I climbed my heart sank, but on entering the offices of the legal firm all was as it should be, a hive of activity in reasonable office-like decor. To descend I took the lift which though speedy was stiflingly hot and once again found myself on the overcrowded pavement. Having signalled the driver we set off for the next appointment, but by now I was in air-conditioned seclusion looking out on the multitudes – a spectacle through the window glass. The driver enthusiastically started to tell me about the cricket and how the first Test against the Australians would soon be taking place – cricket is now also a religion in India. We passed by the Eden Gardens where the game would be played and I thought of the funeral a few months previous of Mother Teresa that had taken place in the same arena, the little old woman now an icon for poor and suffering, and the icons of the sports' fraternity, heroes of bat and ball capable of providing national pride or collective sorrow. When the traffic light created a pause the sellers of strawberries harassed me through the window and I observed a weary rickshaw wallah mopping his brow. Somehow everything and everyone had a bit part in an endless drama, and one minute I felt part of it and in the next was merely an observer.

The birthday party on our first visit was a thoroughly happy affair with lots of little people all intent on stuffing their mouths with crisps and sweeties; the *kooi* (puffed rice) bag strung up on the ceiling was burst and the eager recipients of its little gifts scrambled about the floor picking things up as fast as possible. I recalled my own similar birthdays and the trouble my parents took to make them happy occasions. It was ever thus for the lucky ones. I did the same for my sons in their boyhood, agonising about what shape of birthday cake to devise and inventing games to play and win. At the end of such a day it is always special to see children content, tired and happy, playing with new toys and browsing through books. At Srila and Gopal's it was the same. The little girls helped their father make a list of all the toys that had been received so their donors could be thanked. In making the list each item was inspected and commented upon, but the older girl was quietly curled up already deeply absorbed by a new story. I resolved that in future my gifts would be books.

West Bengal was a very prosperous state and flourished under the British rule; this gave rise in turn to a flowering of culture, and the Bengali language was enriched by poets and writers such as Rabindranath Tagore. Temple building flourished and philosophers appeared – like Ramakrishna and Vivekananda. The British were not however the only colonisers. At Serampore the Danish East India Company had carried on trade from the 17th century till 1845 when they sold their possessions to the British. Subsequently the Serampore College was established and incorporated in 1827 as a university by Danish Royal Charter. This was the first modern university in the whole of Asia. The College is still active and is now a Baptist theological institute.

At Chandernagore there is a gate bearing the motto of the French Republic – *Liberté, Égalité, Fraternité* – and there had been an establishment of learning since 1673 to 1952. Even now though hardly anybody speaks French there is a French atmosphere with a church that resembles a French village church called the Église du Sacre Coeur along with its statue of Joan of Arc and a Lourdes' grotto. My paternal grandmother Aline had family ties here; her father had been an indigo farmer and when they were orphaned the de Veria sisters grew up in Raja Santosh Road in Alipore, a fashionable suburb of Calcutta, where later I was to live as a small child.

The Dutch settled at Chinsura further north and ceded it to Britain in 1826 and there still remain a Dutch barracks, a church and a cemetery. The Armenians built St John's at Chinsura in 1695 and annually in January the Armenians from Calcutta come to hold joint services on St John's day. The Portuguese created the Church of Our Lady of Bandel in 1599 and it was rebuilt after being destroyed by Shah Jahan in 1632. The Portuguese controlled the majority of the trade that passed through West Bengal in the time of the Mughal Empire before the other European nations arrived. Bandel is still the site of an annual pilgrimage and also famous for the local little cheeses that are made there; I was so glad to be able to taste them again when staying with the Basus. At Imambara there is a Shiite mosque and further north of Hooghly are numerous Hindu temples of renown. The surrounding 100 miles around Calcutta have a wealth of holy places to visit and absorb but getting around is challenging and only the most dedicated traveller would probably persevere.

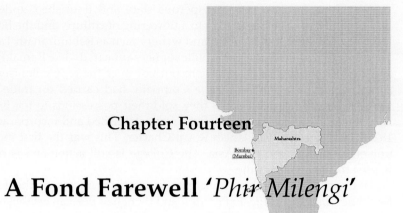

Chapter Fourteen

A Fond Farewell *'Phir Milengi'*

In March I flew on to Mumbai, and Graham and I returned there in May on business. This is an unlovely city and though generally acknowledged to be India's most energetic and successful metropolis, home to the Indian Stock Exchange and centre for a huge film industry that rivals Hollywood in sheer output, I do not enjoy it as a place. By comparison to the other metropolitan cities it is expensive and full of a brashness with no real architectural charm. Arriving in daylight by air fills one with dismay – the shanty towns seem to stretch for miles. The hotels are all very expensive and the fact that it is a favourite leisure venue for the wealthy from the Middle Eastern kingdoms gives it a raffishness that I do not like. Indian society however is full of energy and the hospitality is as generous as ever and indeed we were warmly welcomed on three different occasions.

Travelling by car in Mumbai can take a long time; the city is spread along the coast and a car journey for dinner can easily take up to an hour or more one way. We count ourselves fortunate in having good friends and acquaintances in Mumbai but it will never be a favourite destination, more a base from which to visit Gujarat, Goa and the charming south of India.

The heat and humidity in May was quite simply overwhelming. The dry heat of Rajasthan or Delhi is infinitely preferable to this. As we finally left on a hot sticky night in May I reflected on a year that had seen me travel 50,000 miles on three occasions to and within India. Exhausted but happy I wondered when I would return, but determined to do so.

Beloved Bharat, land of my birth, there is so much yet to explore and experience; fishing on the Cauvery River for *mahseer* in South India, Kerala and its many attractions, Sikkim for its famous flora, Himachal Pradesh for its lush valleys, a return to the source of the Ganges which I have not seen for nearly forty years, the wildlife parks and the great temples of South India, Gujarat and its ancient architecture, a truly marvellous choice, and always with the opportunity to meet up with or make good friends.

Sitting in my study, looking out on the green Peeblesshire hills covered in a light dusting of snow, with the sheep grazing contentedly I look down and see a grey squirrel on the garden wall with two robins fighting for supremacy on the bird table. Raju, my little black cat, stretches and that action somehow reminds me of an Indian garden, with the shy movements of a mongoose venturing out in the morning sunshine; a blackbird enters the bird table impasse but in my mind's eye they are green parakeets and that screeching sound? Surely, that was the call of the peacock.

Chapter Fifteen

2001

Since I completed the book in January 1999 so much has happened personally to us as a family and to the world in general. Now that the book is to be published shortly I thought it appropriate to conclude with my current thinking that is relevant to India.

In the run-up to Christmas 2001, to which we are greatly looking forward, as it will be the first time that our family will all be together for several years and with the addition of our first grandchild, I have been sorting out our book shelves, redistributing the titles and making way for the books we have either received or bought throughout the last year or two. There, in a top corner I found *Malakand Field Force 1897* by W. Spencer Churchill. Ours is a Colonial Silver Library Edition printed in 1901. A century later our televisions have been featuring the 21st century's war in Afghanistan, yet reading Winston Churchill writing over a hundred years ago and looking at the detailed maps, I am forced to murmur "... same country, different protagonists ..."

My thoughts have gone back to December forty years ago when still a schoolgirl, singing carols in an old peoples' home in Winchester along with my peer group. After a rousing session we sat down and talked with the old folk. I had the good fortune to meet a very old gentleman who told me proudly he had fought in the Second Afghan War and he reminisced gently about it. He was thus prompted because I said I would be flying out to India for a family Christmas. I wish I had had the wit to write down what he said but I do remember him talking about harsh terrain, fear, cruelty and barbarism. Yes, indeed, those are words with which we have all become very familiar in the last three months of this year.

Now, tragically, as I am writing the news bulletins give details of a terrorist attack on the Indian Parliament. This could once more bring India and Pakistan to the edge of the abyss. I pray that both countries will behave with restraint and maturity.

Someone once wisely wrote that this quarrel is like a family feud between cousins. It could be said that Pakistan is perhaps the 'cousin' with the negative/poor-relation attitude. India has a powerful idea of its own identity, and is a major force in South Asia, with armed forces totalling 1.26 million and justifiably proud of her huge enduring democracy. Hopefully, diplomacy and a commitment to peace and a desire for coexistence will prevail.

In the decades to come when historians reflect on the 20th century, I think they will categorize it as 'a hundred years' war'. This hundred years' war will have been different from the medieval one, which only encompassed Europe; this one encompassed the world. Curiously though, if you talk to young people about the events and people of the 20th century, among the great leaders and makers of history one man transcends all the others. Why? Because he wanted to change things peacefully. Gandhi's legacy to India is immeasurable and is an example to all of us.

For me it was a very emotional experience to visit Raj Ghat in Delhi and visit the site of Gandhiji's funeral pyre. I most sincerely recommend it as an essential visit to the traveller who visits Delhi. Having driven through the hustle and bustle of the city, when one finally arrives, takes off footwear and walks into the peaceful oasis that is Raj Ghat, there is a serenity and air of friendliness that exemplifies the dichotomy of India. Chaos, confusion, noise and perhaps even aggression on the roads and then silence, birdsong, a gentle smiling greeting from fellow Indian visitors. Sit awhile and look around and read the inscriptions. I found it comforting to purchase a small posy of flowers to lay on the plinth as others do. Watch the *mali* mowing the lawn, in the most timeless way – directing a bullock that is pulling a lawnmower – what could be more Indian or more engaging?

Gandhiji said that 'if we all did a little then a lot would be achieved'. That is not a direct quotation rather a distillation of his thoughts but it is timeless advice. Those of us who have connections with India or just visit can all do a little, or if circumstances allow, much more. The opportunities for practical help are many and varied. When natural disasters strike, the United Kingdom is so generous and prompt in its giving, but on a regular basis there are significant ways to help; be it old people under Help the Aged's Adopt a Granny scheme, which I know to be very worthwhile and rewarding, or whole families picking up their lives after a disaster who can be sponsored through Christian Aid, or most important of all, helping to educate children. A happy childhood is the foundation of life but for a huge number of disadvantaged children, just survival is their aim.

Westerners abhor the idea of child labour but in truth it is a reality for the poor in India. Despite legislation it is known that in the remote villages and rural areas, 80 per cent of children between the ages of six and fourteen are in regular work and do not attend school. Similarly, children you as visitors might see on the streets of the big cities are eking a living, often without support from family and yearn to have the opportunity for schooling.

My gentle suggestion is that if you have the good fortune to go and travel around India, perhaps in some style and comfort, and if you buy a lovely carpet or *dhurries*, think about helping to educate the young folk who very probably wove your new prized possession. Project Mala is just such an action programme for the Scheduled Castes and Tribes, and their students between the ages of nine and eleven have never had the opportunity of formal education. Moreover, Project Mala does not discriminate between boys and girls and the student ratio is approximately fifty–fifty. The great sadness of child labour is that mostly these children grow up illiterate and miss out on their formative years, which has a lasting effect on their personal development. That in turn impacts on the country as a whole. Those of us who may have the opportunity to make a difference can find it infinitely rewarding.

It is estimated that there are over 250 million children deprived of their childhood worldwide, and Asia contributes to 60 per cent of this problem; within India alone there are approximately 60 million child labourers. The garment industry and several others like the diamond and gemstone cutting and polishing units, the manufacture of fireworks and matches, slates and pencils, glass and bangle works, and other traditional manufacturers have historically employed young children. Affluent Indians are also known to employ young children as servants, much as was done in the UK in the 19th century and before. I would like to emphasise that what we Westerners now see as an abomination, we in this country and the rest of Europe have been guilty of in past centuries. Economic prosperity and education will be the dynamic to change this, but pragmatically it will take at least another fifty years to effect.

A very worthy cause is the Butterflies Programme for School and Working Children which is also in New Delhi and struggles heroically to help its young members to be educated and have some stability and security in their dangerous street lives.

India's five star hotels are becoming increasingly famous for their 'out of this world' provision for well-to-do travellers. So many have come into being recently that it would be invidious to recommend any one, but I know personally that they provide unique, friendly luxury and wonderful experiences. The heritage hotels have continued to expand and upgrade and I am continually sent fresh details on the delights that await us on another visit. Indeed, Graham and I plan two visits – one will be to Kerala as we promised ourselves earlier, and the other is to the wildlife and game sanctuaries. Jungle odysseys are readily available at Kaziranga in Assam, or Corbett in the Himalayas, Ranthambhore in Rajasthan or Kanha in central India. They beckon with the promise of wonderful wildlife and that essential feeling of wilderness and timelessness. In the south there is Periyar, which can easily be included in a visit to Kerala.

Last year we travelled 32,000 miles on a tour of Malaysia, both peninsula and Borneo, Singapore, Brunei and Viet Nam. It was a very special and enjoyable trip which I would thoroughly recommend to active and healthy people. Viet Nam is welcoming and interesting but relatively inexperienced in its tourist industry, but they will catch up with the rest of the East very quickly. Malaysia offers both sophistication and primitive experiences to the traveller. However, on reflection I feel that India will always provide a wider choice of antiquity, history, colour, wildlife, beaches, trekking and that intangible quality of spiritual adventure – and perhaps spiritual fulfilment. On a more prosaic note, the variety of shopping is huge and intoxicating.

Finally I would say that those still left with a perception that India is a third world country with a crumbling transport system and people living in poverty, please consider that this is the world's largest democracy of a billion people and the middle classes in India are equivalent to the whole population of the United States. Doctors, scientists, and computer experts, accountants and management consultants from India are in demand all over the world. Materials originating in India influence the clothing industry worldwide, and much of what we wear in the west is manufactured in the subcontinent.

The dichotomy of designer hotels in Delhi or the beach shack restaurants of Goa and Kerala, mist lifting from the lakes at Bharatpur revealing teeming wildlife, the cough of a tiger at Corbett in the undergrowth filling one with excitement and anticipation, watching the sunrise on the mountain peaks in the Himalayan Range, diving off the Lakshadweep Islands; it is all there for you to experience within the constraints of your own personal health, energy and vigour. However sophisticated and efficient the tourist industry might become in India, it is possible to take a side step and experience this vast country's timeless rhythm and fundamental beauty.

I leave you with my abiding memory of a sunset and the peacocks preparing to roost for the night; the dark silhouettes of the birds in the trees, with behind them the crimson glow of the sun setting and slowly descending with a sky gradually becoming deep blue and then black, and tomorrow bringing the promise of a new beautiful day.

December 2001

Part II

Part II

Acknowledgements to Part II

My three books have been welcomed by many people and so I am writing a Part II to this first book for its reissue, which will complete the circle of my writing about the decade between India's 50th and 60th anniversaries of Independence, though I prefer the word Nationhood for such an ancient and great land.

In this last ten years I have made so many new friends through my writing and feel very fortunate to have had this enjoyable continuing opportunity to visit India.

Graham, my husband, always comes in for a very big heartfelt 'thank you' for his enthusiasm and commitment to what I set out to do. He too loves India.

In India, and in other parts of the world, through the books I have met like-minded people and others who simply wanted to help and to them all, old friends and new, I again give my heartfelt thank you.

Aline Dobbie
May 2008

Chapter Sixteen

Delhi in 2008

Here in the Scottish Borders as I write there is a clear blue sky with bright sunshine and the noise outside my study is deafening from the chattering swallows who are inspecting the south-facing eave of our roof for a likely 'des res'; we have been fortunate to host them on two previous summers and now there are even more couples swooping and diving and inspecting and chattering. One pair even mistakenly swooped into the sitting room and I held my breath but they quickly saw it was not a choice and flew out! However there will be most likely at least three mud nests and then the joy of the babies and watching them fledge.

The wild garden still has a late show of daffodils and fritillaries with the cherries and crab apples just coming into late blossom. It has been a cold spring until a few days ago so our *mali* activities (gardeners in Hindi) have been hindered but now all is glorious and 'Mr and Mrs Pheasant' stalk amongst the late daffodils and she has laid a clutch of eggs which will come to nought because she is a silly bird and does not sit on them. Raju, our beloved little black cat, was but a kitten when I wrote the first part of this book and used to sit in my lap or right next to me. He continues to be as loving and companionable and at this time of the year is sitting in his 'boudoir' outside in the dappled shade. The squirrels and rabbits continue to be the bane of Graham's life but somehow despite them we have a beautiful garden which in warm sunny weather is a joy.

Raju has featured in all my books and even has his own folder on my huge website as Dmitry, our talented Russian friend, painted him for us in a lovely portrait in oils; the painting hangs in our family room. He is a firm favourite with our three grandchildren, the youngest of whom, Honor, calls him 'Raju cat' and he understands she is only 18 months old and to be affectionately tolerated. As for Piers and William, well, when they come to stay in 'their room' Raju always likes to settle down for the bedtime story on one of their beds and very often stays until they are fast asleep. Soon I am going to start reading some 'Indian' bedtime stories to them which will be a welcome change for me from the very loved but now mind-numbing (to the adult reader) antics of the various Mister Men!

So much has happened since I first started writing about India in 1998 and the books have led us both on a happy path throughout the wonderful land of my birth. Now we return to India annually and have the happy circumstance that I was invited to become a member of the India International Centre (IIC) in New Delhi, which I mentioned in the first part of this book. The IIC, as I think of it, is a home from home for us now and we so enjoy our stays there. The food is excellent and the staff are welcoming and friendly and the location is superb.

We try to start every day with a walk in the Lodi Gardens after some 'bed tea' and before breakfast; quite often when I awake early here in Scotland and hear the birdsong I think of my walk at sunrise in Delhi where the birdsong is different and rather raucous with the parakeets screeching around me and the little chipmunks devouring a breakfast of corn kernels; the crows are usually having a bath in the pools of water left from the hose.

Having been invited as a guest of the Government of India to attend the Republic Day Ceremonials in India's 60th year of Independence, Graham and I flew out on the 24th January 2007. What a pleasure it was to find ourselves again in Delhi. This was a Delhi bustling with anticipation for the following day's great parade and celebration of the country's anniversary of Republic Day. The security was immense and it was something we encountered from the moment of arrival. Sadly these days with so many intent on evil destruction both the civilian and military arms of government have to take immense precautions which were evident around the wide lovely roads of New Delhi.

On the day itself we left the India International Centre at just after 8.00 am so that we would have plenty of time; as it was the streets and roads were oddly quiet because of the security and the fact it is a national holiday. What I liked was observing the various young contingents being 'bussed' in or walking in columns to the Raj Path area from which they would march or perform for the VIPs and spectators. It was fortunately a lovely morning with early sunshine – at that time of year Delhi can have quite a few foggy mornings but Friday the 26th saw a blue sky and sunshine and Delhi looking lovely in the winter colours of annual flowers on the roundabouts and parks and Lodi Gardens plus a few spring blossoms on the big trees.

Our car was subjected to a most intense search and then sealed. We walked to the ambassadorial enclosure where we were to sit. It was beautifully laid out with carpets and elegant seating and a profusion of elegant flower arrangements and carefully staged bunting and the Republic of India's National Flag. Very sadly, because of the stringent security, we were instructed not to bring anything at all with us but passports and the invitation which meant I could not actually photograph the parade as it unfolded in front of us. We did however take photographs afterwards.

The Parade takes quite a long time and I had wondered typically what people would do for 'conveniences'? Well, that had been factored into the logistics naturally and one could see how it must take a few weeks every year to assemble the whole structure and cater to masses of dignitaries plus the ordinary loyal Indians who would come to rejoice on one of their national days.

We were met by the Chief of Protocol and invited to sit in the front row of seats between Ambassadors from Ghana and other African countries. There was a red carpet in front of us and the actual parade would pass only 10 feet away. A little to the side of us was a group of chairs that were totally different from ours and very soon it appeared that this was for the Russian

The floral map of India for Republic Day Parade on Raj Path 2007.

117

Proud Regiment of the Indian Army.

We paid respects at Gandhiji's Samedhi at the 60th anniversary of his murder in 2008.

contingent. President Vladimir Putin was the Guest of Honour and naturally he had brought along a delegation of high-ranking Russians. As well as looking at all that was going on around me with smart generals and military personnel arriving, I observed the Russians closely. What a cheerless bunch they proved to be. Not a smile or a polite greeting to anyone. Their body language signalled that they were totally unimpressed, did not want to be there, and how would anybody consider a bright sunny day sitting on the side of Raj Path about to witness one of the World's truly great parades an enjoyable thing to do!

The Diplomatic Corps, on the other hand, greeted each other and us and were friendly and warm and used their 'diplomatic' skills for which they are chosen to represent their respective countries. Then a high-ranking American diplomat arrived along with his relatives. He looked slightly miffed that the front row was taken and spied the chairs of the Russians and without thinking decided his party would sit there. The Protocol Chief looked dismayed and had a discreet discussion with a colleague – meanwhile we all observed the dilemma with amusement. He went up to the American and said something like, "Excellency, please would you move from these seats," and gesticulated to the rows in which we were seated. The American lounged back in his seat and said audibly, "Why, these seats are good, I like it here …" to which the Chief of Protocol hissed, "You are sitting amongst the Russians …" Well! He leapt out of his seat and walked off followed by his relatives. The Russians continued to scowl and all of us laughed. The various ambassadors found it a huge source of mirth.

Everything ran to time impeccably and soon at 9.57 am President Abdul Kalam, accompanied by the Chief Guest, President Putin of the Russian Federation, arrived in state. The Prime Minister, Dr Manmohan Singh, received the President and the Chief Guest. The Prime Minister presented to the President and the Chief Guest, the three Service Chiefs and the Defence Secretary. Once they were all seated, the national flag was unfurled. The President's Bodyguard presented the national salute. The band played the national anthem and a 21-gun salute was fired. The parade commenced.

The parade and spectators were showered with rose petals by Indian Air Force helicopters and the various regiments of the Indian Army marched past. It should be remembered that the Indian Air Force was in 2007 celebrating seventy-five years since its inception. There was a huge amount of military hardware also used in the parade and since quite a lot of this had been ordered from Russia, presumably the Russians were pleased to see it. Certainly, to my irritation, one Russian looked at nothing but took a continuous photo of the whole parade. There were mounted columns of cavalry, mechanised columns of tanks and Bofors guns and launchers and light helicopters; these were followed by marching contingents of the

PARA Regiment, the Brigade of Guards, the Rajputs and then very emo-tionally for me, my late father's regiment, the Jats. Captain Sumit Dabral commanded this contingent from the Jat Regiment which was raised in 1795, as I mentioned earlier in the book; the Regiment has taken part in action in post- and pre-Independence periods. The Battle of Dograi fought by the regiment in 1965 has been accepted by analysts as the finest battle fought by an Infantry Battalion. The regiment had been awarded five Battle Honours, eight Maha Vir Chakra, eight Kirti Chakra, thirty-two Shaurya Chakras and thirty-nine Vir Chakras and 170 Sena Medals.

The Border Security Force Camel Contingent was superb; under the command of Deputy Commandant Kamal Singh Rathore these ships of the desert are dependable companions in the inhospitable terrain of Rajasthan and the Rann of Kutch. The camel-mounted troops have been instrumental in successfully tracking down smugglers and extremists in the Rajasthan and Gujarat frontiers. They were followed by the only band of its kind in the world – the Border Security Force Camel Band. Raised in 1986 by the Rajasthan and Gujarat Frontier Force, it is now a permanent feature in all Desert and Marwar Festivals. This was a most wonderful sight.

At this point I observed the Russians had started to become animated and point and smile and enjoy the spectacle. To see a bunch of normally looking disdainful camels being made to 'march' and then the band actu-ally playing on another contingent of marching camels was a rare sight and so colourful.

The Indo–Tibetan Border Police marching contingent in alpine dress known as the 'Himveers' attired in snow combat dress guard the highest and most inhospitable borders in the world and it was a reminder of their lonely duties to see them in Delhi on the Raj Path in white dress uniform with skis on their backs. They play a vital role in India's defences.

When the Cultural Pageant started it too was most interesting and I was so pleased to see Uttarakhand's display of Corbett National Park. The tableau projected the vital importance of conservation of wildlife; the emblematic animal of India is the tiger, followed by the elephant and of course the national bird – the peacock. Jim Corbett was a family friend of whom I wrote extensively in my second book, and it was good to see his vital role in the initial stages of conservation being recognised.

The Children's National Bravery Award Contingent was also breath-taking; all these little heroes and heroines were riding on caparisoned elephants. That too was amusing in that the mahouts had to really make those elephants 'march'!

On a sombre note Teja Sai received the Sanjay Chopra Award posthu-mously as did Durga Doondieswar. These two brave youngsters in 2005 were on an organised picnic from their school when during play a ball fell into the river Munneru in Andhra Pradesh and some of the students tried to retrieve it and were in difficulties. Seeing the plight of their school mates, Durga Doondieswar and Teja Sai jumped into the river and managed to save four children and in the process the strong current washed them both away. They gave their lives for their playmates and have been duly recognised.

At the head of the elephant contingent was Kum Vandana Yadav from Uttar Pradesh who had received the Geeta Chopra Award; while in the fields with her brother, Vandana valiantly resisted three young men who tried to molest her. She was stabbed in the process but thankfully lived and the assailants were caught with the help of nearby people. She led the proud band of Brave Children and received most enthusiastic applause.

Something dear to my heart was the Stree Shakti – Empowering Women tableau. This is the programme of the Government of Delhi aimed at the empowerment of women in the capital, especially those belonging to the more vulnerable sections of society. The tableau portrayed the success stories of the women in various areas of the capital where they have proved themselves worthy and active stakeholders in the development of the city. We found the parade immensely interesting and at times profoundly moving; Vande-Matram, which means Long Live Mother India, is repeated at the end of proceedings and I found myself echoing those words!

When the various guests of honour and the political contingent and diplomatic corps had departed, Graham and I remained and he went and retrieved our cameras from the car. We wandered around and photographed and talked to people and had the rare pleasure of being able to walk down Raj Path to India Gate as it was still closed to traffic. People came up and spoke to us and we engaged with others and it was a happy and relaxed atmosphere. I had complimented the GOC who had commanded the parade and we were talking together when another general came up to us; he had overheard me refer to the Jat Regiment and he introduced himself and said that he too is a 'Jat brat'. Lt General Bartwal and his charming wife invited us to drinks that evening at his home and that meeting was the start of a firm friendship between us.

We did not stay long in Delhi last year because an opportunity arose for us to enjoy one of the very first cruises to the Lakshadweep Islands. India's first cruise ship had just commenced cruises from Goa down the Malabar Coast visiting two islands in the Lakshadweeps and going on to Sri Lanka. It was a wonderful opportunity for which we were very appreciative; I had written a significant amount of the informative material for the passengers' handbook. As I leaned on the ship's rail, looking out to sea with a beautiful sunset beginning to form, there was a pleasant feeling of anticipation and delight at the prospect of fulfilling a long-held dream of visiting the hitherto relatively unknown Lakshadweep Islands on a fortnight's cruise.

Indian Ocean Cruises owns the first ship to have been given permission to visit and land people on the Lakshadweep Islands. The ship took us to two of the Lakshadweep Islands but also showed us the delights of places like Cochin in Kerala and Colombo, capital of Sri Lanka, and inland Sri Lanka. Goa too has its many attractions and we planned to stay on in Goa for four days at our favourite hotel, the Majorda Beach Resort in the south of Goa, when the ship returned us at the end of the voyage. We had visited Goa on two previous occasions, one had been on another cruise ship and another visit was at the end of a long road journey through Karnataka when we visited the abandoned city of Hampi Vijaynagar – all of which I speak of in my third book which was published in October 2006 – *India: The Elephant's Blessing*.

This cruise proved to be very enjoyable and for those who had not had the pleasure of visiting India before I am sure they had some wonderful experiences. For Graham and me however the Lakshadweep Islands of Suheli and Cheriyam proved the greatest attractions of the whole holiday. The ship was well appointed and comfortable and the crew and 'hotel staff' were friendly and welcoming and the food was excellent and plentiful. The crew was truly international and we liked that. The Captain was very approachable and friendly with an enthusiasm which rubbed off on his passengers; moreover he operated an 'open bridge' policy and from time to time it was pleasant to go up and talk to him throughout the journey. A small ship has the advantage of being able to go into small ports and approach really close to coral islands. The Captain was always vigilant for something special like a pod of whales, which he would circle round for his passengers to fully appreciate – he liked to think of it as 'adventure cruising'.

The band played in the lounge at teatime and before dinner daily and was both talented and eager to please; their choice of music was appreciated by most of the passengers, with wonderful old standards and classic pieces plus a few really good raunchy modern tunes that are familiar to most of us.

I particularly liked being up on the mizzen deck early in the morning with a good cup of tea, looking at the ocean, watching for sea life and enjoying the sun's rays before they became too fierce. The Jacuzzis are well positioned on the mizzen deck close to the pool and there is also the opportunity to have an Ayurvedic massage or beauty treatments. I noticed that we had quite a few amateur water colourists on our voyage and they would position themselves under shade on the middle deck and were totally absorbed in their art. Uniquely this ship carried an astrologer. Hesitantly I succumbed to his gentle invitation. I was very tight lipped about my past and any personal details but he proceeded to use my exact time and date and place of birth and plot a chart on his computer which he interpreted extremely accurately – it was amazing. I am yet to find out if one of his important predictions takes place!

The Lakshadweep Archipelago is really an extension of the same one we know as the Maldives, but 200 miles further north. I just loved the pristine white coral sand and the turquoise-blue warm water and the total peace of the place. Everyone has their own priorities but for me just floating in the azure, clean coral lagoon with the blue sky above and the sun overhead was divine. We had visited the Maldives in 2004 which was a wonderful experience but the sobering event of the Asian Tsunami was present in my mind; on that occasion the idyll we had stayed in was decimated and the manager tragically died. The resort Hakura Hura has however been rebuilt.

The ship's chefs and maître'd accompany the guests to each island and proceed to provide a very good barbeque and there are plenty of chilled soft drinks available throughout one's stay. On departure from the islands everywhere is left clean and tidy without any human detritus. Graham and I were the very last people to leave the second island as the sun was setting – it had been such a lovely experience that I left with extreme reluctance and a hope that someday I will return. The lukewarm limpid aquamarine water, the absence of any development and the sun gradually setting in the west was so memorable.

Excursions are laid on for those who feel energetic and want to explore. Cochin has so much to offer the visitor and is aptly named the Venice of the East and is famed for its iconic Chinese fishing nets but we had visited there on two previous occasions which had been immensely enjoyable and which I documented in my third book *India: The Elephant's Blessing*. Local hotels provide a welcome haven to which to gravitate and spend an enjoyable afternoon swimming in the hotel pool and enjoy a taste of India, should one prefer, but from Cochin the ship lays on a tour of the famous Kerala Backwaters which should not be missed. Lazing on a houseboat on the Kerala Backwaters was an amazing experience that we had both loved in 2005 and Graham had woken up on his birthday in the middle of Lake Vembanad and we had sat in the prow and sipped early morning tea and taken in the sunrise; it was a superb, serene and unforgettable experience.

Sri Lanka too is a most beautiful island and the ship is now going to extend its inland tour to fully appreciate the historic and scenic sights around Kandy. Colombo also has elegant hotels nearby if one seeks a change of scene; I particularly love the John Keells Group Hotels like Bentota Beach where we spent a most enjoyable night this time; their hotels have a very good ethos of service and friendliness. There is so much to see in Sri Lanka and it is so pretty that one thinks of it as one huge garden. The historic ancient cities of the north are so interesting and an absolute must for anyone on a Buddhist trail. We had spent ten days in Sri Lanka in January 2004 and absolutely loved all that we experienced. It is a birdwatchers' paradise with the most wonderful birds like the paradise flycatcher, the golden ori-

Wonderful toys made out of wire sold near Gandhiji memorial at Raj Ghat Delhi.

ole and so many others all easily visible; I was speechless when a young farm manager told me to look up into the tree under which we were seated and there was the wonderful paradise flycatcher, then two minutes later I saw a golden oriole. The many kingfishers were in abundance and jacanas and other water birds could be found everywhere you looked. I fell in love with a particular hotel up at Habarana – The Cinnamon Lodge – and would love to revisit one day. We think a week in the Maldives and a week in Sri Lanka is an ideal holiday and it is easily arranged from here in the UK or indeed from India. I am mindful that a civil war continues in Sri Lanka which we know is having a hugely negative impact on her tourism. I so wish it could be resolved peacefully because ordinary Sinhalese are very deserving of security, safety and prosperity – they are the friendliest of people.

In January 2008 we again flew out to Delhi for a five-week stay in India. We stayed at the IIC but on this occasion Delhi became extremely cold and this impacted on everyone and almost everywhere in northern India. To further complicate matters Emirates had for a second time misplaced our luggage and so we were initially much inconvenienced until it finally arrived. The incompetence of their offices in Delhi would have to be experienced to be believed, but there again British Airways currently holds the title for losing the most amount of passengers' luggage. Thankfully, I had travelled in a jacket and cashmere and taken another couple of cashmere sweaters and only had to buy one quilted jacket but Graham was in need of much more as he had never hitherto experienced such dry cold in India. At one point the education authorities in Delhi and its environs closed the primary schools as it was far too cold for little ones to walk to school early in the morning and then possibly sit on ice-cold stone floors for hours and then walk back home.

In Delhi it was lovely once again to meet up with our various friends, and people were very kind and hospitable as ever to us and we returned the hospitality. Our good friend Sam Pachauri's brother Dr Rajendra Pachauri had recently been awarded the Nobel Peace Prize along with ex-Vice President Al Gore for their work on the Intergovernmental Panel on Climate Change and this was a cause for celebration for their family. Sam himself tirelessly works to help promote awareness of India's great ancient buildings and the vital need for conservation. We met General Bartwal and his family again, which was enjoyable; he, in his job as Director General of Military Intelligence for the Indian Government, was preoccupied with the security for the impending Republic Day Parade at which President Sarkozy was to be the special guest. President Sarkozy appeared to be keeping the Indians guessing as to the size of his entourage and he had not yet remarried, which all became the subject of much speculation in social Delhi! Thankfully the parade took place without any problems and we thought of our happy day the year previous.

Satish and Saroj Kumar continue to be busy and proud of their grandchildren and Satish does much good executive work for a medical charity which takes him on international journeys on behalf of that charity. Frank Christopher who is joint director of the Lok Sabha Secretariat made it possible for us to be shown round the relatively new Indian Parliament Museum located in the new Parliament Library of which I wrote in my third book. This exhibition, which is a permanent one, depicts the story of India's democratic heritage and is immensely interesting to visit for anyone really keen to understand and appreciate modern India. It must be a wonderful educational tool for the schools and colleges as they can see and feel and hear of the events that led to India's nationhood in 1947 and how it has evolved since then. From writing my own comments in the visitors' book I could see that many parliamentary delegations have come to inspect it and perhaps produce something similar in their own countries. At a time in the world when democracy seems once again to be under siege from dictators and autocrats and military juntas I think it is excellent that again India, the world's largest democracy, shows how its own road to freedom with democracy evolved.

We paid our respects to Gandhiji at his Samedhi (memorial of the cremation site) at Raj Ghat. I was mindful that the 30th January would make it the 60th anniversary of his cruel assassination. Graham and I had visited previously and I had also taken a friend in 1998 but with this significant anniversary approaching I wanted to return. As ever, there is a peaceful tranquil ambience and people behave in a respectful manner but yet are friendly. I thought of that little man – one of the greats of the 20th century and all he had bequeathed us. John Ruskin, who had been a great influence on Gandhi, had said, "I desire to leave this one great fact clearly stated ... there is no wealth but life." Gandhiji said, "I have nothing new to teach the world. Truth and Non-violence are as old as the hills ... My life is my message."

It has been suggested that John Ruskin and Mohandas Karamchand Gandhi were some of the great seers of the 19th and 20th centuries. Gandhi said that Ruskin's book *Unto This Last* made him reconsider his own life and indeed he went on to say 'it so captured me and made me transform my life'. The values and ideals he imbibed from John Ruskin's book he put into practice when he founded the Phoenix Settlement in South Africa in 1904. The message of Gandhiji already spans the entire world and has been the inspiration for people like Nelson Mandela, the late Martin Luther King, Aung San Suu Kyi of Burma, and maybe now is a talisman for the opposition leaders in Zimbabwe which is being brought to its knees by a dangerous deranged dictator who is flouting democracy whilst the world looks on and waits.

On the 15th June 2007, the UN General Assembly voted unanimously to celebrate the 2nd October, Gandhiji's birthday, from then on as the International day of Non-Violence, in honour of India's greatest son Mahatma Gandhi. In 2006 Graham and I had visited the hallowed precincts of Gandhi Smriti on Tees January Marg; the Smriti is the house which has become a monument to the last 144 days of his life. It was a mansion that belonged to the Birla family but was acquired by the Indian Government in 1971 as a museum. It has become a place of pilgrimage for millions of people from all parts of India and even beyond her shores. Gandhiji's room has been preserved the way it was when he left for his last prayer meeting on that fateful Friday, the 30th January 1948. His worldly possessions are on display here. I most heartily recommend that any newcomer to India should, whilst in Delhi, visit both the Smriti and the Samedhi at Raj Ghat – there is something so special that you will imbibe from those experiences that will stay with you and add to your comprehension and valuation of modern India.

We had always wanted to visit the National Railway Museum in New Delhi and went along on a fine sunny afternoon. Again, for railway buffs I most heartily recommend this but also for anyone with a feel for the days of steam and a bit of grandeur. The museum is in the elegant part of Delhi at Chanakyapuri so easily reached by taxi or auto rickshaw. For

me it was a real trip down memory lane to the steam engines of my childhood in the 1950s but there are also some of the historic coaches used by
erstwhile Indian royalty and people like the Princes of Wales on their per-
ambulations around India in the late 1890s and early 1920s. Very young
visitors would enjoy the tiny train and its carriages that operate within the
museum grounds and from the bank one can see modern trains shooting
through Delhi with all the required noise that they make.

One of my favourite charities is The Brooke Hospital for Animals
which helps healthy working animals in the world's poorest communities. Now one refers to the charity simply as The Brooke and I made it
one of my singled-out charities on my website some years ago. This feel
for The Brooke stems from my early childhood in India when I would
observe weary equines being whipped and shouted at as beasts of burden
or as *tonga* horses or cart horses or little donkeys carrying huge piles
of bricks. I used to rage and boil and put down the window of the car
and shout at the horse's owner that he should not be so cruel – all this
in Hindi but I doubt any of the owners took the slightest bit of notice
of a young white girl child driving by in a car. Now however was my
chance to try and help through visiting and highlighting the work of a
very worthwhile charity. For years my darling mother, who is 97, has
given to The Brooke and now here is my opportunity to give and help
them too.

The Brooke is the UK's largest overseas equine welfare charity. It helps
hundreds of thousands of working horses, donkeys and mules suffering unimaginable distress and pain every year. Founded by horse-lov-
ing English woman Mrs Dorothy Brooke in 1934, in a dusty Cairo back-
street – The Brooke has evolved into an international lifesaver for working
equines.

Today, the charity runs a network of mobile veterinary teams and field
clinics across nine developing countries, including Egypt, Jordan, India,
Pakistan, Afghanistan, Israel and the West Bank, Kenya, Ethiopia and
Guatemala. It reaches hundreds of thousands of equine animals in need
every year – animals that support the livelihoods of over three million people. The Brooke's overseas staff – all nationals of the countries in which
they work – treat equine illnesses and injuries, and nurse casualties back
to health. Brooke vets and education workers deal with a catalogue of har-
rowing cases from heat exhaustion and starvation, to lameness and wounds
caused by beatings. The charity is determined to make sure these animals
have a better life now through free veterinary treatment – and a happier
future by training their owners in good equine care to prevent suffering.
The charity helps communities to understand how to care for their animals
– so that they have regular rest, shade and water and are loaded properly.
This is complemented by vaccination programmes to prevent illness.

The Brooke estimates that 80 per cent of all animal suffering is preventable and The Brooke's animal health teams live in and work with communities so that they are always on hand and good welfare becomes a long-term priority. Helping animals helps people, as a healthy working horse, donkey or mule benefits the poverty-stricken family who depends on it, ensuring they can continue to earn a living. And with an average of six people depending on each animal for an income, The Brooke's work also has profound human consequences. Over the next ten years, the charity hopes to extend its reach to five million working equine animals that desperately need help in the developing world. By ensuring these working animals are healthy and fit for work, The Brooke estimates the livelihoods of nearly four million vulnerable people can be safeguarded.

We asked if we could visit the charity's offices at Preet Vihar in Delhi, which was quite a long drive away in a suburb on the other side of the Jamuna River. Colonel Pundir, a retired Indian Army colonel, is the administration officer and was so enthusiastic and introduced us to his office staff; he then asked us to follow in our car when one of the mobile units went out on a call. This we did after having a welcome cup of tea and looking around the well-appointed offices with illustrations and maps explaining the charity's aims and commitment. Graham, who you will recall is a vet himself, was impressed with The Brooke India's Core Values:

1. Alleviation of animal suffering.
2. Promotion of compassionate care and euthanasia.
3. Involvement of owners/users in decision affecting their animals.
4. Strengthening of local external organisations in their work with equine animals.
5. Maintaining a well-motivated and valued work force.
6. Reinforcing strong intercountry relations with The Brooke Hospital for Animals family.

The five freedoms that the charity considers essential to all animals are:

1. Freedom from hunger and thirst.
2. Freedom from pain and suffering.
3. Freedom from disease and injury.
4. Freedom to express most normal behaviour.
5. Freedom from exposure to adverse climate conditions.

We drove through Delhi's manic traffic into Old Delhi where a *tonga* horse was injured and then right in front of our eyes another horse was injured when a rickshaw piled into him. We were able to observe the procedures undertaken and gauge the feelings of the locals to the charity's ministrations. What has been essential was the appointment of men who work as liaison officers between the vets and the owners and explain what could benefit the animal and how important treatment is and educate the owners so that the vets may do their professional job. Currently the charity has teams in Delhi, parts of Uttar Pradesh, Rajasthan and Andhra Pradesh and also in areas of Uttaranchal and Maharashtra. Each Brooke team in India treats on average 840 cases per month and each Combined Mobile Unit, of which there are eight covering more than 18,000 animals (horses, mules and donkeys) in total, travels on average 100 km in a day to reach these animals in pain and suffering. The Brooke India is entirely funded by The Brooke's London office and the main fundraising team is situated in London but there is another fundraising team in Holland as well; I find it a sobering and wretched thought that so many NGOs who help both humans and animals within India are funded by us who all live in the West. India now has great wealth – but the poor will for ever be present – but those who are prospering within India should now perhaps share their wealth.

Graham and I went on our way after a while spent observing and being closely observed ourselves; I have become inured to people coming right up to me and staring at me and sometimes wanting to touch me – when I feel it is really intrusive I give them a very cold challenging look and it works wonders – Graham had always wondered about that look but when he visited India for the first time with me and saw its efficacy he understood a great deal more – a habit picked up in infancy as a self-defence mechanism in a very crowded country!

A welcome cup of tea at The Imperial seemed called for and besides I had a piece of jewellery to collect from my favourite jeweller Ajay Narain. Ajay Narain's shop used to be within the hotel but now The Imperial is appealing to different sorts of clientele and one of the most important of these are very wealthy Indians who come to shop at the designer boutiques within the hotel. So be it, but for us the contrast from a crowded street in Old Delhi with dreadful electric wiring crossing overhead like so many spiders' webs, shabby shops, surly equine owners and the sheer onslaught of traffic, to the cool calm foyer and marbled rooms of The Imperial was stark. I just wish that some of the young Indians I saw enjoying the hotel could be made to visit the disadvantaged and impoverished of their own city because they are leading parallel lives. Obsequious doormen and the heavy smell of jasmine with powerful and glitzy people coming and going can give the impression that all is well in India; well it is, but they should heed those who have no chance of achieving their humble aspirations for a better life. I will drop in an interesting statistic here: 83 million more mobile cell phone users will be connected within this year in India. This is good news because very ordinary people without property can now be fully in touch and able to pursue their aspirations whereas previously trying to obtain a land line was a complete headache.

Still, after a good cup of tea we went and saw the jeweller; the shop has been squeezed into what long ago was the office of Thomas Cook, to which it was essential to go to change travellers' cheques. That must be a thing of the past now with all the ATMs and credit card transactions but I still like to go to Thomas Cook to change money and I am sorry that they have moved out of The Imperial to another lesser hotel. Ajay's craftsman had made a ring given to me by my mother, which she was given by my father, into a beautiful pendant with great care and attention to detail. I had been present when Pa had bought the ring in Calcutta, now Kolkata, and it is a huge good topaz. So now I had it made into a lovely pendant piece. I would recommend anyone seriously wanting to buy jewellery to go there as they are nice people and will make alterations as well as sell you lovely pieces. Everyone wants to sell you a new piece but it takes a special shop to be bothered to alter something you already own.

We spent a lovely day out at Tikli Bottom of which I wrote at length in my second book *India: The Tiger's Roar*. I love Tikli and our good friends Martin and Annie Howard run such a lovely home stay there. Martin has for ten years worked hard to raise funds to start a private village school for the local villagers to send their children. There is a state school but apparently the state school teachers often do not bother to turn up for their classes and it is badly managed and run. Martin resolved to give the villagers an opportunity to start and run their own school and it started in January 2008, a couple of weeks before we visited. He, with the help of the village headman and elders, has achieved a lot and already the classes are inundated. Moreover, in the afternoons those young people who have missed out on a fundamental primary education turn up in double figures for 'remedial classes' which help them to overcome the huge gaps in their education, or indeed that is actually the start of their education.

It may seem strange that it should be a fee-paying school but Martin knows what he is doing and it is working. When we visited we could see the excellent classrooms and rows of desks and wall posters and aids to teaching; we met the headmaster and saw his house, but work was in progress to build a house for the female teachers who could not live in the same house as the males. The playground has a good solid wall around it; the children can sit under the shade of trees and swing on the swings and a happy little bunch they were on that Saturday afternoon in January of this year. Standing on the roof of the headmaster's house, which is simplicity itself but nevertheless a good clean place to live and work, I looked around to the surrounding village, its pond, the buffaloes and the fields which were green and prosperous looking. India is changing and changing for the better, but it often needs the wisdom and foresight of a man like Martin Howard to motivate a good thing and have the commitment to see it through to fruition.

I was beginning to feel cold so we went to the new Anokhi shop at Gurgaon and I bought a quilted jacket. Thank goodness, little did I know just how cold it was going to become and that jacket was a saviour, which I could have sold many times over it was so admired. Gurgaon is now a city in its own right and so is Noida, from what I could gather; these are modern Indian cities with shopping malls and modern enclaves to which the middle classes aspire. I am glad for those who find security and success in their midst but the scale and speed of development is quite alarming and I just hope that prosperity will ensure that these brash new cities continue to look good and be inspirational in the years to come. I worry that the stark contrast between the haves and the have nots will be exemplified by these concrete canyons.

India has begun preparing for what is one of the world's biggest ever censuses, a survey by millions of volunteers that could affect government policies and reveal how economic growth has affected the population. An army of volunteers and officials has started the long process of mapping cities, towns and villages; the workers will visit every household in the next few years to gather information on jobs, education and quality of life. India's population is projected to grow to 1.19 billion in 2011 from its current 1.13 billion. More than a decade of reform programmes is estimated to have pushed the country's long-term economic growth rate to about 8.7 per cent in 2008. But India urgently requires more infrastructure and creation of new jobs.

India once again faces a general election in 2009 and it will be interesting to see which party becomes the government. One significant change will be the emphasis put on the urban voter. Hitherto Indian politicians have always concentrated on the rural votes but now the huge numbers in the metropolitan cities are determined that their priorities will become the deciding factors; indeed, if India is to continue to grow their demands must be met because without efficient urban infrastructure and facilities big international corporations can decide to remove to another cheaper country where their demands are more likely to be met. India produces 2.5 million graduates annually, but only about 15 per cent are suitable for jobs in technology and outsourcing, the home ministry officials say. Millions of people still live in acute poverty. The last census in 2001 revealed a demographic divide between the poorer states in the north and the better-off south.

When one visits designer boutiques in Mumbai or Delhi if you ask the price of an item such as a linen blazer the arrogant young male assistant raises an eyebrow as if to infer if you need to ask you cannot afford it. Well, he is quite right; a blazer for the equivalent of £3,000 is well beyond our budget! But famous marques have set up shop in India where three quarters of the population live on approximately 25p (in pounds sterling) per day. The pound is roughly equivalent to Rupees 75 as I write. Mumbai is home to one of the few shopping centres to sport a Rolls-Royce showroom, about a 30-minute drive from Asia's largest slum. A famous female designer is considering plans for six stores across the subcontinent and Harvey Nichols is studying a move into the market. One reads that the centre of gravity in luxury retail is shifting east. India will spend about £2 billion on luxury goods this year which might increase to £15 billion by 2015. There are now 54 dollar billionaires in India which is more than currently in Japan. And yet, thousands of people, many wearing only underwear, rioted across northern India this month over power cuts that have left millions without electricity or water, highlighting the yawning gap between the country's superpower aspirations and the realities on the ground. The violence underlined growing public frustration at the Government's failure to improve the basic infrastructure, especially electricity and water supplies, despite the economic boom. The government has pledged to provide power for all by 2012, but analysts say it will struggle to keep up with demand as the appetite of the middle class grows for electronic goods and larger homes. For all the glitz and modern splendour of Gurgaon and Noida and their equivalent in Mumbai, Bangalore or Chennai half of the billion population are not even connected to the electricity network.

During April and May 2008 the world news has been dominated by the Tibetan protests against China, the farce of an election in Zimbabwe and the complete tragedy of a cyclone and its aftermath in Burma and then the terrible earthquake in China. In the background there is always quite a lot of tragic news from the war zones in Afghanistan and Iraq. To compound all that the West is feeling the onslaught of economic crisis brought on by greedy bankers essentially lending money to those in the West, the United States in particular, who did not realistically have the means by which to repay their loans. The lending spree that has dominated the last decade in the UK has finally caught up with a lot of foolish people who allowed themselves to be seduced by easy credit and their desire for material wealth and the need to 'feel good about themselves'. The stupid strap line 'you are so worth it …' is nonsense, if you cannot afford something then it is not worth trying to have that item, holiday, leisure activity or experience until you can actually afford to pay for it.

I personally feel the next great wars will be about water shortages and food shortages. The US Department of Agriculture believes that the world will suffer a 29 million tonne discrepancy in 2008 between what it needs to feed itself and what it can actually produce. Land that might previously have been used to feed people is increasingly planted with crops designed for conversion to biofuels, forcing unexpected price rises in the prices of everything from tofu to instant noodles.

The dramatic improvement in lifestyles and family finances of millions of Chinese and Indians has driven a demand for meat, milk and cooking oils that simply did not exist a decade ago. What has taken most experts aback is the suddenness with which Asia's exposure to a food crisis has emerged. Countries that, until a few weeks ago, could rely on substantial imports of rice from India, Egypt or China are now scrambling to cope with a new reality in which they cannot do so. India – which traditionally has exported millions of tonnes of rice – has decided to set aside a special strategic food reserve on top of its existing wheat and rice stockpiles. Vietnam, the world's third-largest rice producer, has been forced to curb exports and Cambodia has banned them completely. Thailand is the world's largest producer of rice and the price has risen there by 50 per cent and the authorities have stated that there will be enough rice for the kingdom but that does not help other countries normally dependent on imports. Meanwhile in Japan American long grain rice is rotting in grain silos; this is the result of an arcane contract between the USA and Japan; the latter is obliged to buy the US rice annually and apparently never actually uses it and thus it is left to rot or used as animal feed. If this vast amount of rice was put on the open market it could dramatically change the current high price of rice.

In Africa the situation is very grave already; in Sierra Leone, the price of rice has risen 300 per cent and in Senegal and much of the rest of West Africa by 50 per cent. African governments are watching nervously. Food riots have been reported in recent weeks in several countries. Three billion people worldwide rely on rice as a staple food and currently there are 854 million people worldwide who are 'food insecure' which is the euphemism for on the verge of starvation.

Environmental experts in the UK have identified 46 countries – home to 2.7 billion people – where climate change and water-related crises will create a high risk of violent conflict. Janani Vivekananda, one of the authors of the International Alert report, said, 'Water management will be a huge tinderbox in Asia and now is the time for international organisations to come together. Where there is a huge potential for conflict there is potential for co-operation'. What we are talking about is the strong possibility of Water Wars.

In this year of the Beijing Olympics the spotlight has been on China, not just because of the Tibetan protests and brutal response and farcical Olympic torch saga and now the enormous earthquake tragedy. China's environmental problems are mounting. Water pollution and water scarcity are burdening their economy, rising levels of air pollution are endangering the health of millions of Chinese, and much of the country's land is rapidly turning into desert. Preparing for the Olympics has come to symbol-ize the intractability of China's environmental challenges and the limits of Beijing's approach to addressing them. Social unrest over the environmen-tal issues is rising. In 2006 China's top environmental official announced there had been 51,000 pollution-related protests in 2005. That is an enor-mous figure and difficult for us in the West to comprehend. Apparently Beijing city officials are backtracking from their pledge to provide safe tap water to all of Beijing for the Olympics; they now say that they will be able to provide it only for residents of the Olympic Village.

Delhi can feel proud about the city's recent environmental track record; over this last decade the Delhi government has implemented consider-able environmentally friendly legislation and I have written of this in my other books. When one sees that Delhi Corporation buses proudly bear the legend ' Clean Delhi, Green Delhi' it is true as all public transport and auto rickshaws have been converted to CNG – compressed natural gas. The CNG revolution in Delhi's transport energy system implemented by Indraprastha Gas Ltd is probably the world's largest and most success-ful anti-pollution exercise ever. Compressed natural gas has transformed Delhi which was heavily polluted before at the time of writing the first part of this my first book; even by 2002 I could see the improvements and commented upon it in the second book, but now the difference is huge. The authorities are continuing to make plans to expand the piped natural gas business, introduce CNG railway engines, and make use of this fuel for their 60,000 strong light-commercial-vehicle fleet. They have succeeded in creating the world's largest eco-friendly CNG bus fleet and converted thousands of private vehicles to CNG. This is a success story of which they are entitled to feel very proud.

When we were leaving Raj Ghat after paying respects to Gandhiji we came across a young man on the side of the path who was making the most wonderful little toys or models of rickshaws, bikes, motorbikes and other objects from a single piece of coloured wire. I am writing about this now and not at the time when I described our visit to Raj Ghat because then I was in sombre mood and now I want to illustrate how if you look in India you will find something to uplift and amuse – sometimes in the most odd places. We were enchanted with these objects and promptly bought a bike for each of the grandsons. I asked if he thought of making a pram, which would have been just what the granddaughter would like, but he had not, but since I mentioned it he would in the future, he said. We watched and photographed him and it was one of those little experiences that lifted our spirits – India and Indians have so many of those if you keep looking and are alert.

Unexpectedly I was invited to give an address to pupils from Salwan Public School in Gurgaon. The headmistress of this fee-paying school is Dr Indu Kheterpal. She is a charming, capable, talented woman who had been presented very recently with the award for Best Teacher in India by the outgoing President Abdul Kalam. Having been invited at short notice, I thought about what to say to eager young people of 12 to 14 years and a few sixth formers. Then I recalled quite curiously that fifty years ago when experiencing my own first speech day at Saint Swithun's School, Winchester, I had heard a most distinguished guest advise us that our privileged schooling was a passport to the future – in effect an opportunity to learn how to learn. Those words have always stayed with me, so in February I was able to speak to about 70 people and recall that day half a century ago – it was quite extraordinary really. These young-sters were so keen and eager and then questioned me closely at the end about my opinions on a variety of subjects, mostly relating to India and particularly to conservation and India's wildlife. We were then treated to lunch which had been prepared by the school's domestic science students and I was given the most lovely gift of a tray made by a young boy in his carpentry class and a copy of the school's special book. Graham and I thoroughly enjoyed our time with them and I hope we will be invited back sometime; I was very moved by the experience because of the fifty years' anniversary from my own childhood, and I felt cheered that here were lots of young folk who seemed to have the right ideas to help India make the best of her future.

Chapter Seventeen

Akash Ganga
(which means Celestial Ganga –
the Celestial Ganges)

We embarked on a long car journey to see areas of India that Graham had never experienced and that I had not returned to within the last fifty years – ie since I was a child. Even within the last few years the road system has greatly improved and made road travel a lot faster. A decade ago this was still quite a painful way to travel round India though essential for a writer to experience. Now however the various big roads have facilitated long journeys and the road east out of Delhi towards Moradabad is quite pleasurable; you may recall I used this same road to reach Bareilly which is further east from Moradabad in 1998, now here we were ten years on making a similar journey. We were heading to Fort Unchagaon which is 116 km from Delhi. The Unchagaon family is headed by a man who was Foreign Minister long years ago – Surendra Pal Singh. He now is the age of my beloved mother – in his nineties. His young grandsons run Fort Unchagaon. Rupendra Pal Singh and Rajendra Pal Singh and his lovely wife Anushree are creating a rural retreat for foreign and Indian visitors in a serene heritage setting not far from the beautiful Ganga. We arrived in time for lunch on what must be described as the coldest day we had ever experienced in India. I know northern India can be cold in winter but this was the severest cold weather for over forty years and quite challenging even for us hardy Scots!

Fort Unchagaon is in the village of Unchagaon, just about an hour's drive from Garhmukteshwar in Uttar Pradesh. Raja Surendra Pal Singh inherited the Fort in 1927 when he was a child of ten. It enjoys a history that is proud and colourful. Its Jat rulers can trace back their family tree to one of the several prestigious Jat zamindaris which came into prominence during the decline of the Mughal Empire. For years, the family have held a seat of honour in western Uttar Pradesh. For me especially with my family connection with the Jat Regiment I was particularly glad to have been invited to this special family home. The rulers of Unchagaon originally belonged to the village of Pilana in Rajasthan. Their ancestor, Harbal Singh, along with a group of followers, migrated to Bahanpur sometime during the 1730s. However the fort came into the possession of the present family only in 1859. The original owner, a Rajput *zamindar*, lost the fort when he opposed the British during the mutiny of 1857 (or more popularly now known as the First War of Independence). The original fort was a mud fort. Its mud walls were later replaced by brick and the old buildings inside the fort were totally renovated during the 1930s to give it a distinctly colonial look.

We looked at all the silver-framed family photographs of distinguished members of the family and visiting prime ministers and heads of state which vied with the heads of stuffed tigers on the drawing room walls. I commented quite firmly that perhaps to appease the feelings of people like me who do all we can to try and help conserve India's tigers they should explain that these sad trophies are relics of a bygone and wayward era of India's imperial past when Indian and foreigner alike seemed to want to derive their pleasures from killing anything that walked and breathed. Now all of us have a duty to do our best to ensure that India's governing authorities do their utmost with complete commitment to ensure the survival of the few remaining tigers; if they and their countrymen do not then the whole world will condemn India as being careless of her custodianship of all her wonderful unique wildlife. I read that the Prime Minister has also tasked the respective chief ministers of the various states within which tigers still exist that they too must take steps to stop the evil poaching and harassment of the few animals that still are alive.

After a delicious lunch carefully served by very sweet and friendly staff we went for a walk through the village which was interesting; I like to interact with the locals and this is where my rusty Hindi does come in very useful. The potter at his wheel, the toddlers playing in the dust, young schoolchildren returning from lessons, the dhobi ironing outside under a fig tree and a wayward cow which had decided to walk home pulling the cart soon followed by the exasperated owner who had to run to catch up with the beast! There are signs of greater prosperity all around which is heartening but nevertheless there is sadly always evidence of poverty too. I enjoyed walking through the family's mango orchards with Tamta, one

The Fort Unchagaon entrance.

of the domestic staff. He is a charming chap and so eager to please and with him my rusty Hindi made for conversation and companionship.

That evening a small recital of local music was laid on for our benefit. We sat outside under a beautiful full moon, but my goodness was it cold and Graham and I had taken the trouble to dress smartly as we knew it would be noticed and appreciated. I most sincerely enjoyed the little recital but was I glad of going inside at its end. A small fire was helpful but that dry cold made one's concentration wander! In the drawing room we were entertained by Rupendra Pal Singh, the heir, and his sister-in-law Anushree; then Rajendra Pal Singh, the younger brother who is married to Anushree, also joined us. They are charming young people of about the age of our own children and I think they will ensure that the old fort becomes a successful country retreat for travellers.

The following morning we drove down to the banks of the Ganga to watch the sun rise. It was lovely and I suspect the young 'Unchagaons' will wisely promote this activity with careful amenities. To be standing on the banks of the Ganga in complete stillness in weak sunshine in the company of kingfishers, peacocks, seven sisters, crow pheasants, hornbills and lapwings was a huge pleasure. Sometimes one can see a Gangetic river dolphin but we sadly did not. Had it been possible then I would have

Two beautiful elephants saying hi to each other.

loved to breakfast there and further enjoy the experience. For me to put my hands in the Ganga after fifty years was quite moving – in this place there was only a boat being poled across in the distance and no one except our little party of Ajay, our driver, Tamta and ourselves. It was so cold that the fields were still covered in the overnight white frost and the stray dogs were curled up near the temple and refusing to stretch and welcome us. Fort Unchagaon has lovely equine stables and visitors would be able to ride from the property to the river, which in my youth I would have loved to do. Sadly after a very good breakfast we had to take our leave but we would have liked to stay for at least two nights to really relax. It is said that apparently middle class Indians visit country places to relax and drink – with the emphasis on the latter – most of them care nothing for the history and Indian culture and tradition in heritage properties, which is unlike most of the foreign visitors who come to absorb and enjoy the glamour and traditions of India's erstwhile royalty and aristocracy. Only through edu-cation and exposure to a country's distinguished and fascinating past will people find it interesting and value it. Ignorance breeds a careless attitude which has been all too apparent in some aspects of modern life in the UK within the past twenty years.

The drive north to Corbett Wildlife Park is a long one and something we have experienced five years ago – mercifully the road is much improved since then and whereas in the past there were lorries and cars now the plethora of smart cars, motor bikes and four by fours is very obvious; these have to take their chances as ever with bullock carts, buffaloes and horse-drawn vehicles. Well, it would not be India otherwise! Graham was by this time so cold that we stopped in Ramnagar and he bought a very good anorak. We arrived at Corbett Hideaway in mid afternoon and were grateful for a welcoming home-made tomato soup brought to us in little clay vessels in the reception and then a good lunch. The whole resort was bathed in warm afternoon sunshine and we so enjoyed being back after a five-year interval. Good improvements have been made to this property and our lovely suite was warmed by a blow-air heater and thus very relaxing. Walking along the Kosi River was a delight but I am personally dismayed by the amount of development there is. I understand that more and more people within India travel and enjoy these wild places but one has the feeling that the Uttaranchal Government has allowed too much development which in its turn will impact on the wildlife. This is the conundrum: have more people understand and appreciate India's wildlife and the need for conservation or – restrict the masses through exclusivity. Nothing stays the same anywhere and in the long run probably the more that can appreciate their wildlife heritage and the vital necessity for conservation the better for the whole animal kingdom.

One of the highlights of our walk along the banks of the Kosi River was seeing the shoals of mahseer fish in some deep clear pools – it was something I had not experienced previously and because the local village alongside the famous Gargiamata Temple reveres all life, they are protected and a delight to the walker.

Corbett Hideaway was on that occasion filled with Chinese visitors in a large bus party. They are interesting because they go round the world doing what the Japanese used to do and probably still do … .jump out of a coach, ask each other to photograph themselves in front of some world-famous site and then jump back into the coach – been there, done that, bought the T shirt! The world's tourism industry is beginning to depend on these huge numbers but the hospitality and tourism trade of every other country must realise that the Chinese criteria for 'travelling enjoyment' is still in its infancy. I would have dearly loved to ask these Chinese why they are still so foolish and irresponsible about tigers and the use of tiger parts but observing their choice of the extensive buffet menu and how they also greedily helped themselves to extra food, which they took away with them, made me conclude that we would have very little in common with each other!

The next morning we set off at 6.30 am for the jeep journey to within Corbett Park where we would stay for two nights at Corbett Hideaway

Rishikesh where the Ganga comes out of the gorge.

My Mother told me that I first travelled on this carriage 60 years ago as a toddler.

River Lodge. My late father, Frank Rose, and my mother, Barbara, were good friends of the late great Jim Corbett. In my second book *India: The Tiger's Roar* I explore the whole Jim Corbett story. I am so heartened to see his books still in print in India as I grew up on his wonderful stories, the only difference being that I was reading my father's first editions with his various annotations and pasted-in correspondence with Jim Corbett.

When we reached the famous Ramganga River there was the elephant Gulabo crossing the icy water to come and fetch us. Both humans and luggage were transported on the elephant; Gulabo was beautiful but clearly not at all amused at the idea of all this plodding through icy water and she would stop and refuse to budge and the *mahout* would urge her forward and sometimes she would 'harrumph' and I thought if she became really 'vexed' she could have scooped up enough icy water and dowsed her passengers quite effectively! Well, bless her, we reached the other side safely and made the final journey of a few yards in another jeep.

We had a full glorious two days at the River Lodge and I will always treasure them. This camp is the only commercial venture allowed within the Corbett Park and consists of a dozen luxury tents on a five-acre hillside site overlooking the Ramganga River and enclosed by an electrified fence. The tent has an en suite bathroom with good facilities. This experience though very enjoyable and comfortable was about as close as I have come to the camping my parents experienced in the 1940s. In various parts of India tented accommodation is used with all the luxuries of air conditioning and electricity – this is not possible in this out-of-the-way part of Corbett's outer reaches. The lamps are solar source battery powered and electrical equipment is totally useless as there is no electricity. A torch is required in the evening and braziers with log fires are the only real source of heat. In March or April or again in November and December the temperature would be very relaxing. As it was, we experienced the greatest cold for several years and I found myself sleeping with two hot water bottles, fully dressed in everything that I had worn throughout the day. Graham did likewise.

The staff at River Lodge are eager and helpful. Again, this is where my Hindi helps and we were immediately treated as 'insiders'. The food was simple and just what we wanted and the ambience in the thatched dining structure with open sides was relaxed and suitably 'safari-like'. Gulabo, who was one of two elephants, transported us on evening and morning walks through the undergrowth and we spotted the pug marks of a tiger the next morning but never actually saw the animal. I have no doubt however that the tiger was watching us. We saw *sambar*, *chital*, barking deer, monkeys and a wonderful array of birdlife including woodpeckers, bush chats, scarlet *minivet*, kingfishers, hoopoes, fish eagles and river lapwings. I thought of my friend Philip Davis who started and runs the very worth-

General Thimaya driving the Four in Hand at The Saharanpur Remount 1958.

while little charity called Tiger Awareness; these are his words:

'We are a charity that helps to conserve the Tiger in the wild in India. We help with funds at ground level where the funds are needed most. We help support the Forest Guards and also with funds for animal / man conflict situations. The Tiger is the most majestic animal in the wild of which there are only 1500–2000 left in the whole of India. They need our protection urgently. It would be a sad day if the only place we could see a Tiger is in a zoo.'

I came across this charity www.tigerawareness.co.uk through a horrific photograph that appeared in *The Scotsman* newspaper's front page in 2007 showing frozen tigers in a freezer that had been confiscated from poachers and other wicked greedy people dealing in tiger parts to sell to the foolish Chinese, who believe that they will enhance their libido if they consume various bits from a tiger. Police in northern India arrested 16 people in one of the biggest raids on the illegal trade in December 2007. Special agents intercepted a group of hunters in Allahabad who were selling three tiger skins and three skeletons to the country's most notorious trader in wild animal parts. The foremost poacher and dealer is a man who was wanted in connection with at least four wildlife crime cases; he was ready to pay Rs180,000 (£2,250) for each set of skin and bones. The success in finally

143

arresting Shabbir Hasan Qureshi, who was recognised as the man handling a quarter of all the trade in India, did not come too soon. Belinda Wright, the executive director of the Wildlife Protection Society of India, hailed it as a major breakthrough in this endless battle against wildlife crime.

Whilst tigers are seen as 'walking cash registers' because of the value of their skins and body parts for the Tibetan and Chinese peoples, who greedily and cruelly have no sense of responsibility, they are in extreme danger from poaching. Poachers receive up to £10,000 for a tiger skin and £3,000 for a kilogram of tiger bones, used in traditional Chinese medicine. Thankfully, since I wrote *India: the Tiger's Roar* the Dalai Lama has also added his voice of condemnation and that had a significant effect on the Tibetans who were conducting this awful trade. On a programme screened on BBC recently in *The Natural World* series Sir David Attenborough talked of the extreme crisis in tiger numbers throughout India's wildlife parks. Taking part in the programme were Belinda Wright, Valmik Thapar and Rahgunandan Chundawat; all courageous stalwarts in the struggle to save the tiger.

Belinda once again emphasises that India desperately needs a centralised Wildlife Crime Bureau that can co-ordinate the urgent work of detecting and punishing all those involved in this vile trade. It would seem that "The tiger is vanishing and no one is listening," said Hashim Tyabji, one of India's veteran tiger watchers and a conservationist. "Official numbers have been fudged for years, hiding the true extent of the crisis until now."

The tiger numbers are down 70 per cent since 2002 (which is when I researched my second book *India: The Tiger's Roar*). I was led to believe that population pressure was the great threat but in fact the corruption and poaching that have been hidden from the world's eyes is the most serious cause of the fall in tiger numbers. Under the Indira Gandhi Project Tiger we saw their numbers rise from 2,000 to 4,300, but now it is calculated that perhaps only 1500 tigers are left throughout India.

The Wildlife Protection Society of India is Belinda Wright's brainchild through which she has worked with huge energy and commitment to try and help save and conserve India's tiger population. In June 2006 it had been announced that the Indian Army would be enlisted to help to protect the tiger population. "Giving soldiers the power to arrest or even shoot poachers on sight," said Kalpana Palkiwala, the spokesperson for the Ministry of the Environment. There is now even talk of allowing Tiger Farms within India, but this is in emulation of the Chinese and really quite a shameful idea in that by thinking in artificial terms the Indian Government is almost admitting defeat in its half-hearted attempts to continue to save the tiger in the wild. Manmohan Singh, the Prime Minister, give him his due, is trying to do his utmost to help protect the tiger but most tiger watchers feel that he is not actually supported by others who could lend their weight and encouragement. I personally have a huge regard for Manmohan Singh and what he has achieved for India and know him to be

Aline learning to drive a horse and carriage 1959.

a man of integrity and humility and worthy of everyone's respect.

Valmik Thapar who has with equal commitment and energy devoted himself to trying to save tigers said, when questioned recently, the tragedy that has befallen the tiger is that 40,000 tigers existed within India in 1947 and now, at India's 60th anniversary of Nationhood, there are barely 1,500. He urges that politicians must educate themselves about India's wonderful natural world and realise that 600 rivers and streams start their journeys in tiger country – that impacts on everybody; greedy developers would destroy India's whole eco-system if allowed. Politicians must realise the world will condemn them if India's magnificent national animal becomes extinct because of their inertia or greed. The villages within national parks should be relocated and compensated and the forest guards must be trained and armed and given back up to combat violent, ruthless human predators and given public recognition for their dangerous work.

This is exactly where Philip Davis's work with Tiger Awareness fulfils a vital role and I salute Philip for his dedication. As I write in May 2008 Philip is back in India working with forest guards and other individuals who need encouragement and support; one day I would like to accompany Philip to the Sunderbans where his charity has also achieved some practical support for local people. The Sunderbans is the area of the estuary of the Ganga (the Ganges) down in West Bengal where thousands of people eke out an existence amongst the wetlands and mangrove swamps of that area of India. Tiger numbers are quite high in that region, thankfully.

It also behoves the Indian diaspora all over the world and other caring people to show their disgust at this appalling lack of energy and commitment. India wants to be seen as a responsible forward-moving nation; she must act decisively with regard to her wonderful emblematic animal, the Bengal Tiger, and show the world what can be achieved and earn universal respect, relief and approval.

In the new *Saving Planet Earth* television series Sir David Attenborough and Alan Titchmarsh brought tigers to our attention once again in 2007. Fiona Bruce, the BBC television personality, made her first journey to India and visited Bandhavgarh National Park where to her obvious delight and excitement, and some apprehension, she witnessed tigers in the wild and was totally captivated. Dr Ullus Karanth, the dedicated naturalist, explained in conversation with her how the current dire situation could be reversed. This is something we can all make happen with pressure and donations to the various organisations.

Yet again in April 2008 on BBC2 we saw the most enchanting series on a Sunday night of tigers photographed at Pench Wildlife Park with hidden cameras in mocked-up tree trunks, and roots which elephants were used to carry in their trunks and also place on the ground strategically. The series called *Tigers: Spy in the Jungle* followed the life of a tigress who had given birth to four cubs and we, the audience, had the joy of seeing them grow up and overcome various serious challenges and then most wonderful of all, one of them went on to become a mother of cubs herself. It is most rare that all four cubs successfully reach adulthood. I have booked my copy of this wonderful BBC DVD which is to become available in June 2008.

In my three books on India I have spoken about the country's wonderful wildlife and indeed by naming them *India: The Peacock's Call*, *India: The Tiger's Roar* and *India: The Elephant's Blessing*, I used the three most famous creatures in the animal kingdom associated with India! Hopefully now, yet again on the brink of extinction, the tigers of India will be saved and I found a much greater appreciation of the tiger crisis whilst in India earlier this year. Indeed on our last night in Delhi an item on the major television news carried a piece on a wounded tiger and how this animal was going to be treated. My own non-commercial website www.thepeacockscall.co.uk has galleries of photography which is for the most part my own, but sometimes I have been generously loaned photography as in the gallery dedicated to tigers. Indeed on my home page there is a magnificent and unique photograph of a tiger with my words; one simply clicks on that to go through to my galleries and people like Chris Brunskill and Philip Davis have allowed me to use their photography of tigers.

The good news that the authorities have taken the dramatic action of implementing tiger translocation is very heartening. This was announced at the beginning of July 2008 when a male tiger had been airlifted to Sariska Tiger Reserve from Ranthambhore; both reserves are in Rajasthan. A few days later a tigress was flown by helicopter to join the male tiger. Both animals have been fitted with radio collars so that wildlife authorities can monitor their progress. If they settle three more animals could join them over the coming months, and the same techniques could be used in other parts of India. The four-year-old male tiger has made several kills soon after arrival and is adapting well; once he feels secure and his companion the tigress also settles they will hopefully start breeding. This project has been carried out by the Wildlife Institute of India and is the new programme's first real achievement.

It is the first time that such a tiger relocation scheme has been attempted and represents one of the Indian Government's boldest efforts to date to halt the rapid decline in tigers. Belinda Wright thinks there is a very good chance that this is going to work.

Now apparently the Government has vowed to create eight new reserves and a Tiger Protection Force, about which I have already written. It has also pledged $153 million over the next five years to pay for more forest guards, better equipment to track tigers and relocation of 200,000 villagers living inside tiger reserves. I am delighted to have been able to include this encouraging development at the last minute in this book; maybe once again we are back from the brink of extinction for the tigers of India.

On a sober note I have learnt that in the Kruger National Park in South Africa, which we had the great pleasure of revisiting in October 2007, 250 animals have been killed by poachers during the last four years. The dead animals include 44 white rhino, four lions, two elephants and a hippo. Now doubt has been cast on official statistics that suggest 15 out of South Africa's 22 national parks saw no poaching at all. I am so sorry to learn this as truly the management of the SAN Parks, as they are called collectively, is generally very, very high; South Africa learnt its lessons from other developing countries and had the wisdom to see throughout this last decade that they must build on the work that had hitherto gone into preserving their beautiful country's wildlife and general fauna and flora.

The jungle in Corbett was beautiful and we stopped the jeep one morning where the river conjoined with another. The clear waters, river boulders and maidenhair ferns growing on the banks of roads were memorable. We saw three yellow-throated martins, some *khalij* pheasants and a flycatcher. Had it not been so cold I am sure we would have seen more animals and maybe a tiger or two. As it was the two days were a delight and I also have a memory of the staff playing makeshift cricket during the afternoon whilst I lazed in the sunshine. There was an amusing incident which ended well; I saw as I lazed that something was struggling in the perimeter fence and therefore went to look and found a calf enmeshed. I quickly called the staff and Graham came too and the dilemma was how to free the little beast without it becoming more panicky. The staff started to speak to it in Hindi and I said, "Hold on, you are communicating with it as if it is an elephant and understands," and we all burst out laughing. Slowly we were able to help it and it ran away unharmed. On our last night we were joined by three charming travellers, a Bulgarian with his son who is now American and another fellow American. They were experiencing India for the first time and were enchanted notwithstanding the fact that they had been drugged and robbed on the train to Jaisalmer but fortunately not lost their passports. On this occasion whilst crossing the river on Gulabo on their arrival, as indeed we had done, the mahout had an epileptic fit (or something similar) and fell stone cold into the icy water which left them 'driverless' on an elephant on their very first time! Kishore, our young jeep driver, leapt in and rescued the poor mahout and guided the elephant out of the water. These three men were understandably quite shaken but delighting in India with all its diversity nonetheless. They were determined that their various bottles of wine and liquor should be finished by the night's end and I am not much of a drinker but delighted in their red wine; they in turn were very amused to see behind lock and key in a glass cabinet a full selection of rare malt whiskies from Scotland. As they said they somehow did not expect that in the wild interior of an Indian wildlife park – but they perhaps did not appreciate the great Indian tradition of drinking 'Scotch' or indeed Indian whisky. They were delightful people and the conversation ranged over many subjects, and one of them had served in Iraq.

I kept hearing a sort of munching in the night in our tent and was 'not happy'. The next morning we discovered that a jungle mouse had crept onto the dressing table and was nibbling the shortbread biscuits. The following night I left the biscuits on the terrace to deter him – but guess what – he came in all the same, fell over the knife on the plate, which alerted me, and then proceeded to eat Graham's watchstrap! He had to buy a new one in Hardwar when we arrived.

Hardwar was a four-and-a-half-hour journey from Corbett Hideaway; the drive is through rural Uttar Pradesh and Uttarakhand which is apparently the most heavily populated area in the whole world – a depressing statistic. One passes through shabby dirty towns and villages but on the plus side there are good flourishing farms and mango orchards and quite a difference in terrain as one leaves the Kumaon and enters the Gharwal region. I am heartened by the abundance on the fruit and vegetable stalls of grapes, apples, papayas, bananas, cape gooseberries and pomegranates. Arriving at Hardwar was interesting for me after fifty years – the population pressure is severe. Fifty years ago India's population was about 400 million and now the same land mass has three times as many people, the impact of which is seen in certain places like Hardwar.

Graham was fascinated as was I with this place that is so often mentioned in relation to the Kumbh Mela. I was so relieved to see the Ganga looking as I remembered it – beautiful clear and blue/green, which frankly amazed Graham. We were staying at the Haveli Hari Ganga which proved very charming, but again quite cold because most Indian hotels have no concept of efficient heating for when the weather surprises them. It is a thoughtfully renovated old *haveli* – the word means mansion or sizeable house usually with an inner courtyard – with the most beautiful marble floors situated right on the Ganga and we were delighted. There is a little temple within the inner courtyard and in the evening the musician sings *bhajans* – classical Indian songs. After a welcome lunch I managed to encourage the hotel staff to serve me tea as it should be, in a teapot. The disgraceful habit to which so many hotels have succumbed of serving lukewarm water in a cup with an accompanying tea bag completely diminishes India as the land of tea. Thankfully IIC has the highest standards of tea making but perhaps hoteliers think this fashionable, but the ensuing brew is ghastly and lukewarm.

We then went exploring in the lane behind the river which is a complete kaleidoscope of colour and diversity with small shops selling everything imaginable.

Very many stallholders were avidly playing Ludo which was so amusing. There is an element of Venice with the *havelis* being like old palazzos, but sadly that is where the comparison stops. Hardwar is mostly dirty and badly kept and obviously the authorities just rely on its religious importance and care nothing for civic pride or cleanliness which is immensely sad. Prakash, the hotel's guide, took us on an evening walk to experience the Arti that would take place on both banks near the main temple. It was a moving and interesting experience to see the confusion of colour and peoples and fervour of their feeling. One Indian couple 'phoned their son in Italy so he too could experience their joy over the cell phone. Ganga Arti is the act in which the light of *diyas* (wick lights) offered to the Ganga recreates the primeval myth of worshipping nature's life force. The Arti is conducted at the main *ghat* of Hari-ki-Pauri named after a myth about a footprint of Vishnu embedded on a stone in a wall. As the sun sets the temple bells ring in unison. That is the moment when hundreds of lighted *diyas* placed on leaves along with flowers are launched on the river, carrying hopes, prayers and invocations. The river becomes a shimmering surface of light with these little 'vessels of hope and supplication' all bobbing towards the current until they become tiny specks of light.

The following night I had a most endearing experience. I heard the *pujari* (the priest) come to his devotion at the little inner courtyard temple in our *haveli* and I popped out to pay my respects – he turned, beckoned in Hindi and made me go with him to the hotel's own marble steps into the Ganga. He said in Hindi, "You speak my language and now you will do Arti with me," and I did and found his fervour and sweetness profoundly moving. He instructed me gently and I performed the correct rituals in turn with him and then we floated the floral tribute on the Ganga whilst my bare feet were standing in shallow cold water. It was a unique experience for me and as moving as lighting a candle in my Christian faith in a special church or chapel.

To briefly explain the importance of the Ganges – the Ganga: the holy river rises from two sources in the glacial regions of the Himalayas and is known in mythology as the Daughter of the Himalayas. They are the youngest mountain range on earth and date back to approximately 60 million years ago when the subcontinent moved northwards and they continue to grow. The main source of the Ganga is Bhagirathi, named after her human 'progenitor' Bhagiratha. The Bhagirathi rises from the Gangotri glacier, situated in the Uttarkashi district. It comes out as a torrent from the depths of an icicle-filled cave at a height of about 3,900m. This cave is called Gaumukh because it looks like a cow's mouth. From the Satopanth and Bhagirathi-Kharak glaciers located in Chamoli district, beyond Badrinath, arises the second major source of the Ganga, namely the Alaknanda. Like two giant arteries, Bhagirathi and Alaknanda rush down mountainsides swelling with streams and rivers that flow into them at confluences. The most revered shrines of Gangotri, Kedernath and Badrinath fall in the vicinity of these arteries. It is not a coincidence that most shrines and temples are built at the most majestic spots where nature can be seen at her most magnificent. In Uttaranchal the Ganga flows everywhere. It is known by different names, each involving different myths.

To the people in the hill areas, mythology is close to the physical reality they see. They can speak of the names of the seven mythological streams in which Shiva released the Ganga, which spread out as if released from matted locks. Bhagirathi, Jahnavi, Bhilangana, Mandakini, Rishi Ganga, Saraswati and Alaknanda are the seven mythological streams; each has a distinct flow and builds into the big and mighty river known as the Holy Ganga. Flowing southwards the Ganga passes the last stretch of the hills before entering the plains at Hardwar, or Gate of Vishnu (known as Hari), also known as Ganga Dwar, or Gateway to Ganga. From her source to the plains at Hardwar the Ganga covers a stretch of about 225 km and the full length of the river is 2,600 km from her source to her estuary. Five hundred million people live alongside the Ganga's banks, creating a pattern of eco-systems, sacred sites, holy cities and cyclical festivals that make up an intricate web of Hindu–Indian life.

> *To chant her name brings purity*
> *To see her secures prosperity*
> *To bathe in or drink her waters saves*
> *Seven generations of our race*
> **From the Mahabharata**

Tirtha is a place for crossing over from one place to another – a river fording place – thus in religious terms a *tirtha* is a place from where we cross over from our worldly life to a divine sphere – Ganga embodies that concept. The Puranas (the old books of wisdom) stated the belief that continues even now that even the sight of Ganga absolves individuals from their sins and confers blessings. The Braddharma Purana narrates the story of a sinful king whose life was saved because he resided with a merchant who had bathed in the Ganga, and the holy river water is different from any other, presumably because of certain minerals washed down with it from the mountains. There is an ancient saying that goes 'Who dies if Ganga lives, and who lives if Ganga dies?'

We left for Rishikesh the next morning; it is perched on the banks of the full-bodied Ganga at a height of 340 m above sea level in the Shivalik hills. This place is famous for its meditating *sadhus*, ashrams, centres of indigenous health systems, meditation and religious learning. It is also apparently called the Yoga capital of India. It too is horribly overpopulated but Laxman Jhula, the famous suspension bridge over the Ganga which is 450 feet long (approximately 150 metres), proved an enjoyable experience to walk over and happily the poor sad leper colony that used to sit on the banks of the Ganga was relocated to better conditions about ten years ago. Graham was impressed by the green clear water of the Ganga coming out of the gorges. My memory was of fifty years ago when I visited with my parents and I had been appalled and touched by the hundreds of lepers sitting on either side of the swing bridge begging for alms. Leprosy has always had such notoriety through ignorance but is a very disturbing sight and I was only 12 at the time. Curiously on a short visit to Bergen in Norway in August 2007 we visited the very melancholy museum to Norway's Leper Colony with its own hostel and chapel made out of wood. I was horrified that the last inmate only died the year I was born – 1946. I was intrigued to learn that Norwegian scientists discovered the bacterial cause and epidemiology of this terrible disease. Apparently leprosy was quite a significant problem in Norway right through the Middle Ages and into the 19th century – indeed it is thought that the Scots' famous king, Robert the Bruce, suffered from it in later life. Ironically, the museum in Bergen was hosting a shocking exhibition of limbless young people, but they were the victims of land-mines throughout the world – which is a 20th and 21st century man-made affliction.

I gave some money to two *sadhus* and wished them well and received their blessings; in the various tea shops I could see many Europeans all on their backpacking pilgrimages – what a huge difference from my first visit in 1959. The only comforting thought is that the Ganga continues to look beautiful and green and serene.

We drove down to Dehra Dun where we were guests of the Indian Army. It was lovely to be in one of two cantonment areas of Dehra Dun as they are still beautifully maintained and appear to house all the prestigious military academies and the Doon School and various centres of excellence and Raj Bhavan, the governor's residence. The city however is another sad story and contrasted sharply with my memories and is almost unrecognisable. This is the capital of Uttaranchal but the provincial government is merely capitalising on the presence of the various national bodies and not doing anything to enhance their city which is shameful. Mussoorie, which is a hill station further north from Dehra Dun, was where my great-grandparents had a home; I had hoped to visit but it snowed and we were not equipped for any further fall in the temperature.

We were hosted by the Mechanical Engineering School and the colonel, Colonel Tanwar, tasked a dashing young captain to guide and accompany us on a tour. Captain Appala Abhishake, who was soon to be promoted to major, was such a super young man; tall, good looking and full of enthusiasm and knowledge. After a simple lunch we set out on a tour of the locality. We also visited the other cantonment and visited 18 Battalion Jat Regiment, which was a great pleasure. We took tea in the Officers' Mess and ate Jat *churma* which I am told is absolutely essential to the welfare of all Jat officers and men – I had always had the firm impression from my beloved father that *jalebis* filled that requirement! They certainly did for him.

We also visited the Tibetan community and their great temple and statue of Lord Buddha. When I think how the Tibetans have been hounded and brutalized by China I feel such admiration for them as a people. I recall quite clearly in 1959 when we heard the news that the young Dalai Lama had managed to escape from Tibet and was given refuge in India. Now of course he is justly a very famous man and an icon for many, not just Tibetans and Buddhists. His wisdom and integrity shine like a beacon and I so hope he finds a resolution to the Tibetan peoples' problem with their occupying power the Chinese; it could be that the latest huge tragedy of the earthquake will make these intractable rulers more compassionate and understanding of Tibetan aspirations?

It was a huge pleasure to see the military families at an IT tutorial, mothers and children together – that is what is needed to give people a sense of aspiration and encouragement. The men and now the men and women of a nation's armed forces pay the price and suffer the costs of armed conflict. These are our unsung heroes and heroines. Bertold Brecht used the line 'Pity the nation that has no heroes ...' to which the sneering rejoinder was 'Pity the nation that needs heroes ...'. Well, my friends, we all need heroes, to whom we can look up and show respect. Heroes, I repeat, not celebrities; the men and women of our armed forces are unsung heroes and those of the Indian Army in the last century fighting world wars, as I said at the start of this book, were superb. In the horror and turmoil of war acts of great courage and nobility generally go unnoticed – but we must not forget these true unsung heroes. India in 2008 is playing her part alongside other armed forces personnel in the UN peacekeeping forces in Darfur and other places. It is now considered that her army is the second largest in the world.

It seems to me that recently HM Forces have been grossly undervalued and diminished by the current British Government, none of whom have any military experience or training. The war in Afghanistan is now nearly seven years old and we are unlikely ever to actually win there – my ancestors could have told the politicians that! As for Iraq – well, I used the term in my second book that was being written at the time the USA and UK embarked upon that war, 'that the consequences would take a long time to fathom'. What a tragic debacle there has been so far, but as usual politicians can continue to chew the cud about it whilst good men and women pay with their lives and injuries. Only now have the Prime Minister and his part-time Defence Secretary started to value and respect our Armed Services and yet they do not receive adequate amounts of weaponry and equipment with which to fully prosecute an efficient campaign.

It was still immensely cold in Dehra Dun and we had been given the generals' suite in the guest quarters. The two young men who were tasked to look after us were Tulsi, who cooked, and Patel. We had a double bedroom, lounge/study, dressing room and two en suite bathrooms with a downstairs lounge as well. In warm conditions it would have all been glorious but we were freezing and I said to young Patel that I needed heat at which he leapt to the air conditioner and put it on whilst I frantically said, "No, no – heat not cold," but he grinned and said, "Wait, Ma'am, the heat will come. I have flicked the switch ..." and so he had and what bliss. I was able to sit on the bed and write up my notes and drink hot tea. Then little Tulsi called us for dinner at the other bungalow. He was a top-class youngster, ever eager to please and delighted to speak Hindi with me; he offered to bring us our meal but it would have been a lot of extra trouble for him. We went over and ate as fast as possible as the dining room had the chill of a tomb.

The next morning we had our usual omelettes and papaya and tea and when it came to the time of our departure everyone assembled to say farewell. The young captain appeared this time in full dress uniform not fatigues and requested that we take some more photographs – a lovely chap and I foresee him one day as one of India's generals – a man who can both serve and lead. I particularly liked the way he conversed with the driver the day before; some people in authority can be arrogant but he was not and I listened to their Hindi conversation quite easily which was conducted in mutual respect, much as his conversation in English with us. We left some discreet tips for Tulsi and Patel and thanked them all for looking after us. Then Ajay, our own driver, asked that we might drive by the Canteen – which is in fact the Indian Army Stores. He had been assured by Patel that he would be able to buy a tracksuit at a fraction of the going price in Delhi so we went and let him buy what he needed. Ajay had also filled the back of our four by four with flagons of Holy Ganga Water, which is known as Ganga Jal, to take back to his family; this will be dispensed on appropriate occasions like weddings, naming ceremonies of children and death. He too is a nice man with whom we built up a good friendship and his driving was excellent.

We drove down to Saharanpur and were again guests of the Indian Army at the Indian Remount Veterinary Corps and Equine Breeding Station. This was a drive that I could remember and on a nice sunny day Graham saw the best of it as we descended from the hills to the plains. This was a supremely happy experience for me. I last lived in Saharanpur fifty years ago and to visit and see places that have remained as I recalled them is something I treasure. We were most warmly welcomed by the Commandant, Colonel Narbir Singh, and his fellow officers. The Remount has 2,400 acres and over 1,000 equines – stallions, brood mares, horses, and donkeys and mules. We saw foals born within the last hours and beautiful beasts that took me back to my time as a youngster riding at the Remount. The lovely estate is full of peacocks, *nilgai* (the name means blue cow but is in fact a huge antelope), lovely bird life, and beautifully maintained equine breeding buildings and lawns and training grounds. After coffee, upon our arrival, the various senior officers called upon us and we then had lunch and Colonel Narbir Singh had ordered that the four-in-hand carriage be sent for our use and a tour of the whole estate. I knew exactly what was in store for us but Graham was enchanted when the coach arrived resplendent in army livery with two smart liverymen in uniform and its coachman. A young captain was seconded to look after us and as all these officers are vets Graham was in happy company. I had last ridden in that coach in 1959 and had been at Christmas/New Year of 1958/1959 in the company of the famous General Thimaya, then commander in chief of India when he visited the Remount for a fox hunt in which I too participated – I am not sure but I rather think the 'fox' was in fact a jackal! When I recounted all this to Mummy she remembered that I had first sat on that coach in 1948 as a mere toddler going to a children's party. I also learnt to handle a pony and phaeton at the Remount myself and used regularly to ride out, with an accompanying Indian soldier, on the horse loaned to me that I named Blue Grass. The estate is beautiful and seemed to be teeming with peacocks and *nilgai*; I would have remembered them had they been in such large numbers fifty years ago. Colonel Narbir Singh announced that there should be a Mess Night in our honour and that a huge fire should be lit on the lawn with drinks and eats followed by dinner. The road leading into the Officers' Mess had 'welcome' drawn upon it in white chalk. It was a most enjoyable and memorable evening and I met a lovely couple of whom I did not know but with whom I have several mutual friends as it turns out. The officers were almost all colonels; along with the Commandant there were Colonel Dhumal, Colonel Vinod Kumar, Colonel Jagat Singh, Lt Colonel Pawar, Major Sandeep Prakash and Captain Darpan Bedekar. The civilian couple are Beverley and Dinghi Niblet who have a son in the British Army – Dinghi has a private school at which she still teaches but is now going to retire; it had been started by her mother at the time we were children and she has carried it on with great success. I hope one day soon they will be our guests here in Scotland. One of the ladies was an army wife whose husband was away serving with the UN Forces in Darfur and most of the ladies were very qualified themselves, but what was nice was that they brought their children which made it a truly family occasion; fortunately none of the little ones injured themselves on the roaring fire. Was I glad of that fire!

As we lay in bed a pair of jackals took up position and howled and keened under our window in the guest bungalow till we fell asleep. The next morning we rose early and watched the sun rise and the officers riding, as indeed I would have done all those years ago and I showed Graham a particular jump that used to worry me and my horse which was still there and still challenging.

In the evening before the social event we had even managed to locate our old house in the ITC (Indian Tobacco Company) enclave where we had lived and it still is very well maintained with lovely gardens set out by my parents and the mango trees they planted are now mature and fruiting. I was a bit apprehensive about trying to find it as very often revisiting the past can have sad consequences but my memory served me correctly and we found the enclave as I had pictured it and now because of modern times there is a 24/7 security guard. He had to approach his superiors on the telephone to ask permission for us to enter the enclave; this involved me explaining to an unknown man what it was all about but I mentioned enough names for him to be satisfied and the guard led us in. The four houses that were used by senior management of the ITC factory were still in very good condition with beautifully maintained gardens of a couple of acres each – indeed ours had been the largest. As we walked the sun was setting and the peacocks took up their roosting positions in the trees that I remembered from my childhood; it was immensely moving, more so because the date was the 30th January and exactly sixty years ago to that date Gandhiji had been assassinated whilst we lived in Saharanpur. My father had had to think fast and order that Hindus and Muslims leave the factory by different gates as in the immediate aftermath of the assassination no one really knew who had been the assassin and there could have been a sectarian bloodbath. There before me was our house Southside with such happy memories and I took plenty of photographs of it and the garden and explained the story to the security guard and the military official who had accompanied us. The terrace made from bricks designed by my parents, the miniature orange trees, the mature mango trees and the great eucalyptus trees are all still there. On the verandah there are toys belonging to a new generation of children and there was the peace and tranquility of an old garden with just the muted cry of the peacock saying 'goodnight'. I feel so fortunate to have ventured down a memory lane that produced such a happy good experience.

Breakfast was taken by us on the lawn next to the remains of the smouldering fire because the sunshine was warmer than the interior of the Officers' Mess. We then took our leave and drove down to Delhi. I was glad to arrive safely; India's roads may have improved but the driving is still quite challenging and it was good to find ourselves in the IIC once again, and they had turned on their warm air alternative to the air conditioning as well!

Chapter Eighteen

The Golden Temple Mail to Bharatpur, Agra and Dholpur

We arrived back by car from the journey to the Ganga and remained for two nights in Delhi and then set off once again but this time by rail. We had travelled on the Golden Temple Mail in November 2002 when we went to Sawai Madhopur to reach Ranthambhore National Park. I knew that this huge train which starts in Amritzar, the home of the famous Sikh Golden Temple, and continues on through Delhi and down through the eastern reaches of Rajasthan to Mumbai, stops at Bharatpur. It was a pleasant journey travelling first class and Bharatpur has a nice little station at which we were met by a car and driver and driven the very short distance to Laxmi Vilas Hotel.

Laxmi Vilas is a palace belonging to the Maharajah of Bharatpur's family. When I had previously visited Bharatpur and the famous Ghana Keoladeo National Park we had stayed at a very nice heritage *haveli*, of which I wrote in the first part of this book, called Chandra Mahal. We had liked that enormously but we wanted something different this time about which I could write.

Just to refresh your memory, the Kingdom of Bharatpur had been carved out by Badan Singh and Suraj Mal, legendary Jat warriors. You will be aware from my last chapter that the family at Fort Unchagaon are also Jats and indeed the present old Rajah of Unchagaon's wife was a Bharatpur princess. Such was the might of the Jats that Bharatpur came to be known as the impregnable city. In the unsuccessful siege of the Lohagarh fort, the British forces led by Lord Lake suffered heavy casualties and Lord Lake himself was killed. At Deeg (which we visited earlier), the Bharatpur Maharaja's army successfully defeated the might of a combined Mughal and Maratha army of 80,000.

These days, a decade on from my first visit, Deeg has been recognised as a truly worthwhile palace to visit with its clever water features and interesting architecture, but Laxmi Vilas was built in 1887 for Raja Raghunath Singh, the younger brother of the then ruler of Bharatpur, Maharaja Ram Singh. An eclectic and lively fusion of Rajput and Mughal architecture, the palace was earlier called Raghunath Niwas, though the locals always preferred to call it Kakaji Ka Mahal.

For a hundred years the Laxmi Vilas Palace had been the venue for significant events that took place in the princely state of Bharatpur – royal weddings, affairs of the court and royal duck shoots. It has played host to the Duke of Edinburgh, the last Shah of Iran, the Kings of Nepal and the last King of Afghanistan. In those days feasts and festivities lasted for days but since 1994 it has operated as a very attractive and successful heritage hotel.

Graham and I loved it and after a warm welcome we were showed to a beautiful suite which was both elegant and spacious with an excellent modernized bathroom. On one side of the palace there is a large decorative swimming pool and had it been warmer one might have been tempted to swim! The grounds are in reasonable condition but I think could easily be improved. The staff however were a delight and we enjoyed ourselves and after lunch embarked on a trip to the old Fort. We chose, ill advisedly perhaps, to have a rickshaw summoned and set off. Well, I have on and off through my life travelled in rickshaws in India and Viet Nam and amazingly once in central London, but this was the oldest, most shabby and uncomfortable rickshaw that I had experienced and the owner was rather shabby and disadvantaged too. It was an extremely uncomfortable ride but it would have hurt him so much to change to another and besides he quite obviously needed the money. In the end we resolved the problem on our return journey by hiring a second rickshaw and Graham travelled in one and I in the other which seemed to astonish the onlookers, of whom there were plenty.

The Bharatpur Fort is interesting but needs a good deal of renovation and care. I was glad we visited but only because we had previously been to Deeg – I would not give it a moment's thought if I had to choose between the two because of a shortage of time. Indian standards of museums and custodianship are still in many places in their infancy and if the erstwhile ruling family does not take sufficient interest then the place slides into decay – how very different from Jodhpur or Jaipur.

On the way back to the palace we stopped by the side of the road and

The grand salon at the Dholpur Palace.

telephoned home from an international trunk dialling (ITD) booth. In the past there were plenty of these cheap efficient places but now that cell phones have become so common they are beginning to diminish in number. However, we had a good conversation with one of our sons. We actually now own an Indian cell phone for our visits to India and later on that evening used the cell phone to again telephone back to Scotland briefly. They are so cheap to buy in India that it is worth buying one for a long holiday, and in our case for our annual visits. However, the ITD is a fraction of the price for overseas calls.

Sitting on the verandah outside our suite with a welcome cup of tea, we greeted a British couple and started chatting and then ensued a very sociable and pleasant evening. It was their first time in north India and they were enchanted but with some very sensible ideas. Graham ordered a bottle of our favourite red Indian wine, Chantilly, and we socialized in our very spacious suite. India's red wines are delightful for the most part; we particularly like Chantilly and Sula and the important thing is that one feels completely clear headed and there is no 'alcohol punch' which I particularly detest. I so often drink Coke for safety reasons and because I like it but occasionally on a cool evening a glass or two of red wine is very welcome. People were very dismissive of Indian wines until recently but in the last few years there have been huge improvements. Nashik in Maharashtra is the area for viticulture and there are now 50 wineries. Vineyards have been cultivated for over 5,000 years in India apparently. According to the accounts of early European travellers, who visited the courts of the Mughal emperors Akbar, Jehangir and Shah Jahan in the 16th and 17th centuries and reported tasting wines from the royal vineyards, the red wines were produced from the *arkesham* grape and white wine from the *arkawati* and *bhokry* grapes. India now has 123,000 acres of vineyards but only one per cent of this acreage is used for wine, with approximately 400,000 cases produced annually. There are those like the famous and respected Oz Clarke who welcome India's entry into wine production and he is enthusiastic about some of the wines, but though it is a fast-growing market one has to remember that 37 million cases of whisky are consumed annually and 11 million of brandy and 9 million cases of rum!

In those centuries long past of course no one had yet found the dubious delights of whisky, brandy and rum in India. Now ironically it is an Indian who has bought Whyte & Mackay Whisky in Scotland and is thus owner of a great many famous brands, plus a famous beer in India which he was not allowed to advertise so he bought an airline to which he gave the same name – Kingfisher. Dr Vijay Mallya is a very successful businessman and billionaire and member of the Rajya Sabha in India; we found ourselves 'playing' on the same Lakshadweep Island last year which he was visiting on his very sumptuous yacht which is crewed by Europeans and registered in the Isle of Man. Apparently Russia and China are his companies' fast-emerging markets.

The next morning we were up early for our much anticipated return to the Ghana Keoladeo National Park. It was quite simply a total disaster. The entrance is now on a well-made wide road; the naturalists greet you enthusiastically but inside the situation is dire. For three years at least the area has been starved of monsoon and the bird park wetlands have dried up. What water there is has been pumped in by a couple of noisy pumps. Our beautiful memories were shattered. We asked for Devi Singh and were told that he had left and gone to work as a naturalist at Corbett, which was so disappointing for us, but one of his former colleagues had his cell phone number and promptly 'phoned him and when I spoke, quite amazingly he recalled me clearly from ten years ago! Clear as a bell he was speaking down the line and we talked and I told him how I had put him in a book and had just been to Corbett and would love to have met up. I now have his cell phone number and will try and keep in touch. I am so glad in fact that he was able to go to Corbett and find good work because clearly there is nothing happening at Bharatpur.

We spent just about two hours in the park and I photographed what I could but I felt outraged at what was there. It is said that the government

Dholpur Palace.

authorities could dig a canal to the Chambal River and divert water to the national park and thus ensure it does not reach this stage, but, like so much in India, politics enters the arena and nothing has yet been done. I have alerted the various tourism companies and conservation websites because it is only through significant pressure that improvements will be made. In the meantime, it would seem to me that tourism companies who know about this are failing in their duty to their clients in encouraging them or allowing them to make the choice to come to Bharatpur for birdwatching.

I observed quite a few coach loads of tourists and of course other couples for whom it must have been a terrible disappointment. Recalling our pleasure of over a decade ago it was a rather miserable morning and we returned to a poor breakfast which the staff seemed to find an effort to serve. I would say that if that national park turns into dust and scrub they will have very little business in the years to come at Laxmi Vilas because Bharatpur does not have a great deal of charm and people always want value for money, and birdwatchers are dedicated people and will find somewhere else as a focus for their passion. The very capable Chief Minister of Rajasthan should turn her attention to this problem, however tricky the local politics might become, because a practical solution will be of benefit not only to the avian population, but also the local human population who will undoubtedly suffer if tourism and birdwatching goes somewhere else.

We departed from our hotel in a hired car and asked the driver to take us to Fatehpur Sikri. Now this is a success story; ten years on the whole of Fatehpur Sikri is looking really good with excellent conservation and renovation and developed garden areas. The amount of tourists was staggering compared to all those years ago and it was a very pleasant visit. The authorities have even built ladies' beautiful toilet facilities, but, as is so often in India, without adequate supervision and cleaning they will deteriorate. A male attendant sitting outside had the cheek to ask me for some money and I roundly told him yes, if he would clean the place first. I found the various touts on the approaching path really irritating but we pursued our objective which was to make a hurried inspection and take some more digital photography to update our collection. The roads have improved greatly and I was reminded of the last time we were on this road early one morning in November 2002, having travelled from Chandra Mahal on our return from Ranthambhore National Park. We had had the great good fortune to see seven tigers and were elated by our trip. Our journey was to Agra from where we took the Shatabdhi Express to Gwalior for my research for the second book *India: The Tiger's Roar*. The road was so busy with what seemed like the whole Indian Army driving back from the border with Pakistan, having been stood down from the brink of war. Our journey had coincided with our Remembrance Day and I found it very sobering to see literally thousands of men coming back from what could have been a disastrous conflict which was probably provoked by the brutal raid on India's parliament in December 2001. I sincerely hope there are no further Indo–Pakistan conflicts.

How naïve was I to write such a forlorn hope; this month, on the 13th May 2008 seven bomb blasts tore through the walled city of Jaipur. Old Jaipur is a maze of alleyways, crowded with shops and restaurants alongside the city's famous walls and palaces, as I have described earlier in this book. It was obviously a terrorist plot and the culprits are thought most likely to have a Pakistani origin. In 2006, 209 people were killed in bomb explosions placed on the trains of Mumbai. This sort of thing does not however deter me from going to India; we had devastating terrorist strikes on the London Underground in 2005, and during the late 1980s and early 1990s those of us who worked in the City of London were only too well aware of the IRA threats and actual bombings. Now the protagonists are of a different zealous persuasion.

We continued on our way to Agra. It now is approached by good roads but when you enter the environs of the actual city it is so depressing because the roads are still deteriorating and the atmosphere is one of complete shabbiness and decay. I cannot understand why; this city now

Our bedroom at Dholpur Palace!

has three world heritage sites and the Taj Mahal was recently voted as one of the additional 'Seven Wonders of the World'. It is iconic to the image of India and most first-time travellers want to see the Taj. Graham and I are just thankful that we actually experienced Taj ten years ago when there was less emphasis on tourism. I had so hoped that a decade on I would see so much progress about the conservation and clean-up in the area whereas our perception is that there has been a lot of talk. Indeed I am reliably informed that various industries have been compulsorily moved and that renovation on the Taj is taking place, together with the work on the garden for the opposite bank of the Jamuna River as well.

We took a taxi to the spot from where it is obligatory to walk. The area was filthy and covered in touts and beggars whereas curiously in the past where one parked and took an electric vehicle had not been so bad. On this occasion on a warm sunny Sunday afternoon the queues were lengthy and it was reckoned we could waste two hours just standing there. The reason for this is the complete incompetence of the entrance and security authorities. A tout approached us and offered for a sum to expedite our entry through another entrance to which we cautiously agreed. It was the equivalent of about £7 and we paid it on top of the entry fee for foreigners, which is now quite considerable. I am happy to pay the full foreigners' fee but I would like reassurance that it is being used to maintain the Taj Mahal and its environs in a manner befitting this wonderful architectural poem of love and remembrance. Custodianship of the Taj Mahal should be taken over by the Union Government of India since quite obviously the provincial government has no real appreciation of and respect for the treasures in its midst.

We spent a long time at the Taj and took many digital photographs and watched the sun set over the domes and enjoyed observing others' enjoyment and new experience. Once we were ready to leave we had to go and find an ATM with our tout and draw the cash to pay him and retrieve the camcorder, which is not allowed past the Gate of the Taj. These days it is so easy because one 'phones on the cell phone to the taxi driver and he appears very quickly and returns one to the hotel. In the meantime of course he has taken on other fares, but it is a good way of doing business because he had been called by our hotel reception desk and would not want to irritate them or forgo their future business so behaves in a good way.

We were staying at The Grand Imperial which is a relatively new hotel within the heart of the city. I liked it immensely as it is the only heritage hotel in Agra and therefore not too big. The property is a century old and I am told was acquired by the present owner's father in 1944. In the colonial era it had been the home of a senior civil servant or someone of stature and played host to many distinguished people but once acquired during the Second World War it had remained unused. For several decades the lawns of the large front garden, which is walled, were used for the wedding season annually, but about four years ago the present owner and his wife decided to renovate the whole place sympathetically and now it has become a really nice hotel with about 30 rooms. It was built in what is known as Lahori brick, which is the same material used to build the Red Fort and the core of the Taj Mahal complex. There is a charming swimming pool in the enclosed back garden, with a health club, spa and activity room. The multi-cuisine restaurant produced good a la carte food and there are plans to change the bar area into a reading room and library because so many guests once in Agra want to add to their knowledge and this would be a real attraction. I particularly liked our very spacious suite with its original flooring and very comfortable bed and good quality bed linen. In the evening the garden was nicely lit and a fountain played. This hotel is now part of the WelcomHeritage Chain of palaces, forts, *havelis*, resorts and homes. The hotel group is part of the ITC hotel group which belongs to the huge conglomerate for which my late father worked. I have written about some of their other hotels earlier in the book and in my other books but I actually met Mrs Agarwal, who with her husband owns this hotel, when she visited the World Travel Market in London in November 2007. It is worth noting that the Agarwals also own a medium size three star hotel in Mumbai called Parle International which is located quite close to Mumbai's domestic airport. Mumbai is now immensely expensive and I was glad to hear of this reasonably priced hotel.

I specifically returned to Agra to see the Taj Mahal since it has undergone some necessary renovation and to see what progress has been made within the city. I was disappointed on all counts and feel that the Union Government must grasp this nettle because I have read readers' rants in the travel pages of the weekend editions of *The Telegraph* and *The Times* and there are a lot of people who have not enjoyed 'their Taj experience' and that is a very great shame. I was told by a group of distinguished politicians whom I met the following evening that the Uttar Pradesh Government which currently has a woman chief minister is completely disinterested in heritage and its responsibilities. She apparently is appealing to those who come from the most disadvantaged strata of Indian life in Uttar Pradesh and promising 'jam tomorrow' through expedient politics with her sights set on becoming prime minister of India! Uttar Pradesh is the most densely populated state in India and has many social problems but nevertheless the provincial government should look to its responsibilities.

There is however one really good piece of news and animal welfare development since my last visit to this part of India which has cheered us both immensely. Driving along Uttar Pradesh roads in the past, inevitably one saw and grimaced at the spectacle of a dancing bear. This horrible dancing bear tradition in India dates back to the 16th century when bears were forced to perform for the entertainment of the Mughal emperors. In more recent times they have been used by some of the poorest people in India, known as Kalandars, to beg money from tourists. As more and more people took to visiting India, so these wonderful sloth bears could be seen at roadsides all across the country. It wasn't until 1972 that the Indian government introduced the Wildlife Protection Act which finally outlawed this cruel practice. However, at that time there was nowhere to house any bears that were confiscated.

Sloth bears are protected under the Wildlife Protection Act of India (1972) and listed under Appendix 1 of the Convention in International Trade in Endangered Species (CITES) and I have not yet had the good fortune to see one in the wild. In spite of this high level of legal protection, tiny cubs are still poached from the wild every year to be sold on as dancing bears or for bear baiting or the trade in bear parts. Many of them die only days after capture from trauma, dehydration or starvation. The cubs are only months old when they begin training and suffer a punishing regime of beating and starvation to make them submissive to their trainers. As sloth bear cubs spend at least two years with their mothers in the wild, it isn't hard to imagine their fear as they are subjected to an existence which is not only ridden with pain but also totally unnatural.

The cub's muzzle is pierced with a red-hot needle which is forced through the bone, cartilage and nerve membrane in the top of the muzzle, creating a terrible wound. A rope is then pulled up through the nostril and out through the wound. The pain must be excruciating, and even more so when the trainer pulls on the rope forcing the cub to stand upright. The bear is then hit on each hind paw with a stick. To avoid the pain, it lifts each foot in turn. Eventually, the trainer has only to strike the ground for the bear to lift its feet. It is now a dancing bear.

Before the cub is a year old, its teeth are knocked out with a hammer and its claws are pulled out with pliers or cut back to the quick. These mutilations are carried out without any kind of anaesthetic. The bear is fed on chapattis, lentils and sour milk, or given steamed *raji* (dough) balls, wheat *rotis* (flat bread) and bread. Such an inadequate and unnatural diet leads to severe intestinal problems for the bears causing great pain, sometimes blindness, and even death.

Once trained, the bear travels long distances on the hot dusty roads for eight or nine months of the year. When it isn't performing, it remains tied at the roadside on a short length of rope, its miserable existence a far cry from the freedom it was born to enjoy in the wild.

It wasn't until thirty years after the introduction of the Wildlife Protection Act that the first purpose-built bear sanctuary opened its doors in Agra, a few kilometres north of the famous Taj Mahal. During that time the Kalandars were granted licences to continue to 'dance' the bears. However, now that the Agra Bear Rescue Facility is fully equipped, their handlers are required to surrender them in the presence of a government forestry officer. In exchange, they receive a grant for retraining so that they can start up in new businesses and develop better, humane ways of supporting their families. Their new way of life also means that the Kalandar children can go to school.

International Animal Rescue has supported the project since the first six dancing bears were brought in off the streets on Christmas Eve 2002. By 2008 more than 450 bears had been rescued. The majority are housed in Agra, others at a second sanctuary in Bannerghatta near Bangalore. The project is managed by an Indian charity, Wildlife SOS, and funded from the UK and US by International Animal Rescue and from Australia by The Free the Bears Fund. I am filled with admiration for what they have all achieved which has resulted in a 'win-win' situation which is important.

The Agra sanctuary is situated on land within the government-owned Sur Sarovar bird sanctuary. The centre provides a beautiful natural forest habitat where the bears roam freely after an initial period of quarantine and rehabilitation. The socialisation areas which the bear enters at the end of its time in quarantine have freshwater bathing pools, purpose-built dens, feeding and resting areas, as well as climbing frames and other tools of environmental enrichment.

The one positive outcome from Bharatpur's current drought and continuing water problems is that its loss has turned out to be Agra's gain as now all kinds of exotic birds are flocking to the Sur Sarovar sanctuary. Within the sanctuary is a 783 hectare lake. For the past few years all kinds of birds have been visiting this vast expanse of water which has been recognised as a wetland by the National Wetland Commission. Siberian cranes, Chinese coots and flamingos are among the species that are seen regularly in Sur Sarovar.

Named after Surdas, the famous poet of Braj Bhasha, for many years the lake was choked with water hyacinths and weeds. However, thanks to the clearance undertaken by the District Forestry Department for Uttar Pradesh, it now attracts large numbers of birds and birdwatchers. This lovely sanctuary is so close to Agra that I would heartily recommend a visit.

In 2007 International Animal Rescue funded the purchase of an additional area of land across the river from the existing sanctuary, making the centre big enough to accommodate all the bears that are still on the streets. International Animal Rescue and Wildlife SOS are more determined than ever to rescue every dancing bear off the streets of India and bring the curtain down on this barbaric form of entertainment for the very last time and I am so impressed by their determination and commitment: www.internationalanimalrescue.org and www.wildlifesos.org.

I had been invited to visit the Palace of Dholpur in Dholpur which is just within Rajasthan's most eastern border. The Crown Prince of Dholpur is the Yuvraj Dushyant Singh, who is also an MP. Dushyant's mother is, to give her the full title, HH Maharani Vasundhara Raje of Dholpur; she was by birth a princess of the royal family of Gwalior – the Scindias. Gwalior has a fascinating citadel and royal palace which I explored in my second book *India: The Tiger's Roar*. Vasundhara Raje is the Chief Minister of Rajasthan and a very capable and forward-looking woman.

Dushyant, has after careful renovation, recently opened the Raj Niwas Palace at Dholpur as a quiet hotel and has ambitious plans for the palace grounds in which he has built some beautiful cottages, each with their own small swimming pool. I met him in London and he very sweetly urged us to come and stay. He had arranged for one of his palace vehicles to come and collect us from our Agra hotel and the journey was both interesting and comfortable and not long. Leaving Agra, we observed that as usual the military cantonment area of the city was still very well kept and that also led to our dismay at the contrast in the 'civil lines' as they are called.

Dholpur was a Jat principality as was the case with Bharatpur; Dholpur is situated between Agra and Gwalior actually in a part of Rajasthan that separates Madhya Pradesh and Uttar Pradesh. It was near here that Aurangzeb's sons fought a pitched battle to determine who would succeed him as emperor of the rapidly declining Mughal Empire. There is an ancient fort – Shergarh Fort in Dholpur but it is in ruins and I was not taken to see it. We were to be guests at the marvellous and slightly eccentric palace that had been specifically built for the visit of the Prince of Wales in 1876.

The old historic city of Dholpur was initially named 'Dhawalpuri' after the ruler Dhawal Deo who built the city at a site a little south of the present city. Subsequently people started calling it Dholpur. In AD 846 it was ruled by a Chauhan family as a feudatory of Kannauj. It is a very small state but it had a very turbulent history.

Its strategic location on the main route from Kabul and Delhi to the Deccan and its proximity to cities like Gwalior, Agra and Bayana attracted the attention of almost all the powerful kings and rulers of Delhi and Agra. Though the rulers of Dholpur resisted the invasions with valour, it was time and again occupied by the invading forces and plundered and devastated. Sikander Lodi attacked and occupied Dholpur in 1501. His forces plundered the city and even decimated all the gardens that provided shade in this very hot area of central India. Babar also invaded in 1526 and during the rule of Humayun the site of the town was moved northwards to avoid erosion by the Chambal River.

When Shah Jahan fell ill his eldest and most beloved son, Prince Dara Shikoh, was defeated by his younger cruel brother Aurangzeb; the latter served his brother's head on a plate to torture his father whom he hated, which I mentioned earlier. You will recall the story of how his old father, the Emperor Shah Jahan, was then incarcerated in the Red Fort at Agra to live out his life looking at the Taj Mahal. In 1658 at Ran-ka-Chabutra, 5 km east of Dholpur, Aurangzeb's sons Azam and Muazzam fought a war of succession after their father's death.

We visited Machchkund which is about 8 km from the town of Dholpur; it is an ancient sacred place and commands a scenic view. The place is named after Raja Machch Kund, the twenty-fourth king of the Suryavanshi Dynasty (the solar race) which is said to have reigned for nineteen generations before Lord Ram. According to the legend, Raja Machch Kund was sleeping here when a demon, Kaal Yaman, who was pursuing Lord Krishna, accidentally woke him up. The demon was burnt to ashes because of a divine blessing to the Raja. It is now considered a sacred site and attracts a number of pilgrims and it is thought that the enclosures around it were built by the Mughal Emperor Akbar.

About 40 km from Dholpur is a picturesque and historic lake called Talab-e-Shahi. The lake and the palace were built in 1617 as a shooting lodge for Prince Shah Jahan and the palace and the lake were later maintained by the rulers of Dholpur. The lake now attracts a large number of winter migratory fowl and is possibly also another stretch of water compensating for the inadequacies of Bharatpur's bird sanctuary.

It is thought that this area of India together with the lovely Chambal River will be the focus for tourism in the coming years as it is unspoilt. The Chambal is one of five tributaries of the Yamuna River. The river flows north-northeast through Madhya Pradesh, running for a time through Rajasthan, then forming the boundary between Rajasthan and Madhya Pradesh before turning southeast to join the Yamuna in Uttar Pradesh. During the monsoon period it quite frequently floods and creates havoc to the road system and even rail traffic between Madhya Pradesh and Rajasthan. The Chambal is ranked as one of India's cleanest rivers and it is home to the *gharial* – the long-snouted fish-eating crocodile of which there were huge numbers previously but even they have declined in number. The National Chambal Wildlife Sanctuary was created in 1978 and covers 5,400 sq km across the three states of Madhya Pradesh, Rajasthan and Uttar Pradesh with about a 400 km stretch of the Chambal thus protected. The good news is that the rehabilitation programme and captive breeding initiative have resulted in over 5,000 young *gharials* being released into protected areas. The river dolphin and otters as well as wonderful bird life were present in their hundreds in years past, but now they too have been reduced in numbers and the conservation authorities are making attempts to halt the decline. Tourism is however still in its infancy but nevertheless the area is very interesting to visit and I am so glad we were invited to Dholpur. This was however considered to be part of 'bandit country' until recently so I am interested as to how the various hospitality consortiums and owners plan to look after their clients or, maybe in modern India banditry will actually become a horror of the past.

The Raj Niwas Palace itself is built of the local famous red stone; it is huge and imposing and, considering it had lain unused for over forty years until Dushyant and his mother decided to renovate it between 2002 and 2005, is in good condition. The interior is amusing because the Maharajah who built it was obviously greatly enamoured of Victorian tiles and decreed that most of the interior should be fully tiled in those wonderful tiles one still sees from time to time in heritage buildings here in Britain. I think they had their origins in the tile factories in the Midlands near what we now know as Telford, the modern town constructed in the 1980s in beautiful Shropshire. The renovation has been very carefully achieved and the whole place is visually stunning, but nevertheless one feels, when lying on the bed, that perhaps one is at the bottom of a Victorian swimming bath! Our palatial suite comprised a huge bedroom of about 10 metres by 7 metres, with a dressing room which is the size of an average British sitting room and a bathroom that is also huge; all of these rooms are fully tiled to the high ceilings. The bathroom fittings are the originals installed for that princely visit! I think Dushyant has a real headache in devising efficient hot water to these antique bathrooms. I myself like 'heritage' but am not too keen on heritage taken to the extreme – I like a hot shower and I know how frustrated Graham becomes if he does not have sufficiently hot water to shave well. The next suite has a change of design in the tiles and so it continues throughout the palace. The antechambers are also tiled as was the dining room, though the grand salon, or drawing room, is not but is a lovely regal room. I also loved the verandahs which have floors of a mosaic made from broken tiles – this was prevalent in the old mansions in Kolkata which I recalled as a child.

Dushyant's housekeeper is a friendly lady called Bubbles whom we liked and she made us very welcome and comfortable and did the cooking herself which was delicious. The domestic staff would serve us during the day outside in the garden with style on crested Dholpur bone china and breakfast was taken in a more informal dining room. Dushyant drove down from Delhi to meet us and more importantly some distinguished political colleagues who came for dinner when we were there. First we sat outside around a roaring fire out in the garden and they drank whisky and we listened and observed; it was interesting because they are all powerful men, most of them belonged to India's aristocracy and are minor rajahs and had some strong ideas and belonged to the official opposition party. Graham and I drink very sparingly but there were some good 'eats' and it was after ten o'clock before we sat down to eat dinner in the dining room. I observed that whenever one of the domestic staff saw Dushyant for the first time they bowed and touched his feet – so old habits die hard in regal India. I liked some of the guests more than the others and found the ones that made the least noise the most worthy of respect. It was only towards the end of the evening that I let it out that I understand Hindi and that was quite funny – watching the consternation on a couple of faces!

I really wish Dushyant well and hope that his venture into hospitality and tourism works; our memories are of looking out on to the palace gardens from the top verandah with peacocks strutting on the lawns and the Neem trees waving in a little breeze. We were driven back in the evening to Agra railway station from where we took the Shatabdhi Express back to Delhi. We had chosen first class and it was excellent. I have used that service before from Agra and recommend it. The railway station has improved but I was irritated by the lack of any light in the ladies' toilet block. The dilemma about my safety was solved by the porter showing me where it was and standing a little distance away whilst Graham looked after all the luggage. It is however extremely difficult to manage an Indian-style lavatory in complete darkness and shut a door and not have some sort of mishap! I did manage but had I been a lone woman the whole thing would have been very fraught and I would have been vulnerable to attack as I entered or left the conveniences. The porter was rewarded for his care of me when I returned to Graham. On a previous occasion when travelling with a girlfriend we had remained within the ladies' waiting room which had its own WC but that is on the main platform so was not an option for this occasion. Increasingly, lone women have been victims of rape or mugging in India recently so I am pointing out these problems because I am realistic. I cannot say strongly enough that I do not think India is the country to which to travel as a lone female and certainly as a lone, young, perhaps 'blonde bombshell'.

So often I meet people who want to experience Indian railways; well, I would strongly recommend the trip I have just outlined as practical and inexpensive and enjoyable – travelling down to Agra by train and back, or taking in Bharatpur as we did which would give one the added bonus of Deeg, Fatehpur Sikri and the surrounding attractions. The connecting journeys are easily affordable with a hired car and driver organised by the various hotels. Dholpur would be the cherry on the top of such a journey and to be recommended. However you do not need to 'experience' third class train travel as one of our travel acquaintances was planning to do!

Chapter Nineteen

Regal Rajasthan Revisited

Sitting at the Domestic Airport of Delhi, waiting for a delayed flight to Jodhpur was frustrating; the day before, the 6th February, had been a strange, cold, foggy day and had played havoc with the departure and arrival of all domestic flights and this in turn had impacted upon our journey to Jodhpur the next day. The Domestic Airport, which I had known in my youth as Palam Airport, is now altogether a more comfortable and attractive place than a decade ago. Heaven knows it was well overdue for refurbishment and now work is soon to be completed on Indira Gandhi International (IGI) Airport. I started this book by commenting on my immediate perception of the latter upon landing after a 35-year absence from India. Well, in the intervening years it had not improved one iota, but recently because of the Commonwealth Games, which are to be held in Delhi in 2010, and the fact that India is now so popular with industrialists and entrepreneurs from all over the world, some work was being done to repair the first image of this dreadful modern 'Gateway to India'.

This year when queuing at immigration, on arrival we found ourselves behind a man of Middle Eastern origin who had also flown in from Dubai on our flight; he was frankly appalled and asked us hesitantly had we ever been to India before because this was his first visit and he did not like what he saw or was experiencing. I chuckled and reassured him that IGI was actually not an example of the best that India can produce but the worst and that I was sure that very soon when he arrived at his hotel he would change his opinion. There is in fact a whole new international airport being built as I write and I am told it will be excellent; well I cer-

Balasamand Lake Palace staircase.

tainly hope so because when one experiences India's private enterprise in
the form of hotels and company offices and beautiful grand homes and
new temples, the building and finish and maintenance is excellent and
where appropriate actually magnificent, but sadly it would seem government property has not yet entered that category. When I criticize as stri-
dently as I am doing now it is not because I want to make fun or ridicule
India; no, indeed, it is the beautiful land of my birth and I want people to
feel impressed and like what they see and want to experience more of this
huge, amazing, diverse country.

Air travel has burgeoned amazingly in India and the various little
airports have all been developed and improved too. We flew by Indian
Airlines to Jodhpur, which has been subsumed into Air India, and on the
return we were booked on Jet Airways, which I still consider a superb airline and one of the very best in the world for punctuality, comfort and effi-
ciency and charm of its staff. The major new player in India is Kingfisher
Airlines belonging to Dr Vijay Mallya which started in 2005; people say
it is extremely good and very competitively priced – I hear that it has
recently received five star status in the airline world, and has also bought
a huge stake in Air Deccan. Kingfisher has a commitment to start flying
between its bases at Bangalore and Mumbai and London in October 2008;

173

The great Umaid Bhavan Palace of HH Maharajah Gaj Singh of Jodhpur.

hopefully very soon it will also fly between London and Delhi. I have also travelled on Spice Jet which was cheap and cheerful and safe and there are a few others of which I have no experience. Hyderabad has a completely new international airport which opened earlier this year; I wrote about Hyderabad in my third book and consider it is going to be the city of the future in India.

Thankfully the inbound aircraft arrived and we departed several hours late for our destination, Jodhpur. Graham and I were so pleased to be returning to Rajasthan and Jodhpur is a big favourite with us as it is a well-maintained city. I am always enchanted at a daytime arrival at Jodhpur. That evening we arrived as the sun was setting, the pilot banked sharply and the view on the ground was outstandingly beautiful looking down from the aircraft windows as the sun shone its warm reddish-golden light on Umaid Bhavan Palace and the Meherangarh Fort. The airport is dinky and a military one and arriving after ten years I could see that it is still beautifully maintained and a pleasure to use.

We were met by Thakur Sunder Singh's man at the airport and I intimated that though we were so late I wanted to go first to Umaid Bhavan Palace to photograph the sunset. It really was a race against time as the sun was already low in the sky but the driver deposited us at the impos-

HH Gaj Singh's beautiful Marwar mare and foal.

ing portico of Umaid Bhavan and I raced inside and through the marble foyers and circular hall out onto the terrace. Thankfully we managed to film the sun as a glowing red ball going down on the horizon with the palace gardens in the foreground. I think the staff were rather astonished but I explained that sometimes one has to discard other thoughts – who knows if I will have the good fortune to be at Umaid Bhavan again!

We were staying that night at Balsamand Lake Palace and would return on the morrow to Umaid Bhavan. We drove through the gloaming to Balsamand Lake Palace, which is about 9 km northeast of Jodhpur. This lovely summer palace was built on the end of a dam which was first constructed in 1159 by Balak Rao Parihar and this delightful rainwater lake is a cool oasis amidst the rocky hills. The present-day palace hotel was laid out as a summer retreat for Jodhpur's royal family in 1936.

I really wish our plane had not been delayed as I feel cheated of some of my potential enjoyment of such a beautiful place. The welcome was warm and efficient and in no time we had left our car, been garlanded and taken up to the hotel entrance and foyer. The palace was lit by twinkling little lights and there was the promise of so much to see the following morning.

We had been given the most sumptuous of suites with a huge elegant bedroom, most beautifully furnished and with stunning soft furnishings of

The Wilderness Camp of Rohet.

silk with striking Indian designs. There were two bathrooms and I thought they had been well thought out but I just loved the huge shower. It was a bit of a race because we were due for dinner at Thakur Sunder Singh's own family home and this required a full change. On the way to the car we were shown some other rooms in the garden and the outside eating area where chefs were busy preparing delicious tandoori and other delights.

Jodhpur, it was explained to us by Sunder Singh, has benefited hugely from the Chief Minister's ideas – that is Vasundhara Raje who is Dushyant's mother, you will recall. The roads have been widened and shops are not allowed to encroach upon them, roundabouts have been built, the place is cleaned and maintained and, as is always the case, the Indian Army areas which house the Border Security Force are spick and span.

We had a delicious dinner with Sunder and his son Aditya that evening and finally jumped into bed quite late. The sunrise saw me up and dressed to go and watch the sun rise over the Aravalli Hills and photograph the light when it finally shone on the hotel. It was a glorious morning and the lake looked serene in the early morning sunshine with all the bird calls in the trees around me. The hotel's grounds are spacious and attractive and for warmer times it has a beautiful swimming pool with clever colonnades which would give shade from the harsh sun. As it was, that morning there

was a large group of chipmunks totally absorbed in eating their breakfast thoughtfully provided by the ground staff right next to the swimming
pool. There are a jogging track and croquet facilities and an Ayurvedic
Spa, but I did not have the opportunity to use them – though jogging is not
high on my list of things to do when I go travelling, I realise eager younger
souls feel the need for such punishment!

We had an excellent early breakfast with just the two of us sitting on the
terrace overlooking the lake. When we departed we made a point of going
to see the Maharajah of Jodhpur's horses. The stable block is beautifully
maintained and the horseflesh is superb. There were several mares with
their foals and a fine stallion as well. I was left in no doubt that anything
that belongs to HH the Maharajah of Jodhpur is well run and maintained
and a credit to him and to Rajasthan and of course ultimately to India. The
name by which he is known respectfully around Jodhpur is 'Bapji', the
honorific means respectfully 'Fatherji'.

We returned to Umaid Bhavan Palace. This creamy pink sandstone
building set on a hill with elegant grounds leading up to it is the last
and largest palace to be built in India. The palace was commissioned by
Maharaja Umaid Singh with the express purpose of creating jobs for his
people when they had been famine-stricken in the 1920s. It was begun in
1929 and the architect was H. V. Lanchester who had lost out on the commission to design Rashtrapati Bhavan in New Delhi. He was also known
for the Central Hall building in Westminster in London. This attractive
fusion of Rajput, Jain and European Art Deco styles has worked well and
continues to look very imposing, be it from the air or as one surveys it.
Three thousand men took fifteen years to complete the whole building and
19 km of railway had to be laid to bring the sandstone from the quarry.
There are 347 rooms which include eight dining halls, two theatres, a
ballroom, lavishly decorated reception halls and a large beautiful underground swimming pool as well as one in the grounds. At the inauguration
of the building 1,000 people were seated in the central hall under the dome
for dinner.

This heritage hotel is quite simply one of the most stunning I have experienced; the General Manager arranged for us to have a tour of all the principal suites and great rooms and we were bowled over by the attention to
detail and sheer opulence of the place. For me, Art Deco had been part of
growing up in post-war India where so many buildings and mansion flats
belonged to that era; moreover the various relations who had married at
the end of the 1930s had all owned good Art Deco furniture and ornaments
so it was really the norm in many ways. Here the standard of design and
ornamentation in that style was the best that one could have found and
has been well maintained and built upon. I had heard, about a decade ago,
that the palace was looking a little worn and threadbare; well now with

Comfortable bedroom that kept Madonna happy when she visited this year 2008.

clever interior designers it has gone to the top of the tree once again and is magnificent. We were shown the maharajah and maharani suites which are out of this world and the maharajah suite was used by the Prince of Wales and the Duchess of Cornwall on a recent visit. The celebrity wedding of 2007 had part of its celebrations here at Umaid Bhavan and that was a clever piece of hospitality because it ensured that the hotel became known throughout the developed world with the press coverage for that over-the-top nuptial celebration. Subsequently, Condé Nast had a launch party for the *Indian Vogue* magazine. There are apparently 17 Vogues in the world including editions in Russia and China and now there is one in India which is produced and published in Mumbai. One does not however have to be a millionaire or excessively wealthy to stay at Umaid Bhavan and I would most certainly recommend at least one night here if possible. The staff are very well trained and charming and the food is good. I liked the hotel shop too which had interesting elegant bits of clothing and other objets d'art. I actually bought a waistcoat which has since been much admired. Looking out from the dining terrace or the lawns surrounding the swimming pool, one has a superb distant view of the Meherangarh Fort and somehow between the dichotomy of the old with the fort, of which I have already written, and the relatively new palace you feel that

Rawla Narlai which is lovely.

Jodhpur has moved with the times.

Umaid Singh's grandson Gaj Singh II, the present Maharajah of Marwar-Jodhpur, who is head of the Rathore clan, lives in a wing of the palace with his family and no doubt keeps a 'seeing eye' on standards. Currently the Taj Group of Hotels runs the palace for him, whereas Balsamand Lake Palace is run by the WelcomHeritage Group. Graham and I would heartily recommend anyone that can extend their budget to experience these wonderful heritage palace hotels.

We then went and inspected Karni Bhavan, which is the hotel belonging to Thakur Sunder Singh and his son Aditya. This is a lovely property with a three star rating and reasonably priced. It seemed to me that there were all the attentions to detail that are necessary and I liked it immensely as it had all the comfort but was not going to make a hole in your pocket. Too often these days Indian hotels are being overpriced and I warn hoteliers that they will shoot themselves in the proverbial foot but here at least the private ownership understands that there are a lot of people on a medium budget who want to enjoy Rajasthan and they are providing comfort and charm at that level. The bathrooms are good and modern and the outside eating area is made to look like a village – *dhani* is the word in Hindi. There is a good pool and also Ayurvedic massage available. I

179

liked the staff who were so keen to please and enthusiastic about their establishment.

A fifty-minute car journey took us easily to Rohet Garh. It was a delight to return. I had met Sidarth at the World Travel Market a couple of times within the past few years and he had talked with enthusiasm of all the developments at Rohet Garh so it was with pleasurable anticipation that we arrived there. My goodness, there have been developments but all of them good and the place is comfortable and welcoming. We had been given a small suite in the building overlooking the lake which when we last visited in November 1997 had not yet been developed. Now it has become a whole new wing of rooms and even the block looking on to the village has also been developed. It is all done with attractive décor and soft furnishings that are made locally and the court painter has worked his magic with all his lovely murals in each suite and on the outside walls shielded from the rain and sun. I was disappointed as the court painter had gone away on his annual leave but there is now a shop selling his art.

The peacocks strut everywhere and I was conscious that it was these birds, or their close ancestors, that had inspired the title of this my first book. We arrived in time for a late lunch and the maître'd was very polished and fluent in English and I noticed he also spoke good French and German. He was very proud of the fact that Madonna had stayed at Rohet with her family for the recent New Year. When we were last here the court painter was still to complete the murals on the dining room walls, now those are finished and beautiful and there is a second dining room upstairs on the roof of the old one which is reached by some narrow stairs; it however is a clever room made from a huge tent but very elegant as well.

We were at Rohet for three nights which gave us time to really relax but even here the weather was cold and by nightfall most people found they had not brought enough warm clothing. A quiet word with the reception staff resulted in us acquiring an extra *rasai* (Indian-style quilt) each and a hot water bottle. I looked with amusement and sympathy at those who were attired in a blazer for the man and a shrug for the woman – that was not 'doing the business' for anyone whilst we were there!

It was a pleasure to see Sidarth and his family again and I had some conversations with his father who is in fact still the ruler – Sidarth is his heir. The next day he arranged for us to go and visit the Bishnoi once again but then to go on for lunch to the Wilderness Camp that he has developed. The original idea had been for us to spend one night at the camp but having experienced two nights of tented accommodation in the north in the cold I felt I would do it justice by day! We loved our return visit to the Bishnoi and could see the signs of progress and development in that though they still continue to live their village life they have the odd brick-built house

My favourite view of Devi Garh.

too, and now young Bishnoi who have attended the nearby school can continue their education and also find work in Jodhpur to which they travel
by train; they walk to the train, or I did see one or two motorbikes, so progress and prosperity has touched this wonderful proud tribe too. The children were walking to school and stopped to look at us and also converse
– it was so good to see.

We noticed plenty of wildlife and the amount of blackbuck had increased
from our previous visit. There were *nilgai*, camels, birdlife and the blackbuck in their groups of hinds with young and the strutting males with
their magnificent horns. The village folk were shyly welcoming as before
and we reflected that our lives are so different from all this. It seems that
hanging one's clothes on a sort of washing line is the only way to keep
them from the ground but everywhere was very neat and clean. I liked
the fact that there were little earthenware shallow bowls in the scrub filled
with water for the birdlife. In the Brahmin village, which is painted in the
obligatory blue, it too was neat but the emphasis here was on drying red
chillies which made a wonderful photograph – thousands and thousands
of chillies on a charpoy (strap bed) drying in the sun.

We were then driven to the Wilderness Camp and were enchanted. This
has been beautifully done with tented en suite accommodation which is

all white and spacious and then the communal social areas with fireplaces and bright touches in soft furnishings. Lunch had been brought especially for us and we were served with ceremony all on our own. The peace of the desert, the bright sunshine in a clear blue sky and the charm of the place with its bright flowering poinsettias and bougainvilleas worked its magic and we both decided to lie back, each on a charpoy, and enjoy the warm sunshine. Kingfishers dipped and darted nearby and Sidarth has made a natural-looking pond which is the focus for the camp. I hope it receives sufficient rain in the coming monsoon because that is the only way it is filled. He hopes that the famous Demoiselle cranes might also fancy resting here from time to time. Khichan has acquired worldwide fame for the practice of feeding cranes. Khichan is a small Rajasthani town and the surrounding desert plains are visited in winter by thousands of Demoiselle cranes, one of the most elegant species in an already elegant family. They are drawn by the State's many man-made lakes and daily handouts of sorghum grain. Those who belong to the Jain religion consider the cranes' visit a blessing and fulfilment of their religious precepts and they are happy to feed them daily. I consider them very similar to the lovely blue cranes of South Africa – the blue crane is in fact South Africa's national bird and we were fortunate to see many in the wild there in the Cape in October 2007.

I was told with great pride that Madonna had loved the Wilderness Camp and had ridden out to it for her stay at New Year 2007/2008 because of course Rohet has lovely horses and if one is experienced it would make an enjoyable ride. Alishah is Sidarth's fine stallion and he had stood for some of Gaj Singh's mares earlier in the year. The Marwar Horse is a special breed and has ears that curve towards each other and other defining characteristics. We had inspected Alishah back at Rohet and also petted the two young colts in the stable. The breed was known at least as far back as 1212 and it was the ancient breed also known as the Malani from which the warrior mounts for the Rathore rulers were bred and trained. The breed went into decline during British colonial times and immediately post Independence but, thankfully, people like HH Gaj Singh and his late father before him realised that conservation was required and the Institute of Horse Breeding & Research was established at Chopasni near Jodhpur. Now the breed has become a status symbol to own and they can often be seen in cities as they are much in demand for the wedding ceremony that demands a bridegroom ride into the festivities. They also make good polo ponies and are used by the police and the army.

As always with India there is this dichotomy between those who care, have compassion and have foresight, and those who do not. When one considers the Bishnoi and their simple credo for living which has seen them continue for the last five centuries and be worthy of respect in the modern day, and then is informed of the mindless cruelty and neglect that is currently being highlighted within Kerala and other parts of southern India, it is so depressing.

About the time my own third book *India: The Elephant's Blessing* was published Rhea Ghosh published a book on Indian elephants entitled *Gods in Chains*. She was commissioned to write the book by the Wildlife Rescue and Rehabilitation Centre in Bangalore in Karnataka. The foreword to her book is by Professor Raman Sukumar, the director of the Asian Elephant Research and Conservation Centre of Ecological Studies at the Indian Institute of Science which is also in Bangalore. This book leaves one in no doubt as to the bad treatment of domesticated elephants which are used in temple worship and other religious activities as well as for propitious occasions such as marriages and local festivals. I have read extracts from her book and also looked at the Compassion Unlimited Plus Action website of the animal welfare organisation of that name – www.cupabangalore. org. Well the truth is that words fail me when I come across accounts of human cruelty and neglect of animals anywhere in the world, but in India it is particularly galling as the Indian Parliament has passed considerable legislation to counteract neglectful behaviour and stamp out cruelty. Sadly it would seem that seldom are these laws enforced and various officials in states like Kerala appear to ignore them altogether. The elephant is one of the most famous of deities in the Hindu religion and mythology – Lord Ganesh is the most revered and loved of all the gods … yet this continues to happen. I deliberately have given my trilogy titles that involve the creatures that are most associated with India but all three belong in the pantheon of deities which makes them sacred as well as being national emblems symbolic of India the world over. In Kerala currently there is a shameful slaughter of dogs continuing in the most cruel and inhumane way. The outcry reached London with a peaceful demonstration outside India House in London with a petition handed in to the High Commission. Those of us who are veterinary surgeons or veterinary family members such as we are, know only too well that, from time to time in developing countries, local authorities decide to cull the pye-dog population. It is a sad fact of life that rabies is still a huge killer in India and I have had the misfortune to witness a rabid dog as a child which was most frightening – the villagers beat it and drowned it in the village tank (artificial pond). Veterinary authorities and government vets in India are quite capable however of disposing of a surplus dog population humanely but that too requires organisation and discipline and adherence to professional standards; it is on these occasions that India seems to let herself down and then becomes quite grumpy if anyone dares to criticize.

Avis Lyons is a courageous committed British woman who now lives in Kovalam in Kerala and is doing her best to alleviate the suffering of animals and to continue to compel the local authorities to act carefully and responsibly; she is herself being badly treated by the local powers that be which is so short-sighted because her plight and what she is attempting to achieve is now being broadcast through websites worldwide and will bring complete opprobrium on the state of Kerala. www.animalrescuekerala.org is her worthwhile charity and she contacted me because I had signed the petition condemning the cruel form of slaughter of dogs in Kerala.

On an upbeat note I should say that in Delhi when we go for walks around the IIC the pye-dog population are not only tolerated but obviously fed and, at Khan Market in Delhi where I often shop for all sorts of lovely things, in the very cold weather this year the local pye-dogs even had on little dog coats!

We said our farewells to Rohet Garh and thanked them for a most enjoyable visit and looked forward to our next venue. There was however quite a drive and it too proved to be interesting and enjoyable. Our driver, Manohar Singh Bhati, owned his own vehicle and was a good English speaker and knowledgeable about all that was developing in his locality; if I returned to Jodhpur I would most certainly ask to use his service again. We needed cash with which to pay him and now that is no problem at all as there are so many ATMs placed along the main roads. That facility must have made a vast difference to the local population; I know how convenient we find it in the West but for people who have to walk or travel by some form of public transport for long distances, now having the ubiquitous 'hole in the wall' must be magic, along with the cell phone and computers. The latter however are problematical as broadband is still being rolled out in India – as indeed in Scotland – and with the intermittent electricity supply computers can experience a lot of trouble and also 'crash'.

On our way to the erstwhile state of Udaipur from Jodhpur state we stopped at Rawla Narlai. Rawla (which means fortress in the local language) was gifted to Maharaj Dhiraj Sir Ajit Singh by his elder brother HH Maharajah Umaid Singh, who you will recall built the fabulous palace at Jodhpur. This branch of the family also own Ajit Bhavan Palace Hotel in Jodhpur at which we stayed in 1997 and 1998. This charming mansion is lovely as it is situated in the heart of a typical Rajasthani village bustling with activity and colour. The village is dominated by a huge volcanic rock of granite measuring 100 metres in height which is dotted with caves and temples and crowned by a statue of a white elephant and the focus for pilgrims. I liked the village which was much cleaner than a lot of Indian villages and this could be a charming place for two nights. Maharaj and Rani Swaroop Singh and their sons were personally involved with the careful reconstruction and restoration of this fortress with the focus on visual charm, comfort and atmosphere – moreover the bathrooms are good!

Rawla Narlai is about 25 minutes driving from the Ranakpur Temples of which I have written in the first part of this book and is an hour away from Kumbhalgarh Fort which is really massive and impressive.

If one spent time at Jodhpur and then drove here for a couple of days, which could be spent by the beautiful pool or in the quiet courtyard gardens and the odd sortie to a temple or some horse riding, one could then continue on to Udaipur as a destination. It is not overcrowded and does not have coach loads of tourists – some of the resorts rely on coaches of French or German tourists swooping in for lunch or one night which has its drawbacks; they all seem incredibly noisy and do not socialize and are very demanding – a sort of 'been there, seen it, done that …'.

We arrived at our destination Devi Garh in time for lunch. This incredible building is a delight and of immense interest. Devi Garh was built in the 18th century and nestles in the Aravalli hills and commands one of the three main passes into the valley of Udaipur. Sajja Singh, who originated in Gujarat, was awarded this strategically significant principality, in recognition of his bravery and loyalty to Maharana Pratap during the battle of Haldi Ghati. The actual construction of the fort palace started only in the 1760s, under Raghudev Singh II, with further additions made to the structure by following rulers. When Rajasthan was established as a conglomeration of princely states the fort appears to have been abandoned.

Two hundred and fifty years old, the palace was simply a series of small, dark interconnected chambers, infested with bats and birds, when the present owners acquired it in 1984. The entire edifice was falling apart, requiring extensive restoration and rehabilitation work for which conservation organisations were called in to preserve the building. Once the work of strengthening and restoring the palace was complete then the actual work of converting it into a luxurious and elegant hotel began.

Devi Garh has regained its past glory and is once more an imposing, towering and impressive structure as a unique all-suite boutique hotel, with 39 suites furnished in the style of modern India. It is quite visually stunning and decorated in a minimalist but lavish décor with all sorts of quirky, charming, elegant details that make it a delight.

One is welcomed with ceremony and we said farewell to our driver and approached and stood under the main archway from the top of which a shower of rose petals rained down on us and we were given a welcome drink. The management asked us which of two suites we would prefer and Graham and I chose the one facing the sunrise. It was lovely and sophisticated and spacious with its own turret room giving a splendid view of the village and valley and mountains around us. The staff fall over themselves to help and serve you. Our bedroom was spacious; then there was a sitting area with huge television and then a dressing room all done in white marble plus a huge marble bath and then a massive marble shower with small windows looking out, all hundreds of feet above ground-level. There is a lift to these suites but frankly these apartments in the old fort, in my opinion, are not for those who might be infirm or disabled. By the very nature of this strange, high, multi-storied fortress one must be prepared to walk and climb some rather steep ancient steps. It is however all well worth it as long as you are fit. There are superb newly built garden suites near the swimming pool.

There are so many clever decorative ideas used that it defies description but my photography shows it all well. The pool area is big and beautiful with a wonderful panoramic view all round; the pool is heated and elegant tented canopies provide shade and waiters take drinks and light snack orders. There is a beautiful spa and beauty treatment complex situated under the swimming pool. I loved just lazing by the pool and watching the sun set and the light change. Moreover, a place as beautiful as this produces the most excellent tea, which was to our liking! Devi Garh is not however cheap and I think the food is perhaps a little overpriced but the whole experience was a very comfortable and happy one and I would recommend people to visit for two nights as we did.

We took a hotel vehicle and visited the famous temples at Eklingji. The temples are a pleasant 23 km drive away from Devi Garh and on the shores of a lake. They are well preserved and maintained and we both enjoyed the excursion. It is a complex of 108 temples and shrines dedicated to Lord Shiva. This is the site reputed to be where the founder of the Mewar ruling dynasty, Bappa Rawal, received special blessings from a holy man who lived here. The present Maharana continues to attend worship at this temple complex weekly apparently. The main temple was built in the 16th century. We were not allowed to photograph within the temple precincts however and we did not linger. Our preference was Nagda, a short distance away from Eklingji, which has lovely Saas-Bahu temples (which means Mother and Daughter-in-law Temples) which are twin structures dedicated to Lord Vishnu built in the 11th century. There is a finely carved *torana* and the sculptures remind one of Khajuraho and the intricate detail of amorous couples in scenes from the epic *Ramayana*.

When we returned to the hotel it was amusing to see some Japanese being urged to mount a decorated camel for a short walk whilst they continued to wear their mouth masks; the hotel has a sizeable shop but we did not venture further and were content to just soak up the warm sunshine near the pool and enjoy the delights of Devi Garh. One of our most endearing memories is of the parakeets which perched and roosted outside our lovely turret. The turret is decorated beneath its windows by charming glass pieces set in mosaic form depicting the parakeets and here they were chattering and chirping and darting around outside. One little bird kept patting the other on the face with his foot as if to say 'come on, do say yes…'. It was enchanting to watch as they were just a few feet away from us through glass.

Devi Garh is not at all far from Udaipur and now there is a good main road the distance from the new Udaipur international airport is minimal and hotel guests and travellers can arrive by air or leave by air and have but a short transfer to and from the hotel along part of the national high-way which in fact connects Delhi to Mumbai. Udaipur's airport has just opened a new terminal building and there are four new aircraft stands and the improvements mean that it is designated an international airport with customs and immigration facilities, not merely a domestic airport, which again is a sign of the progress that Rajasthan has made.

We had a free night however so we were driven into Udaipur and I arranged for us to stay one night at a guest house. We wanted to stay at one of the luxury hotels but they appeared to be completely booked and as I had a very specific requirement in that I wanted somewhere from where I could photograph the lakes in the sunrise and sunset we decided to try a guest house. The Tiger proved to be good with a recently reno-vated interior with comfortable very clean bedrooms, though the bath-rooms were quite basic; this was another place where beautiful new mod-ern marble floors lifted it into another category. The owners also have a German bakery and coffee shop across the road and a well-regarded res-taurant called Savage Garden. The Tiger is situated at the Gangaur Ghat right where the colourful action takes place daily in Udaipur and it has an adequate restaurant on the top floor with the most beautiful panoramic views and the roof terrace is the cherry on the top. We were delighted because the management was welcoming and the price was very cheap and the food was good.

I have written of my first visit to Udaipur earlier in this book and I can safely say that I think the city has improved in cleanliness and is looking good. The vexed question of the water level in the lakes of course is an ongoing problem but hopefully a good monsoon will see the level rise and the authorities know that any further development is the main reason for the water diminishing – it is their responsibility to ensure Udaipur retains her lakes. A few years ago I saw that the water had completely receded and that the famous Lake Palace Hotel was surrounded by marshland and that will happen again unless they resolve the problem. Graham very sweetly wanted to take me out to dinner at the Lake Palace since it was Valentine's Day but they do not allow casual visitors, even for a full dinner which was sad. The City Palace complex has developed and now there are excellent restaurants in the palace grounds and colonnades of shops fitted in care-fully into the existing buildings with even a very new Anokhi. The city is very popular with international tourists and quite crowded – there are many more westerners in Udaipur than in a place like Jodhpur and it was quite different to see them all eating *café und kuchen* in the Café Edelweiss opposite our hotel which is under the same management; somehow it was rather odd with the elephants and camels that were ambling close by and the delicious fragrance of European patisserie being freshly baked!

We took an auto rickshaw to the Maharana's Vintage Car Collection. This I most heartily recommend as a well-run museum housed in the cars' original garages near another palace hotel. Graham was in his element but so was I because a lot of the beautiful cars were models that I recalled from my childhood. Kolkata had been full of big saloon cars in the late 1940s and 1950s and the Maharana has maintained his collection along with his very special editions of Rolls Royces and especially modified or custom-built vehicles that were obviously commissioned by the royal family. The custodian of the museum is happy to talk to you and tell you a little bit about the vehicles and quite a few of the cars are taken out and driven around in a circle to keep the batteries ticking over. There is a good restaurant to the museum and the service was considerate and the place is very cheap but provides an excellent *thali* (selection of Indian food served on a big brass or stainless-steel circular tray).

We returned by auto rickshaw and asked the owner to take us to a shoe shop of his choice; I wanted to buy some special slippers for our tiny granddaughter. Well we found just the item in pink with sequins and Honor has her very own 'Punjabi slippers' which she can just about say! When they were given to her she was only 16 months and they did not quite fit yet but she loved them and liked to handle them as well.

Rajasthan continues to work its magic on travellers and I think a trip such as I have recently experienced would be enjoyable for anybody. The choice as to how many wonderful old forts, palaces and *havelis* to visit is up to the individual but here one can experience princely India in all its glory yet with the charms and conveniences of modern life and also be aware that some of the Rajasthanis are developing and beginning to receive their fair share of what the modern world has to offer in India.

Chapter Twenty

A Decade of my Writing
about India

In November 1998 our eldest son Hamish was once again deployed to Bosnia. In the first posting in 1996 he had escaped within an inch of his life from an ordnance explosion; now he was back for another six months and we worried. Ten years on there are parents, wives, husbands and families worried about their family members in Iraq and Afghanistan, praying that no tragedy falls on their loved ones. I decided to write a book – this one to take my mind off the situation. The book did not find a publisher till the autumn of 2001 and was published in mid 2002. People seemed to actually enjoy what I had written and it was thought to be a good idea to return to India and research for a second book and then when that was published I was invited to give the Incredible India lecture at the Nehru Centre at its launch in November 2004. The Asian Tsunami struck with all its force on 26th December 2004 and Amitabh Kant, the then Joint Secretary for Tourism for the Indian Government emailed me 48 hours later and said please come and research and write a book about southern India – which I duly did and it was published in October 2006.

Now I have almost come to the end of Part II to be included in the republish of my first book. I have completed a decade of writing about the land of my birth as I see it in the 21st century, striding ahead as one of the new economic superpowers. India's time has come as a democratic huge nation confident and determined to make progress and now that is universally recognised.

Those about whom I care have gone from strength to strength. Project Mala, which is the brainchild of a good man of York, Robin Garland, is doing wonderful things and Project Mala has come a long way since its establishment in 1989. By 2008 they had six primary schools and two middle schools with over 1,100 children in full-time education. They are particularly proud to open the middle schools as it gave an opportunity for the brightest children in their area to reach their full potential. It is also pleasing to know that without Project Mala these children may well have grown up illiterate.

Talking with Robin who is so passionate and committed to his charity, which is registered here in the UK – www.projectmala.org.uk – he makes the point that matters so much to me as well, namely that giving these little ones education gives them some choice in their lives. You are reading this by the very fact that you have bought a book or been given a book and it is assumed we all are literate and have the leisure time to read and enjoy learning. For folk who only exist there is no question of 'life choices' – they do whatever is necessary to continue to live or exist. I know that Graham and I as parents, and indeed our parents before us, made sacrifices and took decisions that gave us, their children, and now us to our children, opportunities that would enable them in their adult lives to make choices. In village India there are still people who have never ever received a letter, travelled to a big city, entered some huge famous building or eaten in a restaurant. Thankfully the great leap forward in electronic technology has meant that the cell phone and the computer are reaching these unsophisticated but good people. However there is a long way to go for them to reach a form of 'lifestyle' that even remotely resembles ours here in the West. I actually dislike the word 'lifestyle' which is so freely used in western advertising to entice foolhardy people to part with their money – or on credit for items of little real 'life-value'!

The curious anomaly is that big charitable foundations want to give to 'people charities' but will not give any funds for what they see as buildings or equipment. It is a peculiar perhaps convenient ploy for them, but without equipment and without a building in which people can assemble and be educated there is not much scope for progress. Frequently NGOs (non-governmental organisations) appeal to the funding bodies and are given money; when it has been used up they can no longer build upon their work and the NGO ceases to exist or does only in name. Project Mala however has flourished with the dogged determination of Robin and his small band of workers and he hopes now that he has proved his charity's sustainability to enter into the business of educating village communities about sanitation and basic hygiene; a lot of chronic health problems would be eliminated were these simple people taught about basic hygiene and healthcare. My mother and Graham and I have had an opportunity to help with funds for specific children and it is a comfort to us that a couple of youngsters now have a basic education and can perhaps make choices. We have no contact with those children but we have received the reports about their individual progress. Robin has sent me photos of the school and I am including these in my DVD. We also have as lovely permanent reminders in our home three *dhurries* made at Project Mala which all bear the charity's logo of a little blackboard in one corner; my favourite of the three is a small *dhurrie* depicting a lotus which is quite unusual.

The Esther Benjamins Trust was started by another special man called Philip Holmes and I first wrote about him and the then new charity in my second book, *India: The Tiger's Roar*; well, Philip and his band of workers are also making the EBT into a successful charity. Since it was founded in 1999, the Esther Benjamins Trust, which is also a UK registered charity, has helped some of Nepal's most vulnerable children to find a happy childhood out of the most desperate circumstances imaginable. It has rescued and rehabilitated over 300 child-trafficking victims from Indian circuses, provided refuge to nearly 100 street children and the children of prisoners and supported education schemes for deaf and disabled young people in Nepal.

Manju is one of a bunch of brilliant young artists able to transform a photograph or a drawing into a beautifully crafted piece of mosaic art. With great dexterity she cuts each tile into shape to take its place in a stunning mosaic. Her natural skills weren't developed on expensive courses in European institutes – they were uncovered in the foothills of the Himalayas in Nepal. Mosaic art was introduced to Manju by Philip Holmes to see if the gentle creative process could aid her recovery from a childhood which left seemingly indelible scars on her. Not only did it have the desired effect, but it unearthed the most incredible talent within a previously shy and damaged young lady. Manju is a survivor of child trafficking. She is one of the children rescued by the Trust from a life characterised by the most hideous abuses imaginable. The charity rescues Nepali children who have been trafficked from their rural villages into lives of bonded labour in Indian circuses. Upon their repatriation, it offers compassionate residential rehabilitation that leads ultimately to their full reintegration into society.

I read an article about EBT in a newspaper article and managed to find an email address and contacted Philip Holmes and was so moved by what I was told that I managed to include a bit about the charity in that second book in 2004. Now four years on their work continues successfully and last year I commissioned a piece of mosaic art to give Graham for a significant birthday! It is a beautiful version of the peacock illustration with which this first book's cover was graced. I will digress a little; when we were trying to design the original first book cover it obviously required a picture of a peacock, but I did not then have a really good photograph and to buy one with a copyright would have been expensive. Then I thought about a most beautiful leather-bound book that I own which is 150 years old called *Game Birds of India Burma and Ceylon*. This book was one of three owned by my father which he and I would go through nearly every night before bedtime, looking at all the beautiful colour plates of birds when I was a tiny child. (In the late 1940s in upcountry India there were no English medium bookshops from which to buy toddlers' books; now we are all so spoilt for choice!) Because the copyright had long since expired we were able to use that depiction of the peacock in 2002 and so I asked that it be reproduced by the young artist in Nepal. Rina's peacock looks lovely hanging in our garden on an ancient stone wall with laburnum blossom and bluebells to complement it behind a favourite bench in the wild area of our property. Philip Holmes has lived in Nepal for some time and is directing the EBT work himself together with his second wife: www.ebtrust.org.uk. You can see more about EBT on my own website: www.thepeacockscall.co.uk.

Martin Bell, the distinguished BBC journalist and reporter, who then went on to become an Independent member of parliament in 1997 and also a UNICEF Ambassador for children, very sweetly wrote a foreword to this book; he once most generously made a journey up to Edinburgh to speak at a fund-raising luncheon at my request. So many people ask to be financially rewarded and he did not and we on that charity were so grateful. He has a great interest in a children's charity that was started in 1994 called Hope and Homes for Children. The charity was started by Colonel Mark Cook, then in command of the British UN contingent in Croatia, after he discovered some 60 children in the basement of a ruined orphanage in the bombed town of Lipic. The charity's Mission Statement says it all: 'to give hope to the poorest children in the world – those who are orphaned, abandoned or vulnerable – by enabling them to grow up within the love of a family and the security of a home, so that they can fulfil their potential'. Now Hope and Homes has spread to other parts of the world doing what they can to fulfil that mission and I for one salute them: www.hopeandhomes.org.

India's new High Commissioner has taken office in London; he is Shiv Shankar Mukherjee and has a distinguished diplomatic career behind him. His predecessor was Kamalash Sharma, who is the new Secretary General of the Commonwealth who is also based in London. My new good friend Ramesh Chandar is the Consul General in Edinburgh and he works tirelessly to promote friendship and interaction between the Indian community in Scotland and those of us who care about and know and love India. The UKIBC is the United Kingdom India Business Council which operates from London, but it too is dynamic in its work to promote business between our two countries. Karan Bilimoria who is the chairman, and was recently made a cross-bench peer in the House of Lords, is a wonderful ambassador for India and his excellent beer is very popular with me too! His late father was a distinguished general in the Indian Army and known to my late father.

There are so many people all determined to foster good relations and also to build upon the work of others. We attended the inauguration of the Kolkata Scottish Heritage Trust in May. A group of Scots headed by Charles Bruce, who is the son and heir of the Earl of Elgin whose ancestor was a Viceroy of India, has decided that the trust should restore and manage the Scottish cemetery in Kolkata and that this would also provide a much needed 'lung' in the heart of Kolkata. They would also try to restore other Scottish monuments and they very much want to establish a training institution for the restoration and preservation of these monuments.

In the first part of this book when I wrote about Kolkata I told you about my recent family history and I spoke of the Scottish church St Andrew's, which is now part of the Church of North India; it is on this church and its umbrella organisation that the Scottish cemetery is dependent. In the Session Room of St Andrew's hangs a large photograph of St Giles' Cathedral in Edinburgh – in which Graham and I were married in 1969 and indeed Graham's great-grandfather had been a minister at St Giles' Cathedral and then went on to be the minister of the Lansdowne Kirk in Glasgow in the 19th century. The cemetery has over 1,600 headstones and monuments, some of Aberdeen granite, but many of brick and lime with marble tablets. My own grandparents and some of their parents before them are buried in that cemetery but I never visited it; my mother who, as I mentioned earlier is 97, said that after her own beloved father George Knox Ord's death she hated visiting but paid someone to maintain the graves, which I doubt actually happened. The graveyard was neglected during the Second World War and became snake infested. What is more, the very poor and destitute colonised it and Mother said that jackals frequented it so that naturally it became a fearsome place to visit and left one with an even more melancholic feeling and she never went back. My clear memory of the cemetery however is from the outside as it is situated in a very good part of town (but not at all near the Scots Kirk) and on my way to school and other activities I was often driven past it.

Sadly the cemetery is now a rare green space in a densely populated part of the city and serves no useful purpose and has become a burden for St Andrew's and the church in general and a matter of concern for the City and State authorities. Yet it is the record of so many generations of Scots. It is generally recognised that the Scots diaspora to Britain's overseas colonies was huge, but in India it is now thought that probably two thirds of the British families were Scots. I really hope that the Trust is successful and

I am sure that the Kolkata authorities will try and be supportive.

We in the West have the dilemma of rising oil prices and equally damaging rises in food prices. These affect India too and she is walking a careful tightrope between her friends in the West, like the United States, and her other interests, like Iran. In fact India has chosen the USA over Iran, and whatever one may think about President George W. Bush he should be credited with the fact that the USA decided to ally herself with India and encourage India in many ways including the nuclear aspect during his 'watch' in the USA. India feels that it would be imprudent to say that one should not engage the United States of America; a strategic partnership with the USA is desirable and important but Asian countries have learned that it is not a good idea to put all the foreign policy eggs in one basket. India is dependent upon Iran as she is on Burma for her hydrocarbon resources. It is because India and China are progressing so rapidly that we now have world shortages and those are increased by greedy speculators who are exploiting these shortages and increasing the prices of oil and food grains.

I am sure the whole world's tourism industry will be affected by the huge oil increases and when people are struggling to live their ordinary everyday lives ideas of exotic holidays remain as pleasant fantasy and do not become reality. I foresee India building on its tourism during the monsoon months of July, August and September when it is of course significantly damp, but with increasingly developed infrastructure the charm of the instant green from the welcome rains makes a wonderful difference; I have experienced the Far East at that time and found it no barrier to having an enjoyable experience.

For the last few years I have used Goaway, a travel agent based in London, and I have found that they do exactly what I ask of them; for me everything has to be tailored to my requirements as I never join a collection of people. Graham and I travel independently and we want scheduled flights, good drivers with roadworthy vehicles, train tickets and domestic flights within India. I have found Goaway to have very reasonable prices and they are pleasant people with whom to do business.

Significantly since 1991 till 2008 there has been a 400 per cent increase in income tax collection in India and it now accounts for 8 per cent of the GDP, whereas in the beginning it was only 1 per cent. Dr Manmohan Singh is undoubtedly the most qualified man to help lead India forward but one has to recognise that it is the businessmen, scientists and entrepreneurs that are actually driving India forward.

The cheerful news is that India received $24.57 billion of foreign direct investment in 2007–2008, prompting the world's second fastest growing economy to set an FDI (foreign direct investment) target of $35 billion for the current fiscal year. In the previous fiscal year of 2006–2007 the inflow was $15.70 billion. Kamal Nath, the Indian Commerce and Industry

Minister, said that, "India remains an attractive investment destination and it will be a good parking lot for money." Barclays Wealth Management has recently published its report titled 'Evolving Fortunes', which signals the rise of emerging markets such as India, displacing more developed economies. This, according to the report, signals a global shift in the distribution of wealth which will result in the terms of the G8 Group being seen as an outmoded categorisation for wealthy economies.

Ratan Tata of the great Tata conglomerate of India has been named as one among the 100 most influential people in the world; his company's launch of the Nano car, which is both small and very cheap, has made it possible for very many ordinary Indian families to aspire to car ownership – of course the impact of that on the pollution growth in India is a severe challenge, but one cannot say to decent hard-working people that you do not have a right to own a car – they too want their slice of the economic good times.

There are so many interesting success stories about Indian industry and commerce and here in Scotland we see the company Tata Consultancy Services has won a £60 million deal to provide information technology applications services to Scottish Water. It has been calculated that this new contract will save Scottish Water a minimum of £8 million in operating expenditure over the next eight years and that is of great interest to me, the average Scottish consumer who pays for this water. As someone whose family was for generations connected to India it is also interesting to note that there are currently 32,000 British people living and working in India.

Amongst all this good economic commercial news however it is worth noting that there is a dynamic for global business leaders to unveil a plan to fight poverty in Africa and Asia. This has to be significant action and not just rhetoric as unless Africa becomes a viable more peaceful continent with its peoples beginning to live stable, decent lives with education and healthcare, the continent will be like a great ugly leaden weight upon the shoulders of those who grow rich.

Those of us who studied the great scramble for Africa in the 19th century as part of our history studies know that there are huge resources in Africa and we in the West mitigated our greed by providing colonial development – hypocrisy is, they say, the homage that vice pays to virtue. In the years to come it will be China, America, maybe Russia and also India who will resume the 'scramble' for Africa's resources and I doubt most of those powers will have many genuine aspirations to develop, educate and improve the lives of African peoples. European powers lost the will to continue in Africa but now in a world that is feeling the pinch in natural resources, with which Africa is richly endowed, the new economic superpowers will very probably have no scruples.

I have come to the end of my trilogy on India; it has been hard work at times but so worthwhile and the annual return visit to India is something to which Graham and I look forward immensely. It could be in the years to come that perhaps you too will be walking in the Lodi Gardens in Delhi and if you see a couple coming towards you with quite a lot of grey hair then it might indeed be us; we shall continue our journeys to India for as long as it is practicable.

It is enormously satisfying for me, a child of India, to see this huge nation taking her place at the world's top table. That is where she should be with all her wisdom, antiquity, beauty, diverse culture, science, technology and research, and not least her spiritual strengths. If we are lucky in life we do not just see nature with our eyes, but with our understanding and our hearts. I know that my privileged and fortunate life has been greatly enhanced by having a dual birthright and knowledge of Mother India. *Vande Mataram*!

Aline Dobbie
May 2008

Aline at the original launch of this book in Scotland – June 2002.

Chapter Twenty-One

Final Word

When writing about India, inevitably events overtake the written word so it is with a sense of sadness that I pen this page. Until now, India has been spared much of the extremist terrorism that has racked much of the Muslim world. Although it has the second largest population of Muslims and has seen regular outbreaks of communal violence, India's Muslim minority has not been radicalised so far by the global jihadist movement. Despite three wars with Pakistan, terrorist infiltration and more than sixty years of tension, India's Muslims have not, on the whole, been seen as a fifth column under the sway of outside agitators. In this past week in Ahmedabad and Bangalore there have been a series of bomb explosions that have left scores of dead and injured, which comes two months after the Jaipur outrage. Just a few weeks ago the terrorist attack against the Indian Embassy in Kabul left many dead and injured. Our world is now a global village – as one who died was the Military Attaché who was the cousin of friends of ours who live in Delhi, so the grief touched us personally too, here in Scotland.

Indian democracy is resilient and has absorbed greater shocks before and the Indian authorities have acted so far with sensible level-headedness. However, any sign that the contagion of extremism has infected India's 160-million-strong Muslim community should be treated with gravity as all India could be at risk. As if this is not bad enough, sadly Indian and Pakistani soldiers have been engaged in cross-border fire across the disputed border once again and these actions threaten a big step backwards in the continuing enmity over Kashmir.

The Prime Minister managed to survive the recent no-confidence vote and has probably, thankfully in my opinion, rescued the new nuclear pact with the USA. There are those passionate objectors to the deal who cite the huge damage it does to the Nuclear Non-Proliferation Treaty – but on balance it is a good move for India and indeed for the whole world order as it will enhance the comity of nations opposed to using nuclear armaments.

In July the seven-year struggle for a global trade agreement that would have opened borders and reduced subsidies broke down finally in Geneva. The Indian Trade Minister was doing his best to justify a wrecking operation but he was not looking at his negotiating partners, the Brazilian, American, European and Argentinian ministers. He was looking to India where the Indian Reserve Bank Governor had raised interest rates and signalled an economic slow down. The Indian rural population numbers 600 million, the last BJP Government was brought down in 2004 for ignoring them and the current Congress Party Government is unlikely to make that mistake as they face the electorate in the first half of 2009. Notwithstanding that the credit crunch may have gripped the economy elsewhere, 'India Inc' is continuing to roar onto the global arena and is all set to become a net exporter of deals to the developed world, according to the global audit and consultancy giant KPMG.

The trade row has however finally destroyed the fiction that is the mantra beloved by development charities and poverty lobbyists that we live in a world divided between North and South or rich and poor. We live on a globe of powerful and conflicting interest groups – Asian peasant farmers in India and China versus Latin American farm labourers and all the rest of us in between.

I wish India well and hope fervently that her leaders, whoever they may be in the coming years, will make wise choices for the people of the world's largest democracy.

On a personal note, we are delighted that Stewart and Corinne's second child – a son – has been born safely, a brother for Honor.

Aline Dobbie
Rosewood
28th August 2008

www.thepeacockscall.co.uk

Contact Details for Those Visiting India

Tikli Bottom (The gracious guest house close to Delhi.)
Martin and Annie Howard
Email: honiwala@vsnl.com
Website: www.tiklibottom.com

Project Mala, UK Charity No 801953
The Project Mala Office
Town Farmhouse, 25 Church Lane, Nether Poppleton
York, YO26 6LF, UK
Tel: + 44 (0)1904 786880
Email: info@projectmala.org.uk
Website: www.projectmala.org.uk

The Esther Benjamins Trust, UK Charity No 1078187
Third Floor
2 Cloth Court
London, EC1A 7LS, UK
Tel: +44 (0)20 7600 5654
Fax: +44 (0)20 7726 6018
Email: info@ebtrust.org.uk
Website: www.ebtrust.org.uk

Hope and Homes for Children, UK Charity No 1089490
Head Office: East Clyffe
Salisbury, Wiltshire, SP3 4LZ, UK
Tel: +44 (0)1722 790111
Fax: +44 (0)1722 790024
Email: hhc@hopeandhomes.org
Website: www.hopeandhomes.org

Tiger Awareness, UK Charity No 1117234
11 Cheney Road
Thurmaston
Leicestershire, LE4 9ND, UK
Tel: +44 (0)116 276 9164
Email: conservation@tigerawareness.co.uk
Website: www.tigerawareness.co.uk

The Brooke Hospital for Animals, UK Charity No 1085760
Broadmead House
21 Panton Street
London, SW1Y 4DR, UK
Tel: +44 (0)20 7930 0210
Fax: +44 (0)20 7868 0828
Email: info@thebrooke.org
Website: www.thebrooke.org

International Animal Rescue, UK Charity No 1118277
Lime House, Regency Close
Uckfield
East Sussex, TN22 1DS, UK
Tel: +44 (0)1825 767688
Fax: +44(0)1825 768012
Email: info@ internationalanimalrescue.org
Website: www.internationalanimalrescue.org

Future Hope, UK Charity No 1001769 (Helping street children of Kolkata.)
6 Queensdale Place
London, W11 4SQ, UK
Tel: +91 33 2485 8391 (The full-time staff are in Kolkata, India.)
Email: timgrandage@vsnl.net
Email: cathy_futurehope@hotmail.co.uk
Website: www.futurehope.net

Dr Graham's Homes Kalimpong, Scottish Charity No 016341
(This charity is over 100 years old and helps street children and orphans.
I use their Christmas cards which are delightful.)
Mrs Jane Steven
Kildarroch, Tweeddale Ave
Gifford, EH41 4QN, Scotland, UK
Tel: +44 (0)845 094 8839
Email: secretary@drgrahamshomes.co.uk
Website: www.drgrahamshomes.co.uk
Responsible Travel
Email: info@responsibletravel.com
Website: www.responsibletravel.com

Goaway and Czech-It-Out, ABTA Membership J1602,
ATOL 5237 and IATA membership
109/111 Bell Street
London, NW1 6TL, UK
Tel: +44 (0)20 7258 7800
Tel: 0870 890 7800
Email: sales@goaway.co.uk
Website: www.goaway.co.uk (Mr Ravi Khurana)

The India Tourist Office
7 Cork Street, London, W1S 3LH, UK
Tel: General enquiries +44 (0)20 7437 3677
Tel: Brochure request 08700 102183
Email: info@indiatouristoffice.org
Website: www.incredibleindia.org

The Royal Burgh of Peebles website: www.peebles.info
(Aline's photography of this beautiful area of the Scottish Borders as well
as galleries of her photography through her own website.)

Aline Dobbie's own non-commercial website:
www.thepeacockscall.co.uk

Bibliography

Ali, Salim, **1941,** *The Book of Indian Birds,* Bombay, The Bombay Natural History Society

Bainbridge Fletcher, T., **1936**, *Birds of an Indian Garden,* Calcutta, Thacker, Spink & Co.

Beach, Milo Cleveland & Ebba Koch, and Wheeler Thackston, **1997,** *The Padshanama King of the World,* A Mughul Manuscript from The Royal Library, Windsor Castle

Mason, Philip, **1974,** *A Matter of Honour – An Account of the Indian Army, its Officers and Men,* London, Jonathan Cape Ltd

Mayo, Katherine, **1935,** *The Face of Mother India,* London, Hamish Hamilton

McCann, Charles, (n.d.), *Trees of India,* Bombay, D. B. Taraporevala Sons & Co.

Miller, Charles, **1977**, *Khyber – The Story of the North West Frontier,* London, Macdonald & Jane's Publishers Ltd

Roberts, Field-Marshal Lord, of Kandahar, VC, GCB, GCSI, GCIE, **1897,** *Forty-one Years in India,* London, Richard Bentley and Son

Rose, Frank D., Lt Col., **1960,** *A Brief Note on the Origin and History of the Jats and the Jat Regiment,* privately published

'Silver Hackle', **1928,** *Man-Eaters and other Denizens of the Indian Jungle,* Calcutta, Thacker, Spink & Co.

Sunity Devee, Maharani of Cooch Behar & Rose, Aline, **1916,** *Bengal Dacoits and Tigers,* Calcutta, Thacker, Spink & Co.

Tillotson, G. H. R., **1990,** *Mughul India,* London, Penguin Books Ltd
Woodruff (Mason), Philip, **1953,** *The Men Who Ruled India,* London, Jonathan Cape Ltd

※ INDIA ※
The Peacock's Call

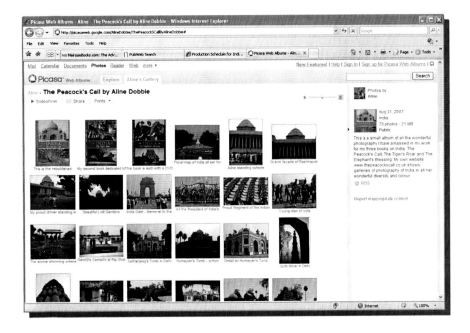

Aline Dobbie's website www.thepeacockscall.co.uk is full of wonderful colourful galleries of her photography and regularly updated with the published articles written by Aline for magazines and newspapers, as well as features on her.

The website is easily accessed and is completely non-commercial with useful links to several worthwhile charities she supports, and to other interesting people whom the reader might find useful if travelling.